RUSSIAN

in 10 minutes a day®

by **Kristine Kershul,** M.A., University of California, Santa Barbara

adapted by Helen Adelbera McIntyre, Ed.D.

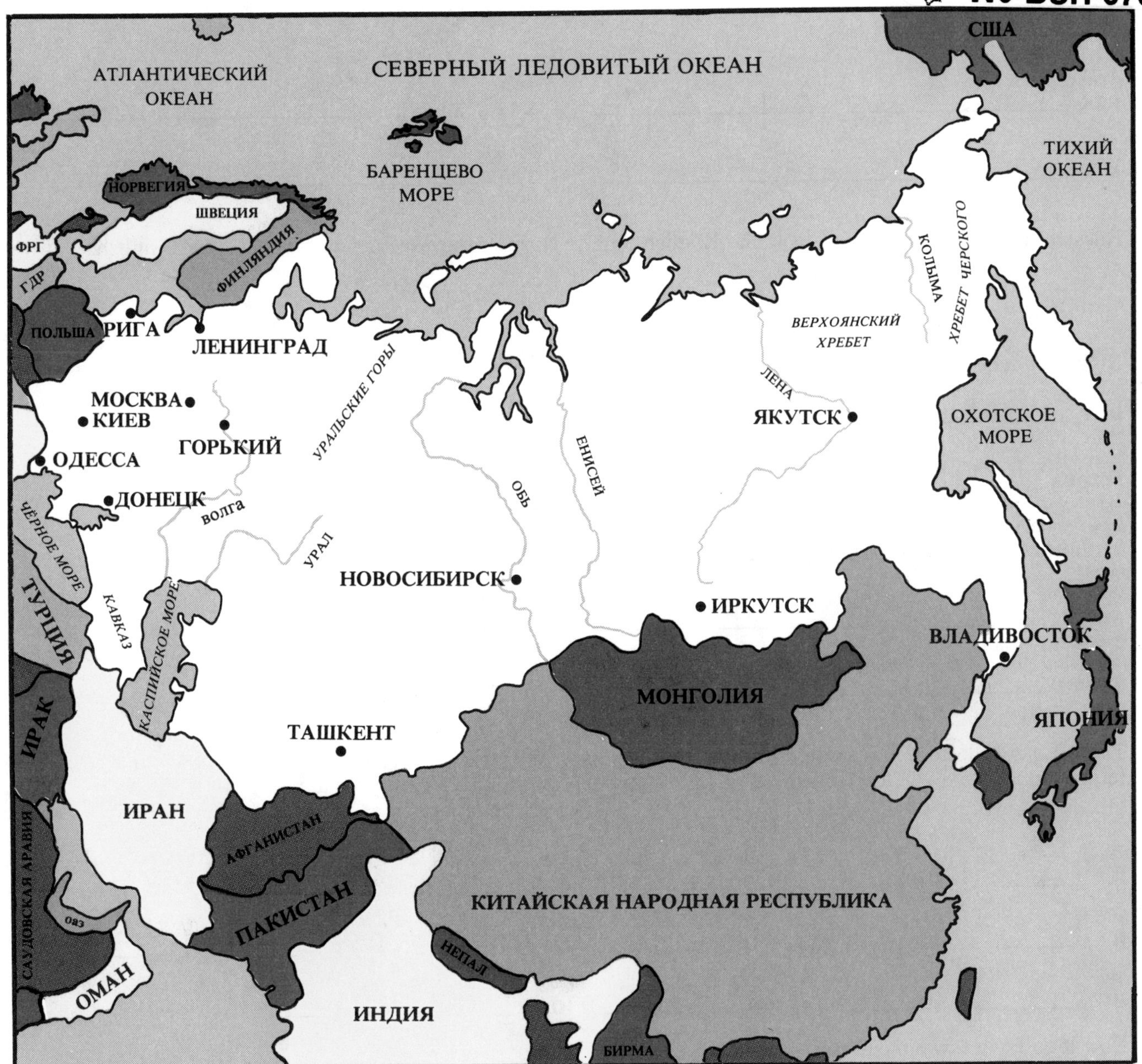

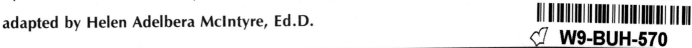

A Sunset Series Lane Publishing Co.
Menlo Park, CA 94025

Third printing May 1990

 ISBN 0-944502-45-8.
Lithographed in the United States.

When you first see words like „**машина**“ and „**когда**“, Russian can appear to be forbidding. However, it is not, when you know how to decode these new letters. To learn these new Russian letters, work through the examples here and on pages 106 and 107. Above all new words is a very easy pronunciation guide. These pages are intended as a guide, so mark them and refer to them whenever you need help. The entire Russian alphabet can be found on page 107.

There are five letters that look and sound like English:

(ah) **А**	*(k)* **К**	*(m)* **М**	*(oh)* **О**	*(t)* **Т**

You can already say:

(kahk) **как** как, как, как, как — how

(ktoh) **кто** ________ — who

(koht) **кот** ________ — cat

(tahm) **там** ________ — there

Russian has seven letters that look like English, but be careful; they are not pronounced like English.

(v) **В**	*(eh/yeh)* **Е**	*(n)* **Н**	*(r)* **Р**	*(s)* **С**	*(oo)* **У**	*(h)* **Х**

Now pronounce these words:

(voht) **вот** ________ — here

(mar-kah) **марка** ________ — stamp

(ahn-tyen-nah) **антенна** ________ — antenna

(kahs-sah) **касса** ________ — cashier

(too-mahn) **туман** ________ — fog

(stoh) **сто** ________ — 100

(sah-har) **сахар** ________ — sugar

(soh-oos) **соус** ________ — sauce

(kar-tah) **карта** ________ — map

(hah-ohs) **хаос** ________ — chaos

These Russian letters look quite different from English. With only a couple of exceptions, they are easy to pronounce once you learn them. Are you ready? First practice writing these new letters.

(b) **б** б, б	*(g)* **г** ____	*(d)* **д** ____	*(yoh)* **ё** ____	*(zh)* **ж** ____	*(z)* **з** ____
(ee) **и** ____	*(l)* **л** ____	*(p)* **п** ____	*(f)* **ф** ____	*(ts)* **ц** ____	*(ch/sh)* **ч** ____
(sh) **ш** ____	*(shch)* **щ** ____	*(eh)* **э** ____	*(yoo)* **ю** ____	*(yah)* **я** ____	

Now let's try a few simple words:

(bahnk) **банк** банк — bank

(zhah-kyet) **жакет** ________ — jacket

(kahg-dah) **когда** ________ — when

(zoh-nah) **зона** ________ — zone

(kahv-yor) **ковёр** ________ — carpet

(tahk-see) **такси** ________ — taxi

 To continue, turn to page 106.

Seven Key Question Words

Step 1

When you arrive in the *(sah-vyet-skee)* **Советский** (Soviet) *(sah-yooz)* **Союз,** (Union) the very first thing you will need to do is ask questions—"Where is the bus stop?" "Where can I exchange money?" "Where *(gdyeh)* **(где)** is the lavatory?" "*(gdyeh)* **Где** (where) is a restaurant?" "*(gdyeh)* **Где** (where) do I catch a taxi?" "*(gdyeh)* **Где** (where) is a good hotel?" "*(gdyeh)* **Где** is my luggage?"—and the list will go on and on for the entire length of your visit. In Russian, there are SEVEN KEY QUESTION WORDS to learn. For example, the seven key question words will help you find out exactly what you are ordering in a restaurant before you order it—and not after the surprise (or shock!) arrives. Notice that "what" and "who" are differentiated by only one letter, so be sure not to confuse them. Take a few minutes to study and practice saying the seven basic question words listed below. Then cover the *(roos-skee)* **русский** (Russian) with your hand and fill in each of the blanks with the matching *(roos-skeem)* **русским** (Russian) *(slohv-ahm)* **словом.** (word)

1.	*(gdyeh)* **ГДЕ**	=	WHERE	где, где, где, где, где
2.	*(shtoh)* **ЧТО**	=	WHAT	________________
3.	*(ktoh)* **КТО**	=	WHO	________________
4.	*(kahk)* **КАК**	=	HOW	________________
5.	*(kahg-dah)* **КОГДА**	=	WHEN	________________
6.	*(pah-chee-moo)* **ПОЧЕМУ**	=	WHY	________________
7.	*(skohl-kah)* **СКОЛЬКО**	=	HOW MUCH	________________

Now test yourself to see if you really can keep these **слова** *(slah-vah)* [words] straight in your mind. Draw lines between the **русскими** *(roos-skee-mee)* [Russian] **и** *(ee)* [and] English equivalents below.

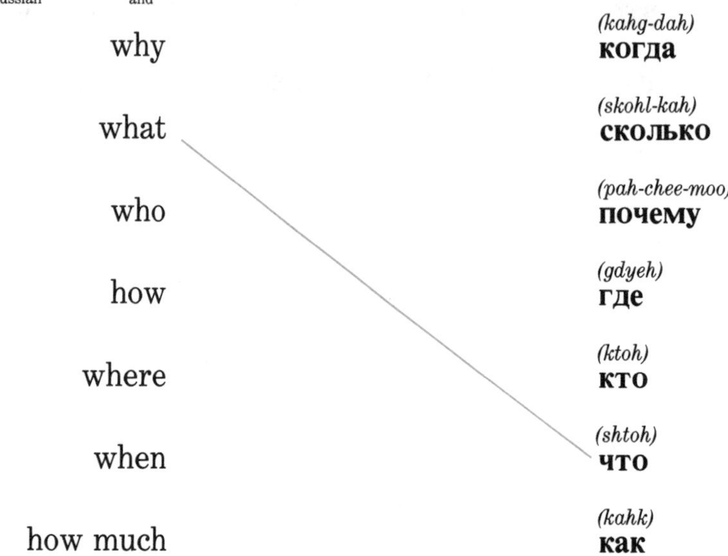

why	**когда** *(kahg-dah)*
what	**сколько** *(skohl-kah)*
who	**почему** *(pah-chee-moo)*
how	**где** *(gdyeh)*
where	**кто** *(ktoh)*
when	**что** *(shtoh)*
how much	**как** *(kahk)*

Examine the following questions containing these words. Practice the sentences out loud **и** *(ee)* [and] then quiz yourself by filling in the blanks below with the correct question **словом.** *(slohv-ahm)* [word]

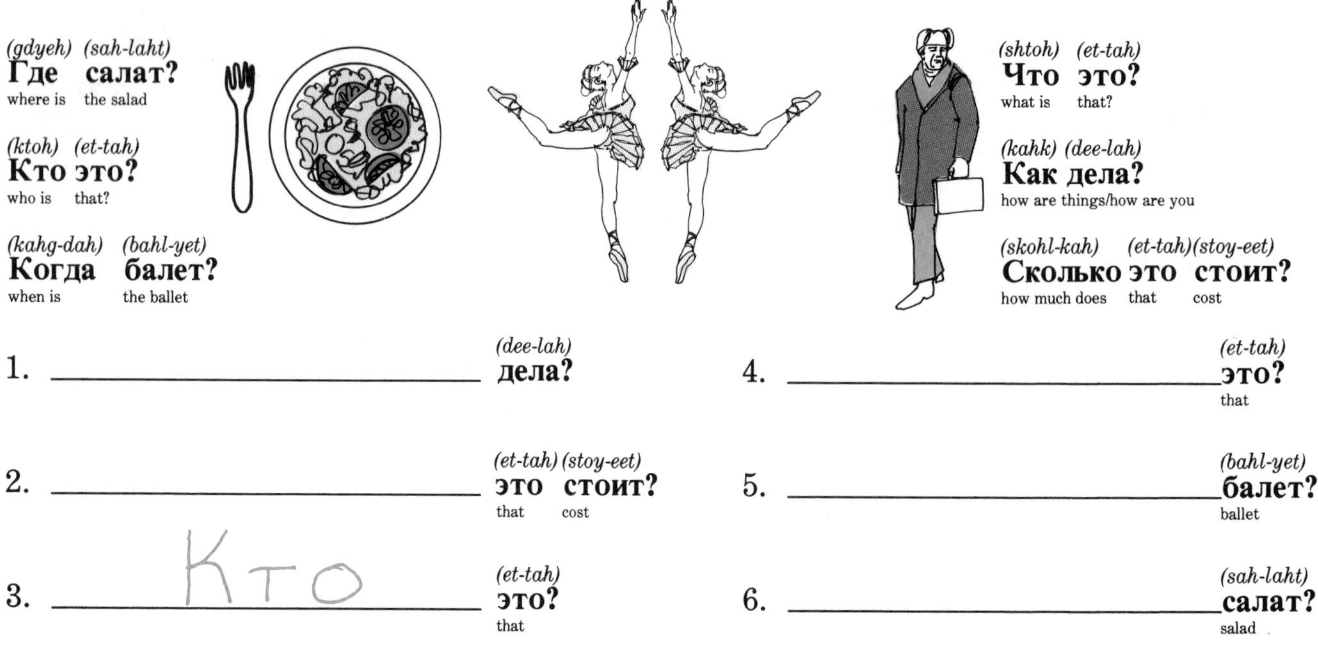

Где *(gdyeh)* [where is] **салат?** *(sah-laht)* [the salad]

Кто *(ktoh)* [who is] **это?** *(et-tah)* [that?]

Когда *(kahg-dah)* [when is] **балет?** *(bahl-yet)* [the ballet]

Что *(shtoh)* [what is] **это?** *(et-tah)* [that?]

Как *(kahk)* **дела?** *(dee-lah)* [how are things/how are you]

Сколько *(skohl-kah)* [how much does] **это** *(et-tah)* [that] **стоит?** *(stoy-eet)* [cost]

1. ________________ **дела?** *(dee-lah)*
2. ________________ **это** *(et-tah)* [that] **стоит?** *(stoy-eet)* [cost]
3. Кто ________________ **это?** *(et-tah)* [that]
4. ________________ **это?** *(et-tah)* [that]
5. ________________ **балет?** *(bahl-yet)* [ballet]
6. ________________ **салат?** *(sah-laht)* [salad]

„Где“ *(gdyeh)* [where] will be your most used question **слово,** *(sloh-vah)* [word] so let's concentrate on it. Say each of the following **русское** *(roos-skah-yeh)* [Russian] sentences aloud. Then write out each sentence without looking at the example. If you don't succeed on the first try, don't give up. Just practice each sentence until you are able to do it easily. Remember **„с“** is pronounced like an "s" **и** *(ee)* **„р“** is pronounced like an "r."

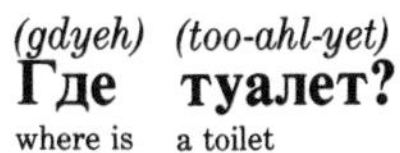
(gdyeh) (too-ahl-yet)
Где туалет?
where is a toilet

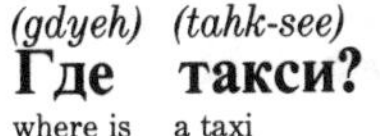
(gdyeh) (tahk-see)
Где такси?
where is a taxi

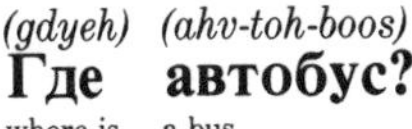
(gdyeh) (ahv-toh-boos)
Где автобус?
where is a bus

______________________ Где такси? ______________________

Где (res-tah-rahn) **ресторан?** (a restaurant)

Где (bahnk) **банк?** (a bank)

Где (ah-tyel) **отель?** (a hotel) / (gah-stee-neet-sah) **гостиница?** (a hotel/an inn)

______________________ ______________________ ______________________

(dah) **Да,** (yes) you can see similarities between (roos-skeem) **русским** (Russian) (ee) **и** (and) (ahn-glee-skeem) **английским** (English), if you look closely. (roos-skee) **Русский** (ee) **и** (and) (ahn-glee-skee) **английский** are not related languages, but some words are surprisingly similar. Of course, they do not always sound the same when spoken by a Russian, but the similarities will certainly surprise you and make your work here easier. Listed below are five "free" (slohv) **слов** (words) beginning with (ah) „**а**" to help you get started. Be sure to say each (sloh-vah) **слово** aloud (ee) **и** then write out the (roos-skah-yeh) **русское** (Russian) (sloh-vah) **слово** (word) in the blank to the right.

☑ **абрикос** *(ah-bree-kohs)*	apricot	**а**	______________
☑ **август** *(ahv-goost)*	August		______________
☑ **авиация** *(ah-vee-aht-see-yah)*	aviation		______________
☑ **Австралия** *(ahv-strah-lee-yah)*	Australia		______________
☑ **Австрия** *(ahv-stree-yah)*	Austria		______________

Free (slah-vah) **слова** (words) like these will appear at the bottom of the following pages in a yellow color band. They are easy—enjoy them! Don't forget to pronounce „**и**" as "ee."

Step 2

Odds 'n Ends

(roos-skee) **Русский** (Russian) *(yah-zik)* **язык** (language) does not have *(slohv)* **слов** (words) for "the" and "a," which makes things easier for you. Russian *(slah-vah)* **слова** (words) also change their endings depending on how they are used, so don't be surprised! Learn *(slah-vah)* **слова** (the words) and be prepared to see their endings change. Here are some examples.

(sloh-vah) **слово** word
(slah-vah) **слова**
(sloh-voo) **слову**
(sloh-vahm) **словом**
(slohv) **слов**
(slah-vah-mee) **словами**

(kuh-nee-gah) **книга** book
(kuh-nee-gee) **книги**
(kuh-nee-geh) **книге**
(kuh-nee-goo) **книгу**
(kuh-nee-goy) **книгой**
(kuh-neeg) **книг**

(stool) **стул** chair
(stool-ah) **стула**
(stool-oo) **стулу**
(stool-ohm) **стулом**
(stool-yeh) **стуле**
(stool-yah) **стулья**

This only appears difficult because it is different from *(ahn-glee-skah-vah)* **английского** (English) *(yah-zih-kah)* **языка.** (language) Just remember the core of *(sloh-vah)* **слова** (the word) doesn't change, so you'll always be able to recognize it. For instance, you will be understood whether you say *(kuh-nee-gah)* **книга** (book) or *(kuh-nee-goo)* **книгу.** Learn to look for the core of the word, and don't worry about the different endings.

Step 3

Look Around You

Before you proceed *(suh)* **с** (with) this Step, situate yourself comfortably in your living room. Now look around you. Can you name the things that you see in this *(kohm-naht-yeh)* **комнате** (room) in Russian? You can probably guess *(lahm-pah)* **лампа** (lamp) and maybe even *(dee-vahn)* **диван.** (divan/couch) But let's learn the rest of them. After practicing these *(slah-vah)* **слова** (words) out loud, write them in the blanks below *(ee)* **и** (and) on the next page.

(kar-tee-nah) *(kar-teen-kah)* **картина/картинка** picture ____________________

(pah-tah-lohk) **потолок** = ceiling ПОТОЛОК, ПОТОЛОК, ПОТОЛОК

- ☐ **автобиография** *(ahv-tah-bee-ah-grah-fee-yah)*. autobiography ____________
- ☐ **автограф** *(ahv-tah-grahf)*.................. autograph ____________
- ☐ **автомат** *(ahv-tah-maht)*.................. automat ____________
- ☐ **автомобиль** *(ahv-tah-mah-beel)*............ automobile ____________
- ☐ **автор** *(ahv-tar)*.......................... author ____________

а

(oog-ahl)
угол = corner

(ahk-noh)
окно = window

(lahm-pah)
лампа = lamp, light лампа, лампа, лампа

(dee-vahn)
диван = sofa

(stool)
стул = chair

(kahv-yor)
ковёр = carpet

(stohl)
стол = table

(dvyair)
дверь = door

(chah-sih)
часы = clock

(zah-nahv-yes)
занавес = curtain

(styen-ah)
стена = wall

(teh-leh-fohn)
телефон = telephone

In Step 2, you learned that *(roos-skee-yeh)* **русские** (Russian) *(slah-vah)* **слова** (words) vary. The correct form of each *(sloh-vah)* **слово** (word) will always be given to familiarize you with the variations. Now open your *(kuh-nee-goo)* **книгу** (book) to the sticky labels (between pages 48 and 49). Peel off the first 14 labels *(ee)* **и** (and) proceed around the *(kohm-nah-tih)* **комнаты** (room) labeling these items in your home. This will help to increase your *(roos-skah-yeh)* **русское** (Russian) *(sloh-vah)* **слово** (word) power easily. Don't forget to say each *(sloh-vah)* **слово** (word) as you attach each label.

Now ask yourself, ,,*(gdyeh)* **Где** *(kar-tee-nah)* **картина?**" (the picture) and point at it while you answer, ,,*(tahm)* **Там** (there is) *(kar-tee-nah)* **картина.**" (the picture) Continue on down the list until you feel comfortable with these new *(slah-vah-mee)* **словами.** (words) Say, ,,*(gdyeh)* **Где** *(pah-tah-lohk)* **потолок?**" (the ceiling) Then reply, ,,*(tahm)* **Там** (there is) *(pah-tah-lohk)* **потолок,**" and so on. When you can identify all the items on the list, you will be ready to move on. Now, starting on the next page, let's learn some basic parts of the house.

- ☐ **агент** *(ah-gyent)*.......................... agent
- ☐ **адвокат** *(ahd-vah-kaht)*.................... advocate, lawyer
- ☐ **адрес** *(ah-dres)*.......................... address
- ☐ **Азия** *(ah-zee-yah)*.......................... Asia
- ☐ **академия** *(ah-kah-dyeh-mee-yah)*............ academy

а

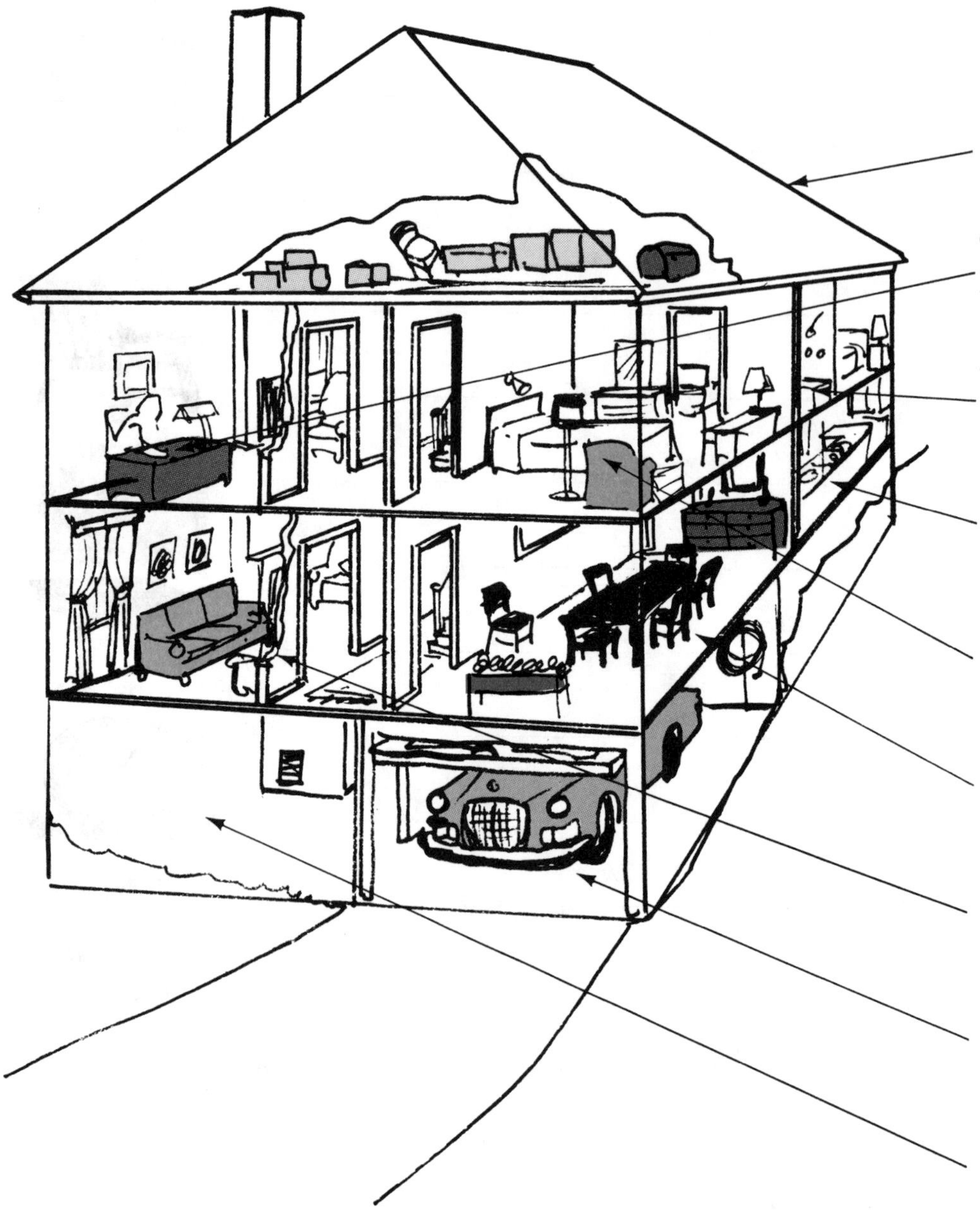

(dohm)
дом = house

(voht) *(dohm)*
Вот дом.
here is the house

(kah-bee-nyet)
кабинет
study

(vahn-nah-yah)
ванная
bathroom

(koohk-nyah)
кухня
kitchen

(spahl-nyah)
спальня
bedroom

(stah-loh-vah-yah)
столовая
dining room

(gah-stee-nah-yah)
гостиная
living room

(gah-rahzh)
гараж
garage

(pahd-vahl)
подвал
basement

While learning these new **слова** *(slah-vah)* (words), let's not forget

(ahv-tah-mah-beel) *(mah-shen-nah)*
автомобиль/машина
automobile/car

(mah-tah-tsee-kul)
мотоцикл
motorcycle

(sah-bah-kah)
собака
dog

__________ МОТОЦИКЛ __________

- ☐ **аккуратный** *(ahk-koo-raht-nee)* .... fastidious, neat
- ☐ **акробат** *(ah-krah-baht)* .... acrobat
- ☐ **акт** *(ahkt)* .... act
- ☐ **актёр** *(ahk-tyor)* .... actor
- ☐ **акцент** *(ahkt-syent)* .... accent

a

(koht)
кот
cat

(sahd)
сад
garden

(poach-tah)
почта
mail

КОТ, КОТ, КОТ

(pahch-toh-vee) (yahsh-chik)
почтовый ящик
mailbox

(tsvet-ih)
цветы
flowers

(zvah-nohk)
звонок
doorbell

Peel off the next set of labels *(ee)* **и** wander through your *(dohm)* **дом** learning these new *(slah-vah)* **слова** (words). Granted, it will be somewhat difficult to label your *(koht)* **кот** (cat), *(tsvet-ih)* **цветы** (flowers) or *(sah-bah-koo)* **собаку** (dog), but use your imagination. Again, practice by asking yourself, „*(gdyeh)* **Где** *(ahv-tah-mah-beel)* **автомобиль?**" (the car) and reply, „*(voht)* **Вот** (here is) *(ahv-tah-mah-beel)* **автомобиль.**"

Now for the following... **Где собака? Где...**

а

- ☐ **алгебра** *(ahl-gyeh-brah)*.................... algebra
- ☐ **алкоголь** *(ahl-kah-gohl)*.................... alcohol
- ☐ **Америка** *(ah-myeh-ree-kah)*................ America
- ☐ **—американец** *(ah-myeh-ree-kah-nyets)*...... American male
- ☐ **—американка** *(ah-myeh-ree-kahn-kah)*...... American female

Step 4

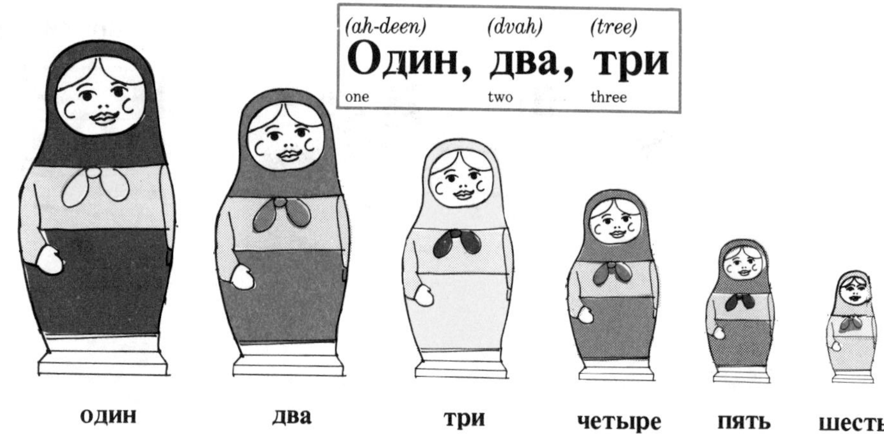

Consider for a minute how important numbers are. How could you tell someone your phone number, your address **или** (ee-lee) [or] your hotel room if you had no numbers? And think of how difficult it would be if you could not understand the time, the price of an apple **или** (ee-lee) [or] the correct bus to take. When practicing the **числа** (chee-slah) [numbers] below, notice the similarities (underlined) between **один** (ah-deen) [one] and **одиннадцать** (ah-deen-nud-tset) [eleven], **три** (tree) [three] and **тринадцать** (tree-nod-tset) [thirteen], and so on.

0	*(nohl)* **ноль**			0	ноль, ноль, ноль, ноль
1	*(ah-deen)* **один**	11	*(ah-deen-nud-tset)* **одиннадцать**	1	
2	*(dvah)/(dveh)* **два/две**	12	*(dveh-nod-tset)* **двенадцать**	2	
3	*(tree)* **три**	13	*(tree-nod-tset)* **тринадцать**	3	
4	*(cheh-tir-ee)* **четыре**	14	*(cheh-tir-nod-tset)* **четырнадцать**	4	
5	*(pyaht)* **пять**	15	*(pyaht-nod-tset)* **пятнадцать**	5	
6	*(shest)* **шесть**	16	*(shest-nod-tset)* **шестнадцать**	6	
7	*(syem)* **семь**	17	*(sim-nod-tset)* **семнадцать**	7	
8	*(voh-syem)* **восемь**	18	*(vah-sim-nod-tset)* **восемнадцать**	8	
9	*(dyev-yet)* **девять**	19	*(div-yet-nod-tset)* **девятнадцать**	9	
10	*(dyes-yet)* **десять**	20	*(dvahd-tset)* **двадцать**	10	

- ☐ **алло!** *(ahl-loh)* .... hello!
- ☐ **Англия** *(ahn-glee-yah)* .... England
- ☐ —where they speak **по-английски** *(pah-ahn-glee-skee)*
- ☐ —**англичанин** *(ahn-glee-chahn-een)* .... Englishman
- ☐ —**англичанка** *(ahn-glee-chahn-kah)* .... Englishwoman

а

Use these *(chee-slah)* **числа** (numbers) on a daily basis. Count to yourself *(pah-roos-skee)* **по-русски** (in Russian) when you brush your teeth, exercise, *(ee-lee)* **или** (or) commute to work. Now fill in the following blanks according to the *(chee-slahm)* **числам** (numbers) given in parentheses.

Note: This is a good time to start learning these two *(oh-chen)* **очень** (very) important phrases.

(yah) (hah-choo) (koo-peet) **я хочу купить**	=	I would like to buy ______
(mwee) (hah-teem) (koo-peet) **мы хотим купить**	=	we would like to buy ______

(yah) **Я** (I) *(hah-choo)* **хочу** (would like) *(koo-peet)* **купить** (to buy) *(et-tah)* **это.** (that)

(yah) **Я** (I) *(hah-choo)* **хочу** (would like) *(koo-peet)* **купить** (to buy) ______ (1).		*(skohl-kah)* **Сколько?** (how many) ______ (2)
		(skohl-kah) **Сколько?** (how many) ______ (1)
Я (I) *(hah-choo)* **хочу** (would like) *(koo-peet)* **купить** ______ (7)	*(mar-ahk)* **марок.** (stamps)	*(skohl-kah)* **Сколько?** (how many) ______ (7)
Я *(hah-choo)* **хочу** *(koo-peet)* **купить** ______ (8)	*(mar-ahk)* **марок.** (stamps)	*(skohl-kah)* **Сколько?** ______ (8)
Я *(hah-choo)* **хочу** *(koo-peet)* **купить** пять (5).		*(skohl-kah)* **Сколько?** ______ (5)
(mwee)(hah-teem) **Мы хотим** (we would like) *(koo-peet)* **купить** (to buy) ______ (9)	*(aht-krit-tahk)* **открыток.** (postcards)	*(skohl-kah)* **Сколько?** ______ (9)
(mwee)(hah-teem) **Мы хотим** (we would like) **купить** ______ (10)	*(aht-krit-tahk)* **открыток.** (postcards)	*(skohl-kah)* **Сколько?** ______ (10)
(mwee)(hah-teem) **Мы хотим** (we would like) **купить** ______ (6).		*(skohl-kah)* **Сколько?** шесть (6)
(yah) (hah-choo) **Я хочу** (I would like) **купить** ______ (1)	*(beel-yet)* **билет.** (ticket)	*(skohl-kah)* **Сколько?** ______ (1)
(mwee)(hah-teem) **Мы хотим** (we would like) **купить** ______ (4)	*(beel-yet-tah)* **билета.** (tickets)	*(skohl-kah)* **Сколько?** ______ (4)
Мы *(hah-teem)* **хотим** (would like) **купить** ______ (11).		**Сколько?** ______ (11)
(yah) (hah-choo) **Я хочу** (would like) **купить** ______ (3)	*(chahsh-kee)* **чашки** (cups of) *(chah-yah)* **чая.** (tea)	**Сколько?** ______ (3)
Мы *(hah-teem)* **хотим** (would like) **купить** (to buy) ______ (4)	*(chahsh-kee)* **чашки** (cups of) *(kohf-yeh)* **кофе.** (coffee)	**Сколько?** ______ (4)

ПАРТЕР

- ☐ **анекдот** *(ah-nyek-doht)*.................... anecdote, joke ______
- ☐ **антенна** *(ahn-tyen-nah)*.................... antenna ______
- ☐ **антибиотики** *(ahn-tee-bee-oh-tee-kee)*........ antibiotics ______
- ☐ **аппетит** *(ahp-peh-teet)*.................... appetite ______
- ☐ **апрель** *(ahp-ryel)*.......................... April ______

а

Now see if you can translate the following thoughts **на** *(nah)* into **русский.** *(roos-skee)* Russian **Ответы** *(aht-vyet-ih)* the answers are at the bottom of the page.

1. I would like to buy seven postcards.

____

2. I would like to buy nine stamps. ______________________________

3. We would like to buy four cups of tea.

Мы хотим купить четыре чашки чая.

4. We would like to buy three tickets.

____

Review **числа** *(chee-slah)* numbers 1 through 20 **и** *(ee)* and answer the following **вопросы** *(vah-proh-sih)* questions aloud, **и** *(ee)* then write the answers in the blank spaces.

Сколько *(skohl-kah)* how many **здесь** *(zdyes)* here **столов?** *(stah-lohv)* tables

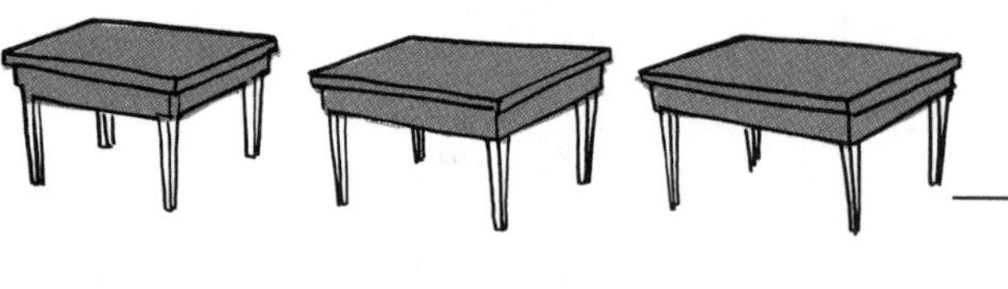

три

Сколько *(skohl-kah)* **здесь** *(zdyes)* here **ламп?** *(lahmp)* lamps

____

Сколько *(skohl-kah)* **здесь** *(zdyes)* **стульев?** *(stool-yev)* chairs

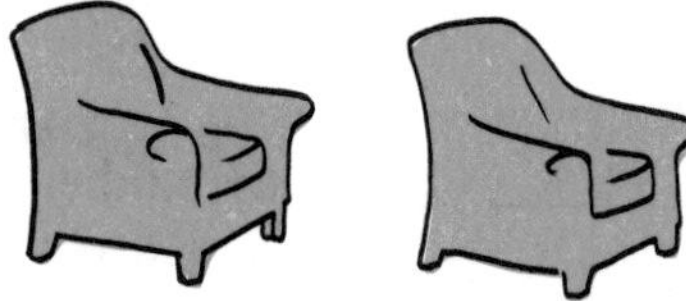

____

ОТВЕТЫ

1. Я хочу купить семь открыток.
2. Я хочу купить девять марок.
3. Мы хотим купить четыре чашки чая.
4. Мы хотим купить три билета.

(skohl-kah) (zdyes) (chah-sohv)
Сколько здесь часов?
how many here clocks

(skohl-kah) (zdyes) (oh-kahn)
Сколько здесь окон?
windows

(skohl-kah) (zdyes) (dyet-yeh)
Сколько здесь детей?
children

три

(skohl-kah) (zdyes) (kuh-neeg)
Сколько здесь книг?
books

(skohl-kah) (zdyes) (lood-yeh)
Сколько здесь людей?
people

(tsvet-ah)
Цвета
colors

Step 5

(tsvet-ah) **Цвета** (colors) are the same *(pah-roos-skee)* **по-русски** (in Russian) as they are *(pah-ahn-glee-skee)* **по-английски** (in English)—they just have different *(ee-myen-ah)* **имена.** (names)

Red is the national *(tsvet)* **цвет** (color) in *(sah-vyet-skahm)* **Советском** (the Soviet) *(sah-yoo-zeh)* **Союзе.** (Union) You will see it everywhere you go—on the flag, which is *(krahs-nee)* **красный** (red) *(ee)* **и** (and) *(zhyol-tee)* **жёлтый,** (yellow) in clothing *(ee)* **и** on banners. Let's learn the basic *(tsvet-ah)* **цвета.** (colors)

Once you have read through the list on the next *(strah-neet-seh)* **странице,** (page) cover the Russian words with your hand, *(ee)* **и** practice writing out *(roos-skah-yeh)* **русское** (the Russian) next to the English.

Once you've learned *(tsvet-ah)* **цвета,** (the colors) quiz yourself. What color are your shoes? Your eyes? Your hair?

а

- ☐ **арена** *(ar-yen-ah)* .... arena ____________
- ☐ **арест** *(ar-yest)* .... arrest ____________
- ☐ **армия** *(ar-mee-yah)* .... army ____________
- ☐ **аспирин** *(ah-spee-reen)* .... aspirin ____________
- ☐ **астронавт** *(ah-strah-nahvt)* .... astronaut ____________

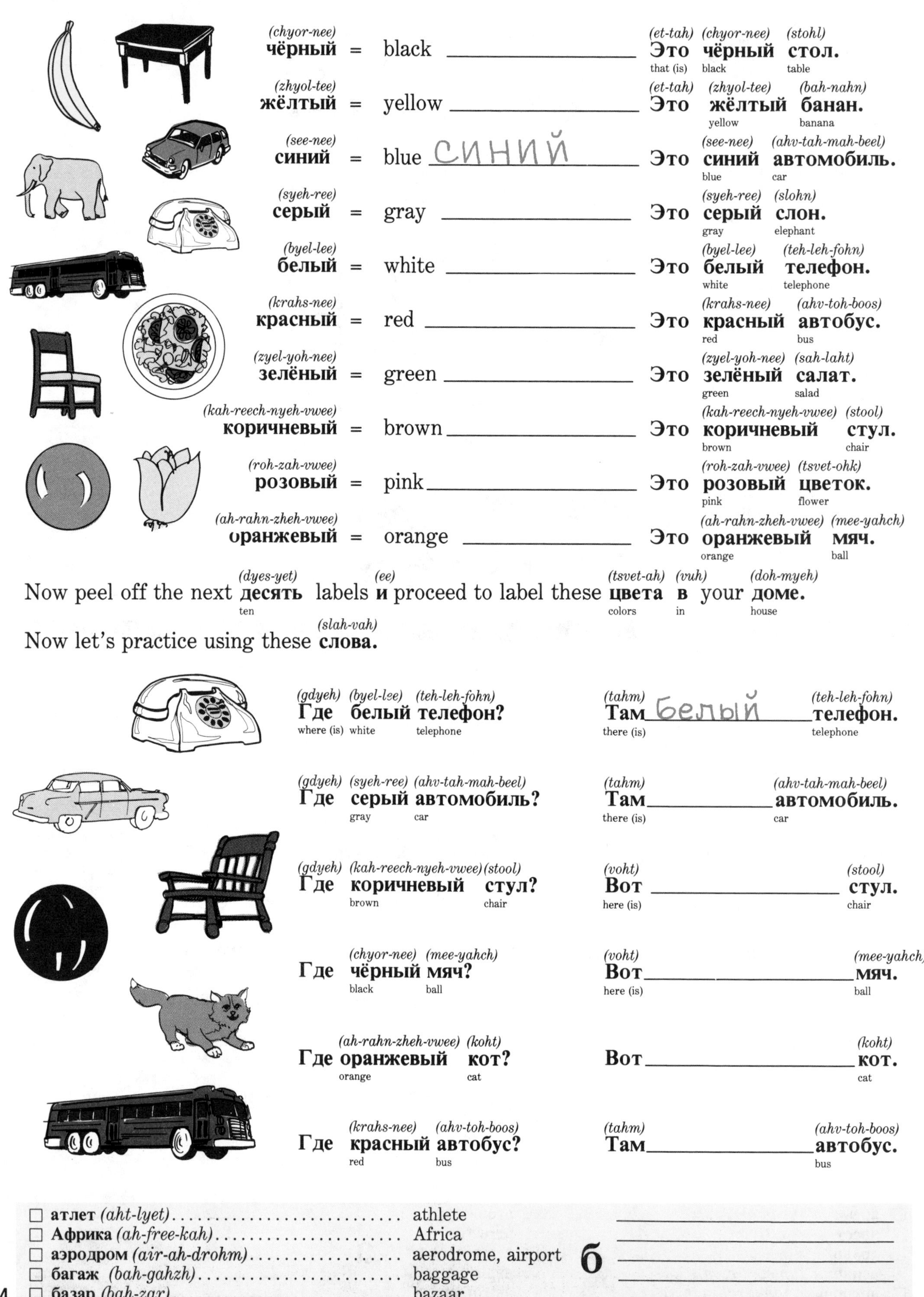

(chyor-nee) **чёрный**	=	black	____________	*(et-tah)* **Это** that (is) *(chyor-nee)* **чёрный** black *(stohl)* **стол.** table
(zhyol-tee) **жёлтый**	=	yellow	____________	*(et-tah)* **Это** *(zhyol-tee)* **жёлтый** yellow *(bah-nahn)* **банан.** banana
(see-nee) **синий**	=	blue	____________	**Это** *(see-nee)* **синий** blue *(ahv-tah-mah-beel)* **автомобиль.** car
(syeh-ree) **серый**	=	gray	____________	**Это** *(syeh-ree)* **серый** gray *(slohn)* **слон.** elephant
(byel-lee) **белый**	=	white	____________	**Это** *(byel-lee)* **белый** white *(teh-leh-fohn)* **телефон.** telephone
(krahs-nee) **красный**	=	red	____________	**Это** *(krahs-nee)* **красный** red *(ahv-toh-boos)* **автобус.** bus
(zyel-yoh-nee) **зелёный**	=	green	____________	**Это** *(zyel-yoh-nee)* **зелёный** green *(sah-laht)* **салат.** salad
(kah-reech-nyeh-vwee) **коричневый**	=	brown	____________	**Это** *(kah-reech-nyeh-vwee)* **коричневый** brown *(stool)* **стул.** chair
(roh-zah-vwee) **розовый**	=	pink	____________	**Это** *(roh-zah-vwee)* **розовый** pink *(tsvet-ohk)* **цветок.** flower
(ah-rahn-zheh-vwee) **оранжевый**	=	orange	____________	**Это** *(ah-rahn-zheh-vwee)* **оранжевый** orange *(mee-yahch)* **мяч.** ball

Now peel off the next *(dyes-yet)* **десять** (ten) labels *(ee)* **и** proceed to label these *(tsvet-ah)* **цвета** (colors) *(vuh)* **в** (in) your *(doh-myeh)* **доме.** (house)

Now let's practice using these *(slah-vah)* **слова.**

(gdyeh) **Где** where (is) *(byel-lee)* **белый** white *(teh-leh-fohn)* **телефон?** telephone	*(tahm)* **Там** there (is) ____________ *(teh-leh-fohn)* **телефон.** telephone
(gdyeh) **Где** *(syeh-ree)* **серый** gray *(ahv-tah-mah-beel)* **автомобиль?** car	*(tahm)* **Там** there (is) ____________ *(ahv-tah-mah-beel)* **автомобиль.** car
(gdyeh) **Где** *(kah-reech-nyeh-vwee)* **коричневый** brown *(stool)* **стул?** chair	*(voht)* **Вот** here (is) ____________ *(stool)* **стул.** chair
Где *(chyor-nee)* **чёрный** black *(mee-yahch)* **мяч?** ball	*(voht)* **Вот** here (is) ____________ *(mee-yahch)* **мяч.** ball
Где *(ah-rahn-zheh-vwee)* **оранжевый** orange *(koht)* **кот?** cat	**Вот** ____________ *(koht)* **кот.** cat
Где *(krahs-nee)* **красный** red *(ahv-toh-boos)* **автобус?** bus	*(tahm)* **Там** ____________ *(ahv-toh-boos)* **автобус.** bus

☐ **атлет** *(aht-lyet)* .... athlete ____________
☐ **Африка** *(ah-free-kah)* .... Africa ____________
☐ **аэродром** *(air-ah-drohm)* .... aerodrome, airport ____________
☐ **багаж** *(bah-gahzh)* .... baggage ____________
☐ **базар** *(bah-zar)* .... bazaar ____________

б

(gdyeh) (zyel-yoh-nee) (beel-yet) (voht) (beel-yet)
Где зелёный билет? Вот _______________ билет.
green ticket

(roh-zah-vwee) (dohm) (tahm) (dohm)
Где розовый дом? Там _______________ дом.
pink house

(zhyol-tee) (bah-nahn) (voht) (bah-nahn)
Где жёлтый банан? Вот _______________ банан.
yellow

(pah-roos-skee)
Note: **По-русски,** "I have" and "we have" are written as follows.

(oo) (men-yah) (yest) (oo)(nahs) (yest)
у меня есть = I have _______________ **у нас есть** = we have _______________

(yah)(hah-choo)(koo-peet) (mwee)(hah-teem) (koo-peet) (oo)(men-yah) (yest)
Let's review „**я хочу купить**" and „**мы хотим купить,**" and learn „**у меня есть**"
I would like to buy; we would like to buy; I have

(oo)(nahs)(yest)
and „**у нас есть.**" Repeat each sentence out loud over and over.
we have

(yah) (hah-choo)(koo-peet) (pee-vah)
Я хочу купить пиво.
I would like to buy a beer

(oo) (men-yah) (yest) (pee-vah)
У меня есть пиво.
I have a beer

(mwee) (hah-teem) (koo-peet) (dvah)(stah-kah-nah)(vee-nah)
Мы хотим купить два стакана вина.
we would like two glasses of wine

(oo) (nahs) (yest) (dvah)(stah-kah-nah)(vee-nah)
У нас есть два стакана вина.
we have glasses of

(yah) (hah-choo) (sah-laht)
Я хочу купить салат.
a salad

(dohm)
У нас есть дом.
a house

(mwee) (mar-ahk)
Мы хотим купить семь марок.
stamps

(men-yah) (yest) (dohm) (vuh)(ah-myeh-ree-kyeh)
У меня есть дом в Америке.
I have a house in America

(oo)(men-yah) (yest) (oo)(nahs) (yest) (yah)(hah-choo) (koo-peet)
Now fill in the following blanks with „**у меня есть,**" „**у нас есть,**" „**я хочу купить**"

(mwee)(hah-teem) (koo-peet)
or „**мы хотим купить.**"

У нас есть_______________ (dyes-yet) (mah-rahk) **десять марок.** stamps
(we have)

_______________ (dvah) (beel-yet-tah) **два билета.** tickets
(we would like to buy)

_______________ (sah-laht) **салат.** salad
(I have)

_______________ (syem) (aht-krit-tahk) **семь открыток.** postcards
(I would like to buy)

☐ **бал** *(bahl)*	ball (dance)	_______________
☐ **балалайка** *(bah-lah-lie-kah)*	balalaika	_______________
☐ **балерина** *(bah-leh-ree-nah)*	ballerina	_______________
☐ **балет** *(bahl-yet)*	ballet	_______________
☐ **балкон** *(bahl-kohn)*	balcony	_______________

б

Теперь *(tyep-yair)* [now] a quick review of **цветов** *(tsvet-ohv)* [colors]. Draw lines between the **русскими** *(roos-skee-mee)* [Russian] **словами** *(slah-vah-mee)* [words] **и** *(ee)* the correct **цветами** *(tsvet-ah-mee)* [colors]. On your mark, get set, *GO!*

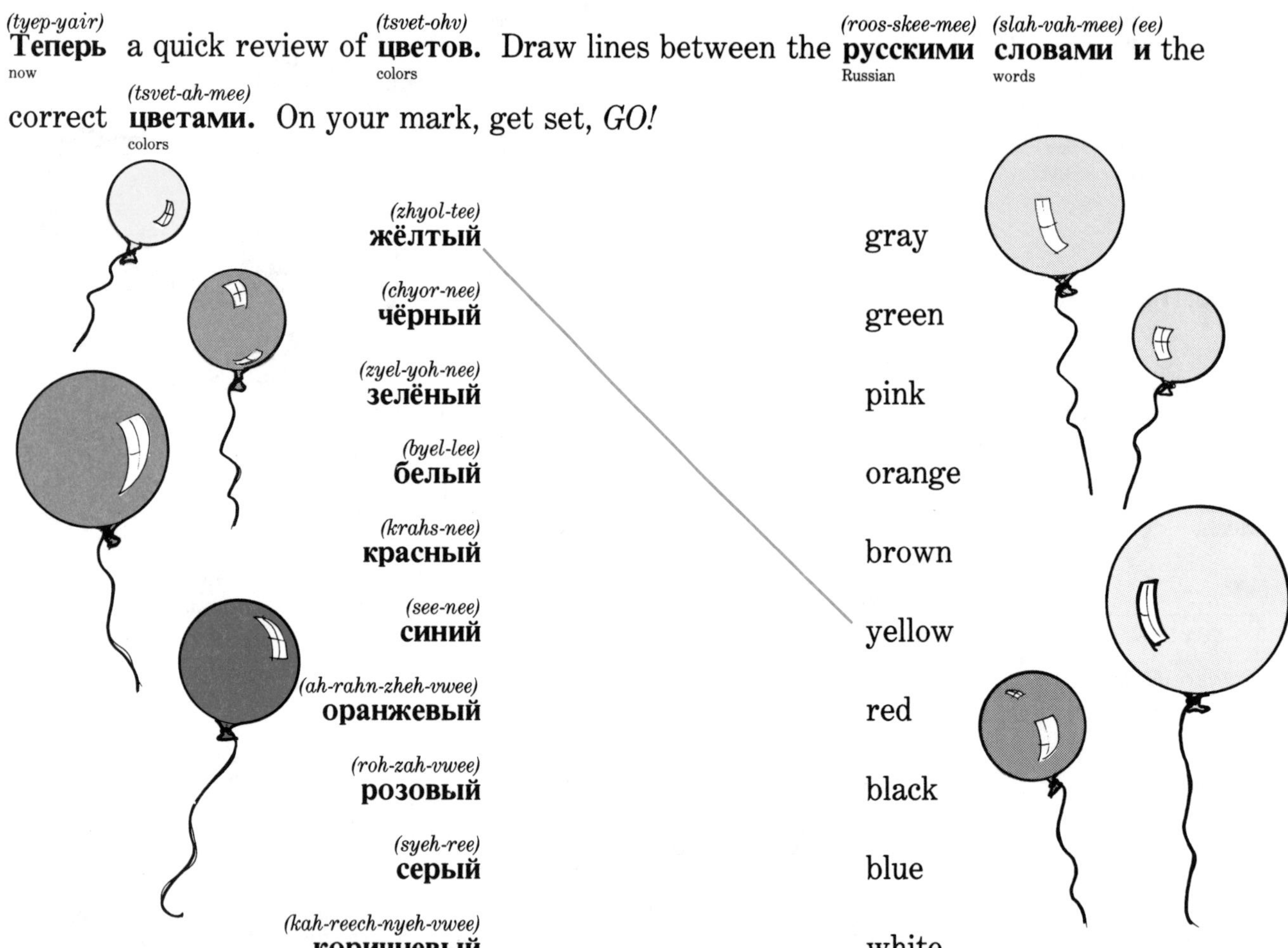

(zhyol-tee) **жёлтый**	gray
(chyor-nee) **чёрный**	green
(zyel-yoh-nee) **зелёный**	pink
(byel-lee) **белый**	orange
(krahs-nee) **красный**	brown
(see-nee) **синий**	yellow
(ah-rahn-zheh-vwee) **оранжевый**	red
(roh-zah-vwee) **розовый**	black
(syeh-ree) **серый**	blue
(kah-reech-nyeh-vwee) **коричневый**	white

По-русски *(pah-roos-skee)* [in Russian], the letter **е** is often pronounced *"yeh"* (as in the English word "yes.") When a letter such as **н, д** or **п** precedes the *"yeh"* sound, they combine to make one sound. For example, the **русское** *(roos-skah-yeh)* [Russian] **слово** *(sloh-vah)* [word] for "no" is **„нет"** pronounced like the **английское** *(ahn-glee-skah-yeh)* [English] **слово** *(sloh-vah)* [word] "net" with a "y": *"nyet."* As you practice each of the following words, combine the sound of *"yeh"* with the letter that precedes it, making one, smooth sound.

(gdyeh) **где** where	*(syem)* **семь** seven	*(kah-bee-nyet)* **кабинет** study
(zdyes) **здесь** here	*(dyev-yet)* **девять** nine	*(byel-lee)* **белый** white
(dyet-ee) **дети** children	*(dyes-yet)* **десять** ten	*(syeh-ree)* **серый** blue

☐ **банан** *(bah-nahn)*.......................... banana ________________
☐ **бандит** *(bahn-deet)*........................ bandit, robber ________________
☐ **бар** *(bar)*................................ bar (restaurant) **б** ________________
☐ **баржа** *(bar-zhah)*.......................... barge ________________
☐ **барьер** *(bar-yair)*......................... barrier ________________

Step 6

Before starting this Step, go back and review Step 4. Make sure you can count to *(dvahd-tset)* **двадцать** (twenty) without looking *(vuh)(kuh-nee-goo)* **в** (at) **книгу.** (the book) Let's learn the larger *(chee-slah)* **числа** (numbers) now, so if something costs more than 20 *(roo-blay)* **рублей,** (rubles) you will know exactly *(skohl-kah)* **сколько** it costs. After practicing aloud *(roos-skee-yeh)* **русские** (Russian) numbers 10 through 1000 below, write these *(chee-slah)* **числа** (numbers) in the blanks provided. Again, notice the similarities (underlined) between *(chee-slah-mee)* **числами** (numbers) such as *(tree)* **три** (3), *(tree-nod-tset)* **тринадцать** (13) and *(treed-tset)* **тридцать** (30).

10	*(dyes-yet)* **десять**	**(пять + пять = десять)**	10 десять
20	*(dvahd-tset)* **двадцать**	**(два = 2)**	20 ____
30	*(treed-tset)* **тридцать**	**(три = 3)**	30 ____
40	*(so-rahk)* **сорок**	*(cheh-tir-ee)* **(четыре = 4)**	40 ____
50	*(peed-dyes-yaht)* **пятьдесят**	*(pyaht)* **(пять = 5)**	50 ____
60	*(shest-dyes-yaht)* **шестьдесят**	**(шесть = 6)**	60 ____
70	*(syem-dyes-yet)* **семьдесят**	**(семь = 7)**	70 ____
80	*(voh-syem-dyes-yet)* **восемьдесят**	**(восемь = 8)**	80 ____
90	*(dyev-yah-noh-stah)* **девяносто**	*(dyev-yet)* **(девять = 9)**	90 ____
100	*(stoh)* **сто**		100 ____
500	*(pyet-soht)* **пятьсот**		500 ____
1000	*(tih-seh-chah)* **тысяча**		1000 ____

Now take a logical guess. *(kahk)* **Как** (how) would you write *(ee)* **и** (and) say the following? *(aht-vyet-ih)* **Ответы** (the answers) are at the bottom of *(strah-neet-sih)* **страницы.** (the page)

140 ____________ 52 ____________

610 ____________ 1100 ____________

ОТВЕТЫ

1100 = тысяча сто
52 = пятьдесят два
610 = шестьсот десять
140 = сто сорок

The unit of currency в (vuh) in Советском (sah-vyet-skahm) the Soviet Союзе (sah-yoo-zeh) Union is the рубль (roo-bil), abbreviated руб. or р. Bills are called рубли (roo-blee) и (ee) and coins are called копейки (kah-pay-kee), abbreviated коп. Just as американский (ah-myeh-ree-kahn-skee) an American или (ee-lee) канадский (kah-nahd-skee) Canadian доллар (dohl-lar) dollar can be broken down into 100 pennies, a рубль (roo-bil) can be broken down into 100 копеек (kah-pyeh-eek). Let's learn the various kinds of рублей (roo-blay) и (ee) копеек (kah-pyeh-eek). Always be sure to practice each слово (sloh-vah) out loud. You will not be able to exchange money before your arrival в (vuh) in Советский (sah-vyet-skee) Союз (sah-yooz), so take a few minutes now to familiarize yourself with Russian currency.

Рубли (roo-blee) rubles

Монеты (mahn-yet-ih) coins

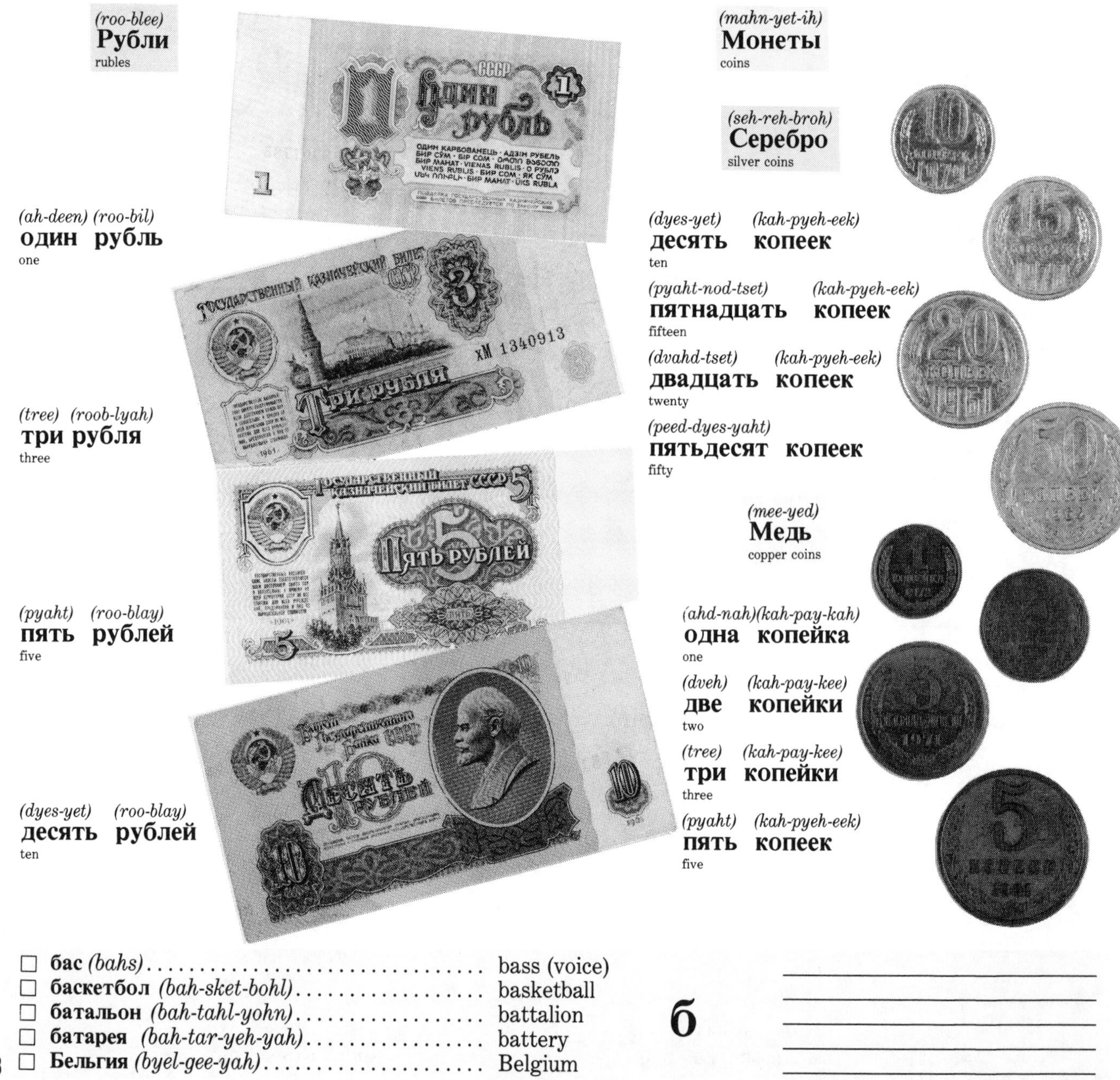

один рубль (ah-deen) (roo-bil) one

три рубля (tree) (roob-lyah) three

пять рублей (pyaht) (roo-blay) five

десять рублей (dyes-yet) (roo-blay) ten

Серебро (seh-reh-broh) silver coins

десять копеек (dyes-yet) (kah-pyeh-eek) ten

пятнадцать копеек (pyaht-nod-tset) (kah-pyeh-eek) fifteen

двадцать копеек (dvahd-tset) (kah-pyeh-eek) twenty

пятьдесят копеек (peed-dyes-yaht) fifty

Медь (mee-yed) copper coins

одна копейка (ahd-nah)(kah-pay-kah) one

две копейки (dveh) (kah-pay-kee) two

три копейки (tree) (kah-pay-kee) three

пять копеек (pyaht) (kah-pyeh-eek) five

- ☐ **бас** *(bahs)* . . . . bass (voice)
- ☐ **баскетбол** *(bah-sket-bohl)* . . . . basketball
- ☐ **батальон** *(bah-tahl-yohn)* . . . . battalion
- ☐ **батарея** *(bah-tar-yeh-yah)* . . . . battery
- ☐ **Бельгия** *(byel-gee-yah)* . . . . Belgium

б

Review **числа** *(chee-slah)* the numbers **десять** *(dyes-yet)* ten through **тысяча** *(tih-seh-chah)* one thousand again. **Теперь,** *(tyep-yair)* now **как** *(kahk)* how do you say "twenty-two" **или** *(ee-lee)* or "fifty-three" **по-русски?** *(pah-roos-skee)* You basically put the numbers together in a logical sequence. For example, 78 (70 + 8) = **семьдесят** *(syem-dyes-yet)* seventy **восемь.** *(voh-syem)* eight See if you can say **и** *(ee)* and write out **числа** *(chee-slah)* the numbers on this **странице.** *(strah-neet-seh)* page **Ответы** *(aht-vyet-ih)* answers are at the bottom of **страницы.** *(strah-neet-sih)*

a. 25 = ______________ (20 + 5)

b. 47 = ______________ (40 + 7)

c. 84 = ______________ (80 + 4)

d. 51 = ______________ (50 + 1)

e. 36 = тридцать шесть (30 + 6)

f. 93 = ______________ (90 + 3)

g. 68 = ______________ (60 + 8)

h. 72 = ______________ (70 + 2)

To ask how much something costs **по-русски,** *(pah-roos-skee)* one asks **„Сколько это стоит"** *(skohl-kah) (et-tah) (stoy-eet)* **Теперь** *(tyep-yair)* now answer the following questions based on **числа** *(chee-slah)* the numbers in parentheses.

1. **Сколько** *(skohl-kah)* how much **это** *(et-tah)* this **стоит?** *(stoy-eet)* costs — **Это** *(et-tah)* this **стоит** *(stoy-eet)* costs ______________ (10) **рублей.** *(roo-blay)* rubles

2. **Сколько это стоит?** — **Это стоит** пять (5) **рублей.** *(roo-blay)*

3. **Сколько стоит** *(stoy-eet)* costs **книга?** *(kuh-nee-gah)* the book — **Книга** *(kuh-nee-gah)* **стоит** ______________ (17) **рублей.** *(roo-blay)*

4. **Сколько стоит карта?** *(kar-tah)* the map — **Карта стоит** ______________ (6) **рублей.**

5. **Сколько стоит картина?** *(kar-tee-nah)* the picture — **Картина стоит** ______________ (110) **рублей.**

6. **Сколько стоит банан?** *(bah-nahn)* the banana — **Банан стоит** ______________ (20) **копеек.** *(kah-pyeh-eek)* kopecks

7. **Сколько стоит открытка?** *(aht-krit-kah)* the postcard — **Открытка стоит** ______________ (12) **копеек.** *(kah-pyeh-eek)*

ОТВЕТЫ

a. двадцать пять
b. сорок семь
c. восемьдесят четыре
d. пятьдесят один
e. тридцать шесть
f. девяносто три
g. шестьдесят восемь
h. семьдесят два
1. десять
2. пять
3. семнадцать
4. шесть
5. сто десять
6. двадцать
7. двенадцать

Step 7

(see-vohd-nyah) **Сегодня,** today	(zahv-trah) **Завтра** tomorrow	(ee) **и** and	(vchee-rah) **Вчера** yesterday

(kah-lyen-dar)
Календарь
calendar

(syem) **Семь** seven (dnay) **дней** days **в** in (nee-dyel-yeh) **неделе.** week

(pah-nee-dyel-neek) **понедельник** Monday	(vtor-neek) **вторник** Tuesday	(sree-dah) **среда** Wednesday	(chet-vyairg) **четверг** Thursday	(pyaht-neet-sah) **пятница** Friday	(soo-boh-tah) **суббота** Saturday	(voh-skree-syen-yah) **воскресенье** Sunday
1	2	3	4	5	6	7

(oh-chen) **Очень** very (vahzh-nah) **важно** important to know the days of the week (ee) **и** the various parts of the day. Let's learn them. Be sure to say them aloud before filling in the blanks below. (roos-skee-yeh) **Русские** Russians begin counting their week on Monday with (pah-nee-dyel-neek) **„понедельник."**

(pah-nee-dyel-neek) **понедельник** Monday ______________________

(vtor-neek) **вторник** Tuesday ______________________

(sree-dah) **среда** Wednesday среда, среда

(chet-vyairg) **четверг** Thursday ______________________

(pyaht-neet-sah) **пятница** Friday ______________________

(soo-boh-tah) **суббота** Saturday ______________________

(voh-skree-syen-yah) **воскресенье** Sunday ______________________

If (see-vohd-nyah) **сегодня** today (sree-dah) **среда,** Wednesday then (zahv-trah) **завтра** tomorrow (boo-dyet) **будет** will be (chet-vyairg) **четверг** Thursday and (vchee-rah) **вчера** yesterday (bil-lah) **было** was (vtor-neek) **вторник.** Tuesday (tyep-yair) **Теперь** now you supply the correct answers. If (see-vohd-nyah) **сегодня** today (pah-nee-dyel-neek) **понедельник,** Monday then (zahv-trah) **завтра** tomorrow (boo-dyet) **будет** ______________________ and (vchee-rah) **вчера** yesterday (bil-lah) **было** was ______________________. Or, if (see-vohd-nyah) **сегодня** today (pah-nee-dyel-neek) **понедельник,** Monday then завтра (boo-dyet) **будет** will be (vtor-neek) **вторник** Tuesday and ______________________ (bil-lah) **было** (voh-skree-syen-yah) **воскресенье.** (shtoh) **Что** what is (see-vohd-nyah) **сегодня?** today **Сегодня** ______________________.

(tyep-yair) **Теперь,** now peel off the next (syem) **семь** labels **и** put them on (kah-lyen-dar) **календарь** calendar you use every day. From now on, Monday is (pah-nee-dyel-neek) **понедельник.** Notice that Friday—(pyaht-neet-sah) **пятница**—is the fifth day of the week **и** contains the **слово** for five—(pyaht) **пять.**

- ☐ **Библия** *(bee-blee-yah)* .... Bible
- ☐ **бинокль** *(bee-noh-kil)* .... binoculars
- ☐ **бланк** *(blahnk)* .... blank (form)
- ☐ **бокс** *(bohks)* .... boxing
- ☐ **Болгария** *(bahl-gar-ee-yah)* .... Bulgaria

б

____
____
____
____
____

There are **четыре** (cheh-tir-ee) [four] parts to each **день** (dyen) [day].

morning	=	**утро** (oo-trah)	____________
afternoon/daytime	=	**день** (dyen)	____________
evening	=	**вечер** (vyeh-cher)	____________
night	=	**ночь** (nohch)	____________

Notice that **„в“** means "on." For example, **„в воскресенье** (voh-skree-syen-yah) **утром“** (oo-trahm) means on Sunday morning." **Теперь,** (tyep-yair) [now] fill in the following blanks **и** then check your answers at the bottom of **страницы.** (strah-neet-sih) [page] Don't be surprised that the words change slightly.

a. on Sunday morning = ____________

b. on Friday morning = ____________

c. on Friday evening = ____________

d. on Saturday evening = ____________

e. on Saturday morning = ____________

f. on Wednesday morning = ____________

g. on Wednesday afternoon = ____________

h. on Thursday afternoon = ____________

i. on Thursday evening = ____________

j. yesterday evening = ____________

k. yesterday afternoon = ____________

l. yesterday morning = ____________

m. tomorrow morning = ____________

n. tomorrow afternoon = ____________

ОТВЕТЫ

a. **в воскресене утром**
b. **в пятницу утром**
c. **в пятницу вечером**
d. **в субботу вечером**
e. **в субботу утром**
f. **в среду утром**
g. **в среду днём**
h. **в четверг днём**
i. **в четверг вечером**
j. **вчера вечером**
k. **вчера днём**
l. **вчера утром**
m. **завтра утром**
n. **завтра днём**

So, with merely eleven **слова,** *(slah-vah-mee)* [words] you can specify any **день** *(dyen)* [day] of **недели** *(nee-dyel-ee)* [week] **и** any time of **дня.** *(den-yah)* [day]

Сегодня, *(see-vohd-nyah)* [today] **завтра** *(zahv-trah)* [tomorrow] **и вчера** *(vchee-rah)* [yesterday] will be **очень** *(oh-chen)* [very] **важные** *(vahzh-nih-yeh)* [important] **слова** for you in making reservations **и** appointments, in getting **билеты** *(beel-yet-ih)* [tickets] for **театр** *(tee-ah-ter)* [theater] **и** for many other things you will want to do. Knowing the parts of **дня** *(den-yah)* [day] will help you to learn **и** [and] understand the various **русские** *(roos-skee-yeh)* [Russian] greetings below. Practice these every day until your trip.

good morning	=	*(doh-brah-yeh)(oo-trah)* **доброе утро**	
good day good afternoon	=	*(doh-brih) (dyen)* **добрый день**	
good evening	=	*(doh-brih) (vyeh-cher)* **добрый вечер**	добрый вечер
good night	=	*(spah-koy-nih) (noh-chee)* **спокойной ночи**	
How are you?	=	*(kahk) (dee-lah)* **Как дела?**	

Notice that "good afternoon" and "good day" are the same **по-русски:** *(doh-brih) (dyen)* **„добрый день"**

Take the next **четыре** *(cheh-tir-ee)* [four] labels **и** stick them on the appropriate things in your **доме.** *(doh-mee)* [house] How about the bathroom mirror for *(doh-brah-yeh)(oo-trah)* **„доброе утро"?** **Или** *(ee-lee)* [or] the front door for *(doh-brih) (dyen)* **„добрый день"?** **Или** *(ee-lee)* [or] your alarm clock for *(spah-koy-nih) (noh-chee)* **„спокойной ночи"?** **Или** your kitchen cabinet for *(kahk) (dee-lah)* **„Как дела"?** You are about one-fourth of your way through **эту** *(et-too)* [this] **книгу** *(kuh-nee-goo)* [book] **и** it is a good time to quickly review **слова** you have learned before doing the crossword puzzle on the next **странице.** *(strah-neet-seh)* [page] **Удачи!** *(oo-dah-chee)* **Или,** as we say **по-английски,** *(pah-ahn-glee-skee)* [in English] "good luck to you!"

ОТВЕТЫ TO THE CROSSWORD PUZZLE

ACROSS

1. банк
3. гостиница
6. купить
8. страница
10. нет
12. кухня
13. стена
14. зелёный
15. два
16. Советский Союз
21. оранжевый
23. где
25. копейки
27. стоит
28. почему
30. открытка
32. лампа
34. доллар
36. кофе
37. четырнадцать
39. утро
40. картина
43. стол
44. это

DOWN

2. когда
4. телефон
5. такси
6. коричневый
7. туалет
9. банан
11. американский
12. кто
17. синий
18. занавес
19. пятьдесят
20. дверь
22. автомобиль
24. сколько
26. как
29. один
31. почта
33. пять
35. или
36. красный
38. цвет
41. ноль
42. окно

CROSSWORD PUZZLE

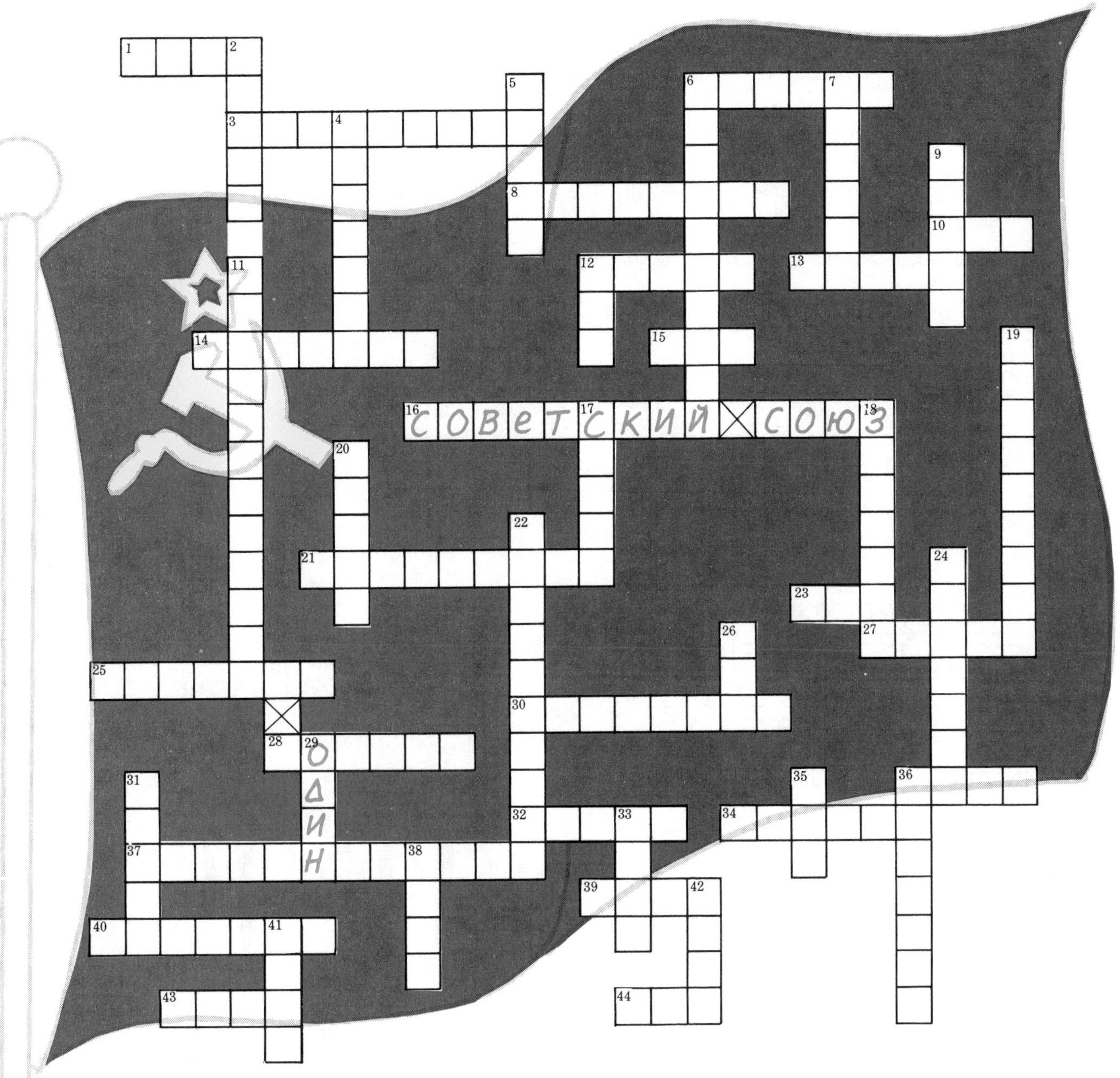

ACROSS

1. bank
3. hotel/inn
6. to buy
8. page
10. no
12. kitchen
13. wall
14. green
15. two
16. Soviet Union
21. orange
23. where
25. kopecks
27. costs
28. why
30. postcard
32. lamp
34. dollar
36. coffee
37. fourteen
39. morning
40. picture
43. table
44. this

DOWN

2. when
4. telephone
5. taxi
6. brown
7. toilet
9. banana
11. American
12. who
17. blue
18. curtain
19. fifty
20. door
22. automobile
24. how much
26. how
29. one
31. mail
33. five
35. or
36. red
38. color
41. zero
42. window

Step 8

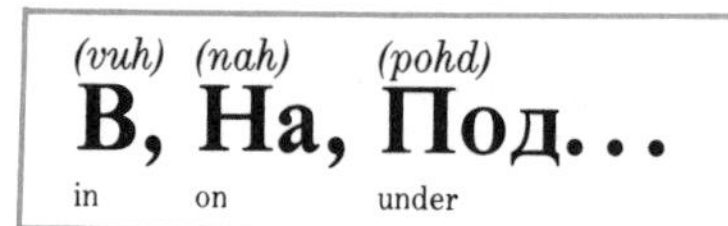

(vuh) (nah) (pohd)
В, На, Под...
in on under

Русские *(roos-skee-yeh)* Russian prepositions (words like "in," "on," "through" and "next to") are easy to learn **и** *(ee)* they allow you to be precise **с** *(suh)* with a minimum of effort. Instead of having to point **шесть** *(shest)* six times at a piece of yummy pastry you would like, you can explain precisely which one you want by saying it is behind, in front of, next to **или** *(ee-lee)* under the piece of pastry that the salesperson is starting to pick up. Let's learn some of these **маленькие слова** *(mah-lyen-kee-ee)* little words by studying **примеры** *(pree-myair-ih)* examples below.

из *(eez)* = out of/from		**рядом с** *(ryah-dahm) (suh)* = next to		**под** *(pohd)* = under	
в *(vuh)* = into/in				**над** *(nahd)* = over	

Мужчина *(moozh-chee-nah)* man **вышел** *(vih-shel)* comes **из** *(eez)* out of **гостиницы.** *(gah-stee-neet-sih)*

Женщина *(zhen-shchee-nah)* woman **идёт** *(ee-dyoht)* goes **в** *(vuh)* into **гостиницу.** *(gah-stee-neet-soo)* hotel

Врач *(vrahch)* doctor **в** *(vuh)* (is) in **гостинице.** *(gah-stee-neet-syeh)* hotel

Картина *(kar-tee-nah)* picture **над** *(nahd)* (is) over **столом.** *(stah-lohm)* table

Картина *(kar-tee-nah)* picture **рядом с** *(ryah-dahm) (suh)* (is) next to **часами.** *(chah-sah-mee)* clock

Собака *(sah-bah-kah)* dog **под** *(pohd)* (is) under **столом.** *(stah-lohm)*

Часы *(chah-sih)* clock **над** (is) over **столом.** *(stah-lohm)*

Часы рядом с *(ryah-dahm) (suh)* (is) next to **картиной.** *(kar-tee-noy)* picture

☐ **Боливия** *(bah-lee-vee-yah)*.................... Bolivia
☐ **бомба** *(bohm-bah)*.................... bomb
☐ **борщ** *(borshch)*.................... borsch (beet soup)
☐ **бронза** *(brohn-zah)*.................... bronze
☐ **брюнет** *(broo-nyet)*.................... brunette (male)

б

Fill in the blanks below *(suh)* **с** (with) the correct prepositions according to *(kar-teen-kahm)* **картинкам** (pictures) on the previous *(strah-neet-seh)* **странице.** (page)

(moozh-chee-nah) **Мужчина** (man) *(vih-shel)* **вышел** (comes) ____________ (out of) *(gah-stee-neet-sih)* **гостиницы.**

(sah-bah-kah) **Собака** (dog) ______под______ (under) *(stah-lohm)* **столом.** (table)

(chah-sih) **Часы** (clock) ____________ (over) **столом.** (table)

(vrahch) **Врач** (doctor) ____________ (in) *(gah-stee-neet-syeh)* **гостинице.**

Часы ____________ (next to) *(kar-tee-noy)* **картиной.** (picture)

Картина (picture) ____________ (over) **столом.**

Стол (table) ____________ (under) **картиной.**

Картина ____________ (next to) *(chah-sah-mee)* **часами.** (clock)

(zhen-shchee-nah) **Женщина** (woman) *(ee-dyoht)* **идёт** (goes) ____________ (into) *(gah-stee-neet-soo)* **гостиницу.**

Стол ____________ (under) **часами.**

(tyep-yair) **Теперь,** (now) answer *(vah-proh-sih)* **вопросы** (questions) based on *(kar-teen-kahk)* **картинках** (pictures) on the previous *(strah-neet-seh)* **странице.** (page)

(gdyeh)(vrahch) **Где врач?** (doctor) ____________________

(sah-bah-kah) **Где собака?** (dog) Собака под столом.

Где стол? (table) ____________________

(kar-tee-nah) **Где картина?** (picture) ____________________

(shtoh) **Что** (what) *(dyeh-lah-yet)* **делает** (does) **эта** *(zhen-shchee-nah)* **женщина?** (woman) ____________________

Что *(dyeh-lah-yet)* **делает** (does) *(et-tut)* **этот** (this) *(moozh-chee-nah)* **мужчина?** (man) ____________________

(chah-sih) **Часы** ((is) clock) *(zyel-yoh-nih-yeh)* **зелёные?** (green) ____________________

Собака ((is) dog) *(syeh-rah-yah)* **серая?** (gray) ____________________

☐ **бульвар** *(bool-var)*	boulevard		____________
☐ **бюрократ** *(byoo-rah-kraht)*	bureaucrat		____________
☐ **ваза** *(vah-zah)*	vase	**В**	____________
☐ **вальс** *(vahls)*	waltz		____________
☐ **Ватикан** *(vah-tee-kahn)*	Vatican		____________

(tyep-yair) / (roos-skee-mee)

Теперь (now) for some more practice with **русскими** (Russian) prepositions!

(nah) **на**	= on
(myezh-doo) **между**	= between
(pyeh-red) **перед**	= in front of
(zah) **за**	= behind

(stah-kahn) (vah-dih) (nah) (stohl-yeh)
Стакан воды на столе.
glass of water (is) on table

(kar-tee-nah) (styen-yeh)
Картина на стене.
picture (is) on wall

(lahm-pah) (zah) (stah-lohm)
Лампа за столом.
lamp (is) behind table

(stohl) (pyeh-red) (kroh-vaht-yoo)
Стол перед кроватью.
table (is) in front of bed

(lahm-pah) (myezh-doo) (kroh-vaht-yoo)
Лампа между столом и кроватью.
lamp (is) between table and bed

(stah-kahn) (vah-dih)
Стакан воды на______________ **столе.** (table)

Картина ______________ **стене.** (wall)

Лампа ______________ **столом.** (table)

Стол ______________ (kroh-vaht-yoo) **кроватью.** (bed)

Лампа ______________ **столом и кроватью.**

Answer the following (vah-proh-sih) **вопросы,** (questions) based on (kar-teen-kahk) **картинках,** (pictures) by filling in the blanks (suh) **с** the correct prepositions. Choose the prepositions from those you have just learned.

(gdyeh) (kuh-nee-gah)
Где книга? (book)

Книга ______________ (on) (stohl-yeh) **столе.**

(ahv-toh-boos)
Где автобус? (bus)

Автобус ______________ (in front of) (gah-stee-neet-say) **гостиницей.** (hotel)

- ☐ **веранда** *(vee-rahn-dah)*.................... veranda
- ☐ **витамин** *(vee-tah-meen)*.................... vitamin
- ☐ **водка** *(vohd-kah)*.................... vodka
- ☐ **волейбол** *(voh-lay-bohl)*.................... volleyball
- ☐ **Волга** *(vohl-gah)*.................... Volga River

В

____
____
____
____
____

(teh-leh-fohn) *(kahv-yor)*
Где телефон? telephone **Где ковёр?** carpet **Где картина?** picture

(syeh-ree) **Серый** gray **телефон** ______________ (on) *(styen-yeh)* **стене.** wall

Серый телефон рядом с (next to) *(kar-tee-noy)* **картиной.** picture

Серый телефон ______________ (over) *(stah-lohm)* **столом.** table

(zyel-yoh-nee) **Зелёный** green *(kahv-yor)* **ковёр** carpet ______________ (under) **столом.**

Картина picture ______________ (on) **стене.**

(tyep-yair) **Теперь,** now fill in each blank on *(gah-stee-neet-seh)* **гостинице** hotel below *(suh)* **с** the best possible preposition.

The correct *(aht-vyet-ih)* **ответы** answers are at the bottom of *(strah-neet-sih)* **страницы.** page Have fun!

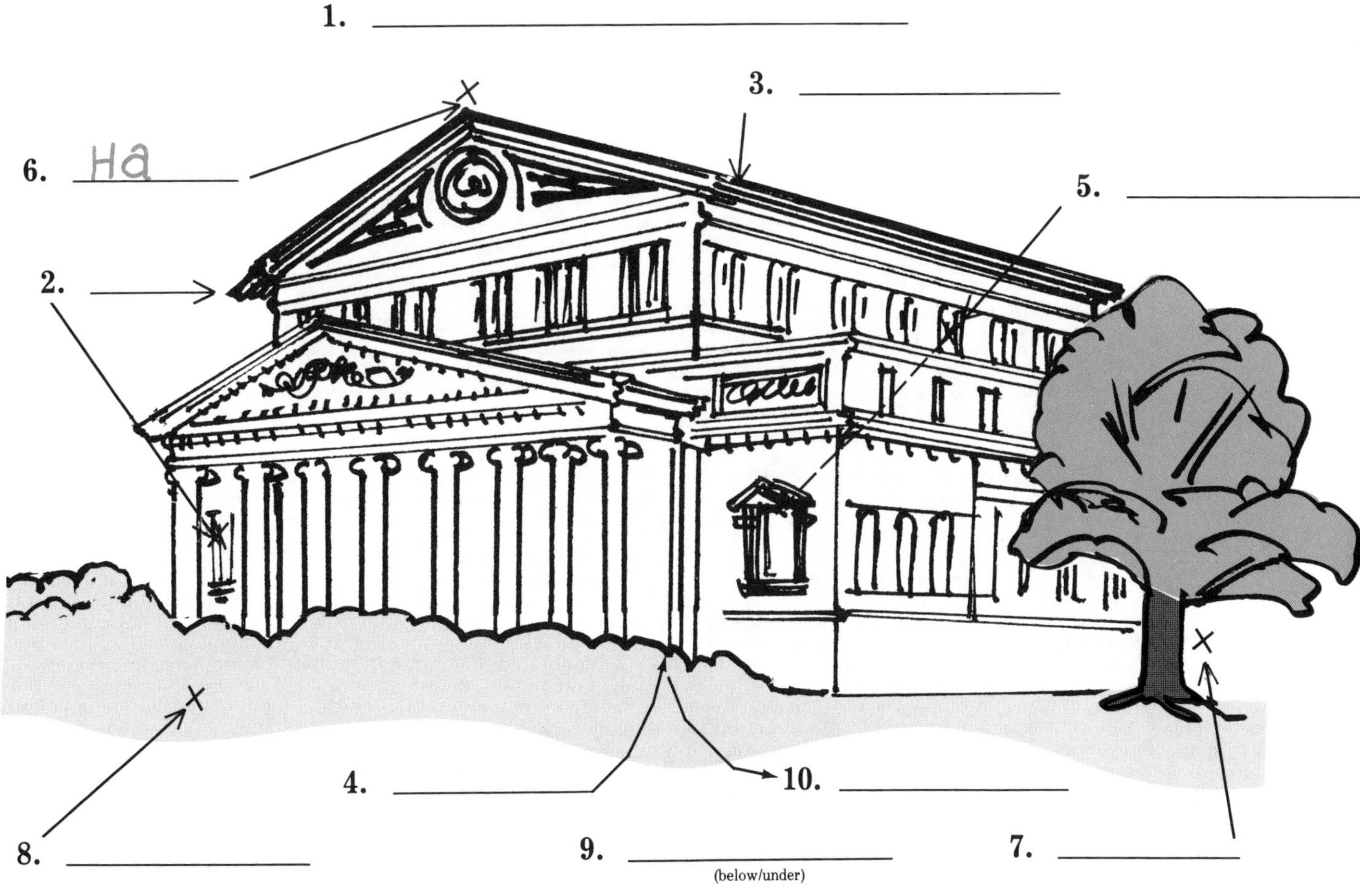

ОТВЕТЫ

1. **над** 3. **за** 5. **в** 7. **рядом с** 9. **под**
2. **между** 4. **в** 6. **на** 8. **перед** 10. **из**

Step 9

(vuh) *(yahn-var-yeh)* *(fyev-rahl-yeh)* *(mart-yeh)*
В Январе, Феврале, Марте
in January February March

(treed-tset) *(dnay)* *(syen-tyah-bree-yeh)* *(ahp-ryel-yeh)*
Тридцать дней в сентябре, апреле,
thirty days September April
(ee-yoon-yeh) *(nah-yah-bree-yeh)*
июне, и ноябре.
June November

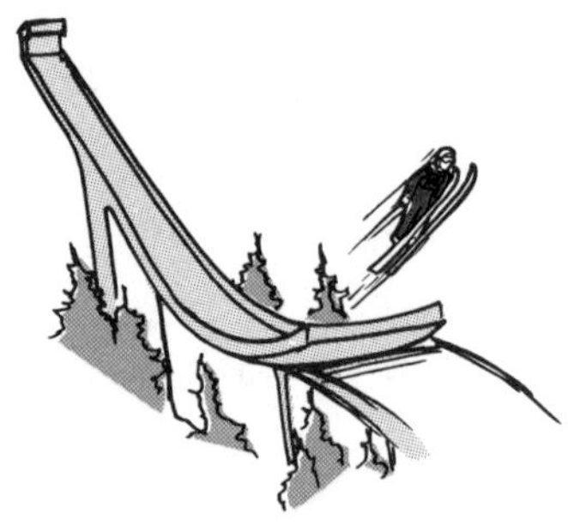

Sound familiar? You have learned **дни недели** *(dnee) (nee-dyel-ee)* (days of week), so now it is time to learn **месяцы года** *(myes-yet-see) (go-dah)* (months of year) **и** all the different kinds of **погоды** *(pah-go-dih)* (weather). **Например,** *(nah-pree-myair)* (for example) you ask about the **погоде** *(pah-go-dyeh)* (weather) **по-русски** *(pah-roos-skee)* (in Russian) just as you would **по-английски** *(pah-ahn-glee-skee)*: **„Какая сегодня погода?“** *(kah-kah-yah) (see-vohd-nyah) (pah-go-dah)* (how is today weather) Practice all the possible answers to this **вопрос** *(vah-prohs)* (question) **и тогда** *(tahg-dah)* (then) write the answers in the blanks below.

(kah-kah-yah) *(see-vohd-nyah)* *(pah-go-dah)*
Какая сегодня погода?

(see-vohd-nyah) (ee-dyoht) (dohzhd)
Сегодня идёт дождь. ______________________
today it is raining

(ee-dyoht) (snyeg)
Сегодня идёт снег. ______________________
it is snowing

(zhar-kah)
Сегодня жарко. Сегодня жарко.
hot

(hoh-lahd-nah)
Сегодня холодно. ______________________
cold

(hah-roh-shah-yah) (pah-go-dah)
Сегодня хорошая погода. ______________________
good weather

(plah-hah-yah) (pah-go-dah)
Сегодня плохая погода. ______________________
bad weather

(too-mahn)
Сегодня туман. ______________________
fog

(vyet-ren-ah)
Сегодня ветрено. ______________________
windy

(tyep-loh)
Сегодня тепло. ______________________
warm

Теперь, *(tyep-yair)* (now) practice **слова** on the next **странице** *(strah-neet-seh)* **и тогда** *(tahg-dah)* (then) fill in the blanks **с** *(suh)* the names **месяцев** *(myes-yet-sev)* (of months) **и** the appropriate weather reports.

- ☐ **газ** *(gahz)*. . . . . natural gas ______________
- ☐ **газета** *(gah-zyet-ah)*. . . . . gazette, newspaper ______________
- ☐ **—газетчик** *(gah-zyet-cheek)*. . . . . newspaper man **Г** ______________
- ☐ **галерея** *(gahl-yair-eh-yah)*. . . . . gallery ______________
- ☐ **генерал** *(gee-nee-rahl)*. general ______________

(vuh) (yahn-var-yeh) **в январе** ______ (in January)	(vuh) (ee-dyoht) (snyeg) **В январе идёт снег.** ______ (in January it snows)
(fyev-rahl-yeh) **в феврале** ______ (February)	**В феврале идёт снег.** ______ (February it snows)
(mart-yeh) **в марте** ______ (March)	(dohzhd) **В марте идёт дождь.** ______ (it rains)
(ahp-ryel-yeh) **в апреле** ______ (April)	(dohzhd) **В апреле идёт дождь.** ______
(mah-yeh) **в мае** В мае (May)	(vyet-ren-ah) **В мае ветрено.** ______ (windy)
(ee-yoon-yeh) **в июне** ______ (June)	(vyet-ren-ah) **В июне ветрено.** ______ (June)
(vuh) (ee-yool-yeh) **в июле** ______ (July)	(zhar-kah) **В июле жарко.** В июле жарко. (hot)
(ahv-goost-yeh) **в августе** ______ (August)	**В августе жарко.** ______ (hot)
(syen-tyah-bree-yeh) **в сентябре** ______ (September)	(hah-roh-shah-yah) (pah-go-dah) **В сентябре хорошая погода.** ______ (September good weather)
(ahk-tyah-bree-yeh) **в октябре** ______ (October)	(too-mahn) **В октябре туман.** ______ (fog)
(nah-yah-bree-yeh) **в ноябре** ______ (November)	(hoh-lahd-nah) **В ноябре холодно.** ______ (cold)
(dee-kah-bree-yeh) **в декабре** ______ (December)	(plah-hah-yah) **В декабре плохая погода.** ______ (bad)

(tyep-yair) (vah-proh-sih) (kar-teen-kahk)
Теперь, answer the following **вопросы** (questions) based on **картинках** (pictures) to the right.

(kah-kah-yah) (pah-go-dah) (vuh) (fyev-rahl-yeh)
Какая погода в феврале? ______
how is / February

(ahp-ryel-yeh)
Какая погода в апреле? В апреле идёт дождь.
April

(mah-yeh)
Какая погода в мае? ______
May

(ahv-goost-yeh)
Какая погода в августе? ______

(see-vohd-nyah) (hah-roh-shah-yah) (plah-hah-yah)
Какая погода сегодня? Хорошая или плохая? ______
bad

Г

- ☐ **Греция** *(gret-see-yah)* . . . . Greece ______
  —where they speak **по-гречески** *(pah-greh-chee-skee)*
- ☐ **география** *(gee-ah-grah-fee-yah)* . . . . geography ______
- ☐ **геология** *(gee-ah-loh-gee-yah)* . . . . geology ______
- ☐ **—геолог** *(gee-ah-lohg)* . . . . geologist ______

Теперь for the seasons of **года...** (year)

(zee-moy) **зимой** in winter	*(lyet-ahm)* **летом** in summer	*(oh-syen-yoo)* **осенью** in autumn	*(vees-noy)* **весной** in spring

(zee-moy) (hoh-lahd-nah) **Зимой холодно.**	*(lyet-ahm) (zhar-kah)* **Летом жарко.**	*(oh-syen-yoo) (vyet-ren-ah)* **Осенью ветрено.** (windy)	*(vees-noy) (ee-dyoht)* **Весной идёт дождь.**

At this point, it is *(hah-roh-shah-yah)* **хорошая** (good) idea to familiarize yourself *(suh)* **с** *(roos-skee-mee)* **русскими** *(tyem-pee-rah-too-rah-mee)* **температурами.** (temperatures)

Read the typical weather forecasts below **и** carefully study the thermometer because *(tyem-pee-rah-too-rih)* **температуры** (temperatures) *(vuh)* **в** *(sah-vyet-skahm)* **Советском** *(sah-yoo-zeh)* **Союзе** are calculated on the basis of Celsius (not Fahrenheit).

(fah-ren-gate) **фаренгейт** Fahrenheit	*(tsel-see)* **цельсий** Celsius	
212° F	100° C	*(tyem-pee-rah-too-rah)(kee-pyeh-nee-yah)* **температура кипения** boiling point
98.6° F	37° C	**температура** *(nar-mahl-nah-yah)* **нормальная** normal
68° F	20° C	
32° F	0° C	**температура** *(zah-myair-zah-nee-yah)* **замерзания** freezing point
0° F	-17.8° C	
-10° F	-23.3° C	

(tyem-pee-rah-too-rah) **Температура в** *(lyen-een-grahd-yeh)* **Ленинграде:** (Leningrad)

(hoh-lahd-nah) **холодно.** (cold)

температура: (temperature) **пять** (five) *(grah-doo-sahv)* **градусов** (degrees)

Температура в *(mahsk-vyeh)* **Москве:** (Moscow)

(zhar-kah) **жарко** (hot)

температура: *(dvahd-tset)* **двадцать** (twenty) **градусов**

- ☐ **геометрия** *(gee-ah-myet-ree-yah)*........... geometry
- ☐ **Гибралтар** *(gee-brahl-tar)*................ Gibraltar
- ☐ **гид** *(geed)*............................. guide
- ☐ **гимнастика** *(geem-nah-stee-kah)*........... gymnastics
- ☐ **гитара** *(gee-tah-rah)*...................... guitar

Г ____________________

(syem-yah) Семья: *(koohk-nyah)* Кухня, *(tsair-kahv)* Церковь, и *(dyet-ee)* Дети
family, kitchen, church, children

One of the charming aspects *(vuh)* **в** *(sah-vyet-skahm)* **Советском** *(sah-yoo-zeh)* **Союзе** concerns names. A father's first name becomes the middle name for both his sons **и** daughters. Daughters add *(ohv-nah)* **-овна,** *(yev-nah)* **-евна,** or *(eech-nah)* **-ична** to the father's first name **и** sons add *(ah-veech)* **-ович** *(yev-eech)* **-евич** or *(eech)* **-ич.** Both the given first name **и** the father's name (patronymic) are constantly used *(pah-roos-skee)* **по-русски.** Mastering these will help you master the language. Study *(kar-teen-kee)* **картинки** (pictures) below **и** *(tahg-dah)* **тогда** (then) practice these new names on the next *(strah-neet-seh)* **странице.**

Семья

(ahn-nah) **Анна** *(pee-trohv-nah)* **Петровна** — *(nee-kah-lie)* **Николай** *(bah-ree-sah-veech)* **Борисович**

(gleb) **Глеб** *(vlah-dee-mee-rah-veech)* **Владимирович** — *(mah-ree-yah)* **Мария** *(nee-kah-lah-yev-nah)* **Николаевна**

(ee-vahn) **Иван** *(nee-kah-lah-yev-eech)* **Николаевич** — *(nee-nah)* **Нина** *(ah-lek-say-yev-nah)* **Алексеевна**

(mee-hah-eel) **Михаил** *(gleb-ah-veech)* **Глебович** — *(tah-mah-rah)* **Тамара** **Глебовна**

(oh-leg) **Олег** *(ee-vahn-ah-veech)* **Иванович** — *(zee-nah-ee-dah)* **Зинаида** **Ивановна**

- ☐ **грамм** *(grahm)*. . . . . gram
- ☐ **гранит** *(grah-neet)*. . . . . granite
- ☐ **группа** *(groop-pah)*. . . . . group
- ☐ **ГУМ** *(goom)*. . . . . department store in Moscow
- ☐ **гусь** *(goose)*. . . . . goose

Г

(rohd-stveen-nee-kee)
родственники
relatives

(dyed)
дед ______________________
grandfather

(bah-boosh-kah)
бабушка ______________________
grandmother

(dyet-ee)
дети
children

(sin)
сын сын, сын, сын, сын
son

(dohch)
дочь ______________________
daughter

(rah-dee-tee-lee)
родители
parents

(aht-yets)
отец ______________________
father

(maht)
мать ______________________
mother

(rohd-stveen-nee-kee)
родственники
relatives

(dyah-dyah)
дядя ______________________
uncle

(tyoh-tyah)
тётя ______________________
aunt

(sin) *(dohch)* *(braht)* *(see-strah)*
Сын и дочь = брат и сестра!
brother sister

Let's learn how to identify *(syem-yah)* **семья** (family) by name. Study the following examples carefully.

(kahk) **Как** (how) *(zah-voot)* **зовут** (is called) *(aht-tsah)* **отца?** (father)

(aht-tsah) **Отца** (father) *(zah-voot)* **зовут** (is called) ______________________.

(kahk) **Как** (how) *(zah-voot)* **зовут** (is called) *(maht)* **мать?** (mother)

Мать (mother) *(zah-voot)* **зовут** (is called) Нина Алексеевна.

(kahk) **Как** (how) *(zah-voot)* **зовут** (is called) *(sin-ah)* **сына?** (son)

Сына зовут (is called) ______________________

(kahk) **Как** *(zah-voot)* **зовут** *(dohch)* **дочь?** (daughter)

Дочь зовут (is called) ______________________

Как (how) *(zah-voot)* **зовут** (is called) *(dyed-ah)* **деда?** (grandfather)

Деда зовут ______________________

Как зовут *(bah-boosh-koo)* **бабушку?** (grandmother)

Бабушку зовут ______________________

Как (how) *(vahs)* **вас** *(zah-voot)* **зовут?** (are you called)

(men-yah) **Меня** *(zah-voot)* **зовут** (I am called) ______________________ (your name)

Д

- ☐ **дама** *(dah-mah)*........................ dame, lady, woman
- ☐ **дата** *(dah-tah)*........................ date
- ☐ **Дания** *(dah-nee-yah)*.................... Denmark
- ☐ —where they speak **по-датски** *(pah-daht-skee)*
- ☐ **делегат** *(dyel-eh-gaht)*.................. delegate

(koohk-nyah)
Кухня
kitchen

Study all these *(kar-teen-kee)* **картинки** (pictures) **и** then practice saying *(ee)* **и** writing out **слова.**

Это *(koohk-nyah)* **кухня.** (kitchen)

(hah-lah-deel-neek)
холодильник
refrigerator

____

(plee-tah)
плита
stove

____

(vee-noh)
вино
wine

____

(pee-vah)
пиво
beer

____

(mah-lah-koh)
молоко
milk

____

(mah-slah)
масло
butter

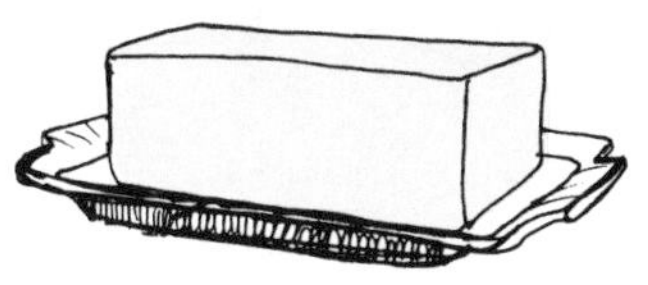

масло

Answer these *(vah-proh-sih)* **вопросы** (questions) aloud.

(gdyeh) **Где** *(pee-vah)* **пиво?** (beer) . . . . **Пиво в** *(vuh)(hah-lah-deel-neek-yeh)* **холодильнике.** (refrigerator)

Где *(mah-lah-koh)* **молоко?** (milk) — **Где** *(vee-noh)* **вино?** (wine) — **Где** *(bah-nahn)* **банан?**

Где *(mah-slah)* **масло?** (butter) — **Где** *(sah-laht)* **салат?** (salad) — **Где** *(ah-bree-koh-sih)* **абрикосы?** (apricots)

Д

- ☐ **демонстрация** *(dyeh-mahn-straht-see-yah)*. . . demonstration ______________________
- ☐ **джаз** *(dzhahz)*. . . . . jazz ______________________
- ☐ **джин** *(dzheen)*. . . . . gin ______________________
- ☐ **диагноз** *(dee-ahg-nohz)*. diagnosis ______________________
- ☐ **диаграмма** *(dee-ah-grahm-mah)*. . . . . diagram, blueprint ______________________

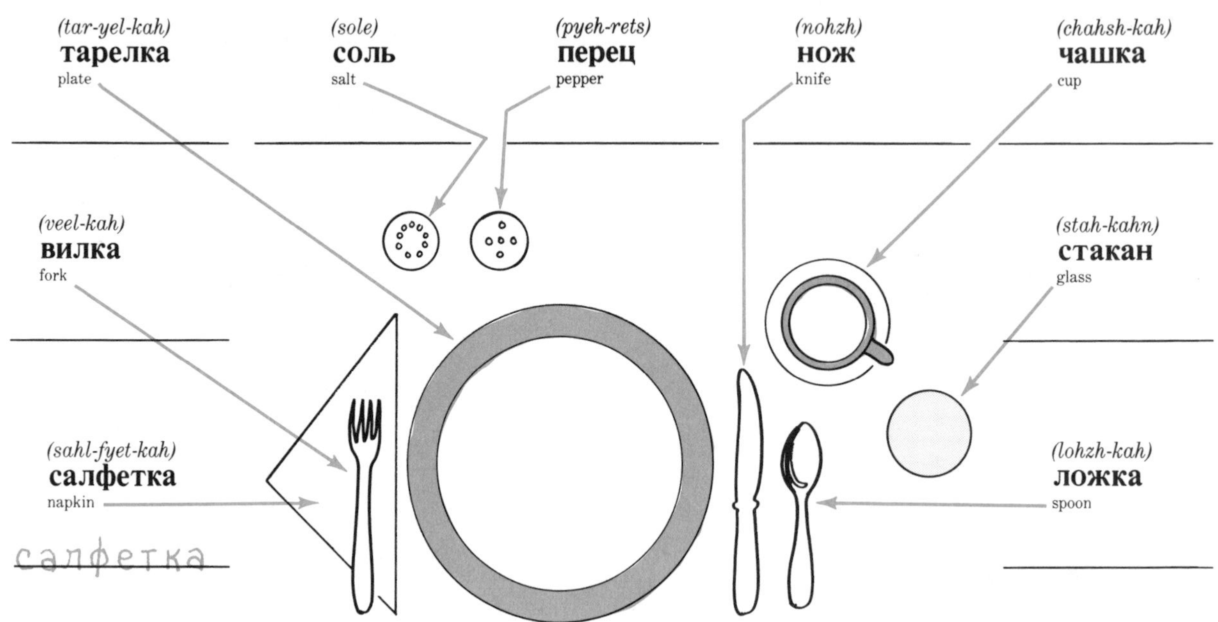

И more…

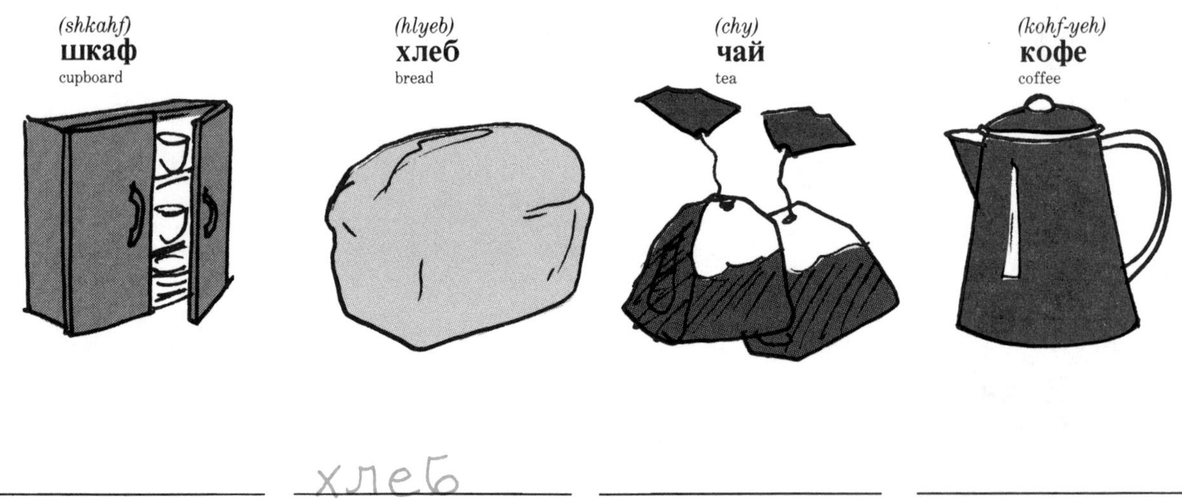

Где *(gdyeh)* **хлеб?** *(hlyeb)* bread **Хлеб в** *(vuh)* in **холодильнике.** *(hah-lah-deel-neek-yeh)* refrigerator **Где чай?** *(chy)* tea **Где кофе?** *(kohf-yeh)* coffee **Теперь** open your **книгу** *(kuh-nee-goo)* book **на** *(nah)* to **странице** *(strah-neet-seh)* **с** *(suh)* the labels **и** remove the next **девятнадцать** *(div-yet-nod-tset)* labels **и** proceed to label all these things in your **кухне.** *(koohk-nyeh)* kitchen Do not forget to use every opportunity to say these **слова** out loud. **Это очень** *(oh-chen)* very **важно.** *(vahzh-nah)* important

Д

- ☐ **диван** *(dee-vahn)*.......................... divan, couch
- ☐ **дизель** *(dee-zyel)*.......................... diesel
- ☐ **диплом** *(dee-plohm)*.......................... diploma
- ☐ **дипломат** *(dee-plah-maht)*.......................... diplomat
- ☐ **директор** *(dee-rek-tar)*.......................... director

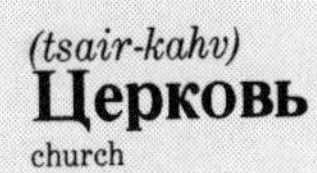

(tsair-kahv)
Церковь
church

(vuh) (sah-vyet-skahm) (sah-yoo-zeh) **В Советском Союзе,** there is a wide variety of *(ree-lee-gee-ee)* **религий** (religions). A person's *(ree-lee-gee-yah)* **религия** (religion) is usually one of the following.

1. *(prah-vah-slahv-nah-yah)* **православная** (Orthodox woman) / *(prah-vah-slahv-nee)* **православный** (Orthodox man) ____________
2. *(yev-ray-kah)* **еврейка** (Jewish woman) / *(yev-ray)* **еврей** (Jewish man) ____________
3. *(kah-tah-leech-kah)* **католичка** (Catholic woman) / *(kah-toh-leek)* **католик** (Catholic man) ____________
4. *(moo-sool-mahn-kah)* **мусульманка** (Moslem woman) / *(moo-sool-mah-neen)* **мусульманин** (Moslem man) ____________

(tsair-kahv) **Церковь** (church) *(vuh)* **в Москве.**

Это (is it) *(prah-vah-slahv-nah-yah)* **православная** (Orthodox) *(tsair-kahv)* **церковь?**

Это (is it) *(no-vah-yah)* **новая** (new) **церковь?** *(nyet)* **Нет,** (no) *(stah-rah-yah)* **старая.** (old)

You will see *(mnoh-gah)* **много** (many) *(krah-see-vihk)* **красивых** (pretty) *(tsair-kvay)* **церквей** (churches) like this during your holiday *(vuh)* **в** *(es-es-es-air)* **СССР.** (U.S.S.R.)

Теперь, let's learn how to say "I am" *(pah-roos-skee)* **по-русски:**

I am = *(yah)* **я** ____________

Practice saying *(yah)* **„я“** *(suh)* **с** the following **словами. Теперь** write each sentence for more practice. Make sure you understand what you are saying.

Я (I am) *(kah-tah-leech-kah)* **католичка.** ____________

Я *(prah-vah-slahv-nah-yah)* **православная.** ____________

Я *(yev-ray)* **еврей.** ____________

Я *(ah-myeh-ree-kah-nyets)* **американец.** (American) ____________

Я *(vuh)* **в** *(es-es-es-air)* **СССР.** ____________

Я *(kah-nahd-yets)* **канадец.** (Canadian) Я каналец.

Я *(ahv-strah-lee-yets)* **австралиец.** (Australian) ____________

Я *(ahn-glee-chahn-kah)* **англичанка.** (English) ____________

Д

- ☐ **дискуссия** *(dee-skoos-see-yah)* .... discussion ____________
- ☐ **доктор** *(dohk-tar)* .... doctor ____________
- ☐ **документ** *(dah-koo-myent)* .... document ____________
- ☐ **доллар** *(dohl-lar)* .... dollar ____________
- ☐ **драма** *(drah-mah)* .... drama ____________

Я *(yah)* I am **в** *(vuh)* in **церкви.** *(tsair-kvee)* church ________________

Я в кухне. *(yah) (koohk-nyeh)* ________________

Я мусульманин. *(moo-sool-mah-neen)* ________________

Я еврейка. *(yev-ray-kah)* ________________

Я в гостинице. *(gah-stee-neet-seh)* hotel ________________

Я в ресторане. *(res-tah-rahn-yeh)* restaurant ________________

Я голоден. *(go-lah-dyen)* hungry ________________

Я хочу пить. *(hah-choo) (peet)* thirsty ________________

Теперь identify all **людей** *(lood-yeh)* people **на картинке** *(kar-teen-kyeh)* below by writing **правильное** *(prah-veel-nah-yeh)* correct **русское** *(roos-skah-yeh)* **слово** for each person on the line with the corresponding number **под** *(pohd)* under **картинкой.** *(kar-teen-koy)* picture

1. ________________
2. ________________
3. ________________
4. ________________
5. ________________
6. ________________
7. Михаил Глебович
8. ________________
9. ________________
10. ________________

Are **вы** ready for a Russian rhyme?

Это *(et-tah)* **Коля** *(kohl-yah)* Kolya **с братом** (his) brother **Васей.** Vasya **Коля в школе** *(shkohl-yeh)* school **в пятом** *(pyah-tahm)* fifth **классе.** *(klas-seh)* class

Ж

- ☐ **жакет** *(zhah-kyet)*........................ jacket (woman's) ________________
- ☐ **жасмин** *(zhahs-meen)*........................ jasmine ________________
- ☐ **желе** *(zhyel-yeh)*........................ jelly ________________
- ☐ **журнал** *(zhoor-nahl)*........................ journal, magazine ________________
- ☐ **—журналист** *(zhoor-nah-leest)*........................ journalist ________________

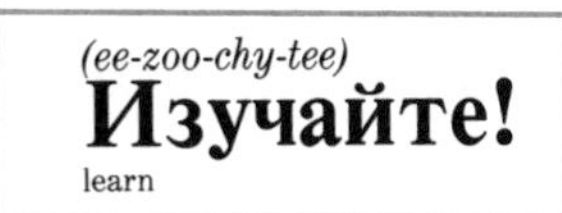

Step 11

You have already used the verbs **у меня есть** (oo)(men-yah) (yest) I have, **я** (yah) I **хочу** (hah-choo) would like and **идёт** (ee-dyoht) goes. Although you might be able to get by with these verbs, let's assume you want to do better. First a quick review.

How do you say "I" **по-русски?** (pah-roos-skee) ________ How do you say "we" **по-русски?** ________

Compare these **два** (dvah) two charts **очень** (oh-chen) very carefully **и** learn these **шесть слов** (shest) six (slohv) on the right.

I	=	**я** (yah)
he	=	**он** (ohn)
she	=	**она** (ah-nah)

we	=	**мы** (mwee)
you	=	**вы** (vwee)
they	=	**они** (ah-nee)

Not too hard, is it? **Теперь** draw lines between the matching English **и русские** (roos-skee-yeh) **слова** (slah-vah) below to see if you can keep these **слова** straight in your mind.

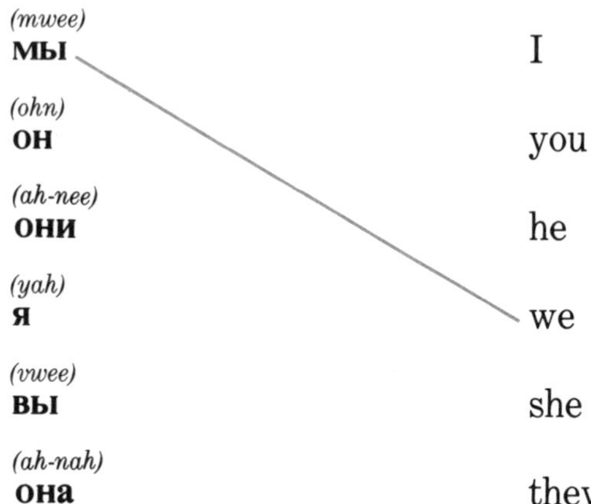

Теперь (tyep-yair) close **книгу** (kuh-nee-goo) **и** (ee) write out both columns of the above practice on **бумаге** (boo-mahg-yeh) paper. How did **вы** (vwee) you do? **Хорошо** (hah-rah-shoh) good **или** or **плохо?** (ploh-hah) bad **Хорошо** (hah-rah-shoh) good **или нет?** (nyet) not **Теперь** that **вы** (vwee) you know these **слова**, **вы** (vwee) you can say almost anything **по-русски** with one basic formula: the "plug-in" formula. With this formula, **вы** (vwee) you can correctly use any **слова вы** wish.

- ☐ **зона** *(zoh-nah)*.......................... zone ________
- ☐ **зоопарк** *(zah-ah-park)*.................... zoo ________
- ☐ **импортный** *(eem-part-nee)*................ imported ________
- ☐ **Индия** *(een-dee-yah)*...................... India ________
- ☐ **индустриальный** *(een-doo-stree-ahl-nee)*..... industrial ________

З

To demonstrate, let's take **шесть** (shest) [six] basic **и** practical verbs **и** see how the "plug-in" formula works. Write the verbs in the blanks below after **вы** have practiced saying them out loud many times.

(zah-kah-zih-vaht) **заказывать** = to order/reserve	*(pah-koo-paht)* **покупать** = to buy	*(ee-zoo-chaht)* **изучать** = to learn
заказывать	__________	__________
(pahv-tar-yaht) **повторять** = to repeat	*(pah-nee-maht)* **понимать** = to understand	*(gah-vah-reet)* **говорить** = to speak
__________	__________	__________

Study the following patterns carefully.

(yah) **я**

(zah-kah-zih-vah-yoo) **заказываю**	=	I *order*
(pah-koo-pah-yoo) **покупаю**	=	I *buy*
(ee-zoo-chah-yoo) **изучаю**	=	I *learn*
(pahv-tar-yah-yoo) **повторяю**	=	I *repeat*
(pah-nee-mah-yoo) **понимаю**	=	I *understand*
(gah-vah-ryoo) **говорю**	=	I *speak*

(ohn) **он** / *(ah-nah)* **она**

(zah-kah-zih-vah-yet) **заказывает**	=	he/she *orders*
(pah-koo-pah-yet) **покупает**	=	he/she *buys*
(ee-zoo-chah-yet) **изучает**	=	he/she *learns*
(pahv-tar-yah-yet) **повторяет**	=	he/she *repeats*
(pah-nee-mah-yet) **понимает**	=	he/she *understands*
(gah-vah-reet) **говорит**	=	he/she *speaks*

Note:
- With all these verbs, the first thing you do is drop the final „**ть**" from the basic verb form.
- With **я,** you add **ю** (yoo) or **у** (oo) to the basic verb form. This is basically the sound "*oo.*"
- With **он** or **она,** you add the sound "*yet*" **(ет)** to the basic verb form or the sound "*eet*" **(ит).**

Some verbs just will not conform to the pattern! But don't worry. Speak slowly **и** clearly, **и** you will be perfectly understood whether you say **изучаю** (ee-zoo-chah-yoo) or **изучает** (ee-zoo-chah-yet). **Русские** [Russians] will be delighted that you have taken the time to learn their language.

- ☐ **инженер** *(een-zhyen-yair)*.................. engineer __________
- ☐ **инспектор** *(een-spyek-tar)*.................. inspector __________
- ☐ **институт** *(een-stee-toot)*.................. institute __________
- ☐ **инструктор** *(een-strook-tar)*.................. instructor __________
- ☐ **инструмент** *(een-stroo-myent)*.............. instrument __________

И

Here's your pattern for *(mwee)* **мы** (we). Add the sound *"yem"* **(ем)** or *"eem"* **(им)**.

мы	*(zah-kah-zih-vah-yem)* **заказываем**	=	we *order*	**мы**	*(pahv-tar-yah-yem)* **повторяем**	=	we *repeat*
	(pah-koo-pah-yem) **покупаем**	=	we *buy*		*(pah-nee-mah-yem)* **понимаем**	=	we *understand*
	(ee-zoo-chah-yem) **изучаем**	=	we *learn*		*(gah-vah-reem)* **говорим**	=	we *speak*

Here's your pattern for *(vwee)* **вы**. Add the sound *"yet-yeh"* **(ете)** or *"eet-yeh"* **(ите)**.

вы	*(zah-kah-zih-vah-yet-yeh)* **заказываете**	=	you *order*	**вы**	*(pahv-tar-yah-yet-yeh)* **повторяете**	=	you *repeat*
	(pah-koo-pah-yet-yeh) **покупаете**	=	you *buy*		*(pah-nee-mah-yet-yeh)* **понимаете**	=	you *understand*
	(ee-zoo-chah-yet-yeh) **изучаете**	=	you *learn*		*(gah-vah-reet-yeh)* **говорите**	=	you *speak*

Finally, here's your pattern for *(ah-nee)* **они** (they), which calls for the sound *"yoot"* **(ют)** or sometimes *"yaht"* **(ят)**.

они	*(zah-kah-zih-vah-yoot)* **заказывают**	=	they *order*	**они**	*(pahv-tar-yah-yoot)* **повторяют**	=	they *repeat*
	(pah-koo-pah-yoot) **покупают**	=	they *buy*		*(pah-nee-mah-yoot)* **понимают**	=	they *understand*
	(ee-zoo-chah-yoot) **изучают**	=	they *learn*		*(gah-var-yaht)* **говорят**	=	they *speak*

Теперь it is your turn to practice *(shtoh)* **что** (what) *(vwee)* **вы** have learned. Fill in the following blanks **с** the correct form of the verb. Each time **вы** write out the sentence, be sure to say it aloud.

(zah-kah-zih-vaht)
заказывать
to order/reserve

(yah) **Я** __________ *(stah-kahn)* **стакан** (glass) *(vah-dih)* **воды.** (water)

Он / Она __________ **стакан** *(vee-nah)* **вина.**

(mwee) **Мы** __________ **стакан** *(mah-lah-kah)* **молока.**

(vwee) **Вы** заказываете *(chahsh-koo)* **чашку** (cup) *(chah-yah)* **чая.** (tea)

(ah-nee) **Они** __________ **чашку** *(kohf-yeh)* **кофе.**

(pah-koo-paht)
покупать
to buy

Я __________ *(kuh-nee-goo)* **книгу.** (book)

Он / Она покупает **салат.**

Мы __________ *(lahm-poo)* **лампу.**

Вы __________ *(chah-sih)* **часы.** (clock)

Они __________ *(beel-yet)* **билет.** (ticket)

- ☐ **интеллигент** *(een-tyel-lee-gyent)*. . . . . intellectual
- ☐ **интервю** *(een-tyair-view)*. . . . . interview
- ☐ **интерес** *(een-tyair-yes)*. . . . . interest
- ☐ **интернациональный** *(een-tyair-naht-see-ah-nahl-nee)* international
- ☐ **информация** *(een-far-maht-see-yah)*. . . . . information

И __________

(ee-zoo-chaht)
изучать
to learn

Я	______	*(roos-skee)* **русский.** Russian
Он / Она	______	**русский.**
Мы	______	*(ahn-glee-skee)* **английский.** English
Вы	изучаете	**английский.**
Они	______	*(nee-myet-skee)* **немецкий.** German

(pahv-tar-yaht)
повторять
to repeat

(yah) **Я**	______	*(sloh-vah)* **слово.**
Он / Она	______	*(aht-vyet-ih)* **ответы.** answers
Мы	повторяем	**ответы.**
Вы	______	*(chee-sloh)* **число.** number
Они	______	*(vah-proh-sih)* **вопросы.** questions

(pah-nee-maht)
понимать
to understand

Я	понимаю	*(pah-ahn-glee-skee)* **по-английски.**
Он / Она	______	**по-русски.**
Мы	______	*(pah-nee-myet-skee)* **по-немецки.** German
Вы	______	*(pah-frahn-tsoo-skee)* **по-французски.** French
Они	______	*(pah-ee-spahn-skee)* **по-испански.** Spanish

(gah-vah-reet)
говорить
to speak/say

Я	______	*(pah-roos-skee)* **по-русски.** Russian
Он / Она	______	**по-английски.**
Мы	______	*(pah-ee-tahl-yahn-skee)* **по-итальянски.** Italian
Вы	______	**по-русски.**
Они	говорят	**по-английски.**

(voht) (shest)
Вот шесть more verbs.
here are six

(yek-haht) **ехать** = to go (by vehicle)

______

(pree-yez-zhaht) **приезжать** = to arrive

______

(vee-dyet) **видеть** = to see

______

(zheet) **жить** = to live/reside

жить

(zhdaht) **ждать** = to wait for

______

(ees-kaht) **искать** = to look for

______

At the back of *(kuh-nee-gee)* **книги, вы** will find *(syem)* **семь** *(strah-neets)* **страниц** (pages) of flash cards to help you learn these *(noh-vih-yeh)* **новые** (new) **слова.** Cut them out; carry them in your briefcase, purse, pocket **или** knapsack; **и** review them whenever *(vwee)* **вы** have a free moment.

- ☐ **Исландия** *(ees-lahn-dee-yah)*............... Iceland
- ☐ **история** *(ees-toh-ree-yah)*................... history
- ☐ **Италия** *(ee-tah-lee-yah)*...................... Italy
- ☐ —where they speak **по-итальянски** *(pah-ee-tahl-yahn-skee)*
- ☐ **кабина** *(kah-bee-nah)*......................... cabin, booth

К

Теперь fill in the following blanks with the correct form of each verb. Be sure to say each sentence out loud until **вы** (you) have it down pat!

(yek-haht)
ехать
to go

Я *еду/* ______ **в** (to) *(vuh) (es-es-es-air)* **СССР.** (U.S.S.R.)

Он / Она *едет/* ______ **в** *(mahsk-voo)* **Москву.**

Мы *едем/* ______ **в** *(lyen-een-grahd)* **Ленинград.** (Leningrad)

Вы *едете/* ______ **в** *(gah-stee-neet-soo)* **гостиницу.** (hotel)

Они *едут/* ______ **в** *(gor-kee)* **Горький.** (Gorki)

(pree-yez-zhaht)
приезжать
to arrive

Я *приезжаю/* ______ *(eez)* **из** (from) *(mahsk-vih)* **Москвы.**

Он / Она *приезжает/* ______ *(eez)* **из** *(kah-nah-dih)* **Канады.** (Canada)

Мы *приезжаем/* ______ *(eez)* **из** *(es-es-es-air)* **СССР.**

Вы *приезжаете/* ______ **из** *(lyen-een-grah-dah)* **Ленинграда.** (Leningrad)

Они *приезжают/* ______ **из** *(ahv-strah-lee-ee)* **Австралии.** (Australia)

(vee-dyet)
видеть
to see

Я *вижу/* ______ *(gah-stee-neet-soo)* **гостиницу.** (hotel)

Он / Она *видит/* ______ *(tahk-see)* **такси.** (taxi)

Мы *видим/* ______ *(res-tah-rahn)* **ресторан.** (restaurant)

Вы *видите/* ______ *(bahnk)* **банк.** (bank)

Они *видят/* ______ *(mahsk-voo)* **Москву.**

(zheet)
жить
to live/reside

Я *живу/* ______ **в** *(vuh) (es-es-es-air)* **СССР.**

Он / Она *живёт/* ______ **в** *(ah-myeh-reek-yeh)* **Америке.** (America)

Мы *живём/* ______ **в** *(kah-nahd-yeh)* **Канаде.** (Canada)

Вы *живёте/* ______ **в** *(ahn-glee-ee)* **Англии.** (England)

Они *живут/* ______ **в** *(ahv-strah-lee-ee)* **Австралии.** (Australia)

(zhdaht)
ждать
to wait for

Я *жду/* ______ *(tahk-see)* **такси.**

Он / Она *ждёт/* ______ *(ahv-toh-boo-sah)* **автобуса.** (bus)

Мы *ждём/* ______ *(ee-vah-nah)* **Ивана.** (Ivan)

Вы *ждёте/* ______ *(ahn-noo)* **Анну.** (Anna)

Они *ждут/* ______ *(myen-yoo)* **меню.** (menu)

(ees-kaht)
искать
to look for

Я *ищу/* ______ *(mar-koo)* **марку.** (stamp)

Он / Она *ищет/* ______ *(tsvet-ih)* **цветы.** (flowers)

Мы *ищем/* ______ *(too-ahl-yet)* **туалет.**

Вы *ищете/* ______ *(dohm)* **дом.** (house)

Они *ищут/* ______ *(kuh-nee-goo)* **книгу.** (book)

☐ **камера** *(kah-myair-ah)*.................... camera
☐ **Канада** *(kah-nah-dah)*.................... Canada
☐ **канал** *(kah-nahl)*.................... canal
☐ **канарейка** *(kah-nah-ray-kah)*.................... canary
☐ **кандидат** *(kahn-dee-daht)*.................... candidate

К ______

Теперь take a deep breath. See if *(vwee)* **вы** can fill in the blanks below. The correct **ответы** are at the bottom of *(et-toy)* **этой** (this) **страницы.**

1. I speak Russian. ______________________
2. He arrives from America. ______________________
3. We learn Russian. ______________________
4. They repeat the number. ______________________
5. She understands English. ______________________
6. We go to the U.S.S.R. Мы едем в СССР.
7. I see the hotel. ______________________
8. I live in Canada. ______________________
9. You buy a book. ______________________
10. He orders a glass of water. ______________________

(dah) **Да,** (yes) it is hard to get used to all those *(noh-vim)* **новым** (new) **словам.** But just keep practicing *(ee)* **и,** before *(vwee)* **вы** know it, **вы** will be using them naturally.

In the following Steps, *(vwee)* **вы** will be introduced to more **и** more verbs **и вы** should drill them in exactly the same way as *(vwee)* **вы** did in this section. Look up *(noh-vih-yeh)* **новые** (new) **слова** in your *(slah-var-yeh)* **словаре** (dictionary) **и** make up your own sentences using the same type of pattern. Try out your *(noh-vih-yeh)* **новые** (new) **слова** for that's how you make them yours to use on your holiday. Remember, the more *(vwee)* **вы** practice *(tyep-yair)* **теперь,** the more enjoyable your trip will be. *(oo-dah-chee)* **Удачи!** (good luck)

Теперь is a perfect time to turn to the back of this *(kuh-nee-gee)* **книги,** clip out your verb flash cards **и** start flashing. Also, don't skip over your free **слова.** Be sure to check them off in the box provided as **вы** *(ee-zoo-chah-yet-yeh)* **изучаете** (learn) each one.

ОТВЕТЫ

1. Я говорю по-русски.
2. Он приезжает из Америки.
3. Мы изучаем русский.
4. Они повторяют число.
5. Она понимает по-английски.
6. Мы едем в СССР.
7. Я вижу гостиницу.
8. Я живу в Канаде.
9. Вы покупаете книгу.
10. Он заказывает стакан воды.

Сколько Времени? (skohl-kah) (vreh-mee-nee) — what time is it

Step 12

Вы (vwee) know как (kahk) to tell дни (dnee, days of) недели (nee-dyel-ee, week) и месяцы (myes-yet-sih, months of) года (go-dah, year), so now let's learn to tell time.

As a traveler в (vuh) СССР, вы need to be able to tell time in order to make резервацию (rez-yair-vaht-see-yoo, reservations) и to catch поезда (poh-yez-dah, trains) и автобусы (buses). Вот (voht, here are) the "basics."

o'clock/hour	=	**час** (chahs) ________
minutes	=	**минут** (mee-noot) ________
half	=	**половина** (pah-lah-vee-nah) ________
minus	=	**без** (byez) без, без, без

What time is it?	=	**Сколько времени?** (vreh-mee-nee)
		Который час? (kah-toh-ree) (chahs)
special endings	=	**-ого** (oh-vah/ah-vah)
		-его (yeh-vah)

Теперь, как are these **слова** used? Study **примеры** (pree-myair-ih, examples) **внизу** (vnee-zoo, below). When **вы** think it through, it really is **не** (nyeh, not) too difficult. Just notice that the pattern changes after the halfway mark.

Пять часов. (chah-sohv, o'clock)

Десять минут шестого. (dyes-yet, ten) (mee-noot, minutes (toward)) (shest-oh-vah, sixth hour) = 5:10

Двадцать минут шестого. (dvahd-tset, twenty) (mee-noot, minutes (toward)) (shest-oh-vah, sixth hour) = 5:20

Половина шестого. (pah-lah-vee-nah, half (of)) (sixth hour) = 5:30

Без двадцати шесть. (byez, minus) (dvahd-tset-ee, twenty (from)) (shest, six) = 5:40

Без десяти шесть. (dyes-yet-ee, ten (from)) = 5:50

Шесть часов. (chah-sohv)

Семь часов. (syem) (chah-sohv)

Двадцать минут восьмого. (dvahd-tset, twenty) (minutes (toward)) (vahs-moh-vah, eighth hour)

Половина восьмого. (pah-lah-vee-nah, half (of)) (vahs-moh-vah, eighth hour)

Без двадцати восемь. (dvahd-tset-ee, twenty (from)) (voh-syem, eight)

Восемь часов. (chah-sohv)

Теперь fill in the blanks according to **время** (vrem-yah, time) indicated on **часах** (chah-sahk, clocks). **Который** (kah-toh-ree) **час?** (chahs)

1. ____________________
2. Семь часов.
3. ____________________
4. ____________________

ОТВЕТЫ

1. Восемь часов.
2. Семь часов.
3. Половина восьмого.
4. Четыре часа.

Вот more time-telling **слова** to add to your vocabulary.

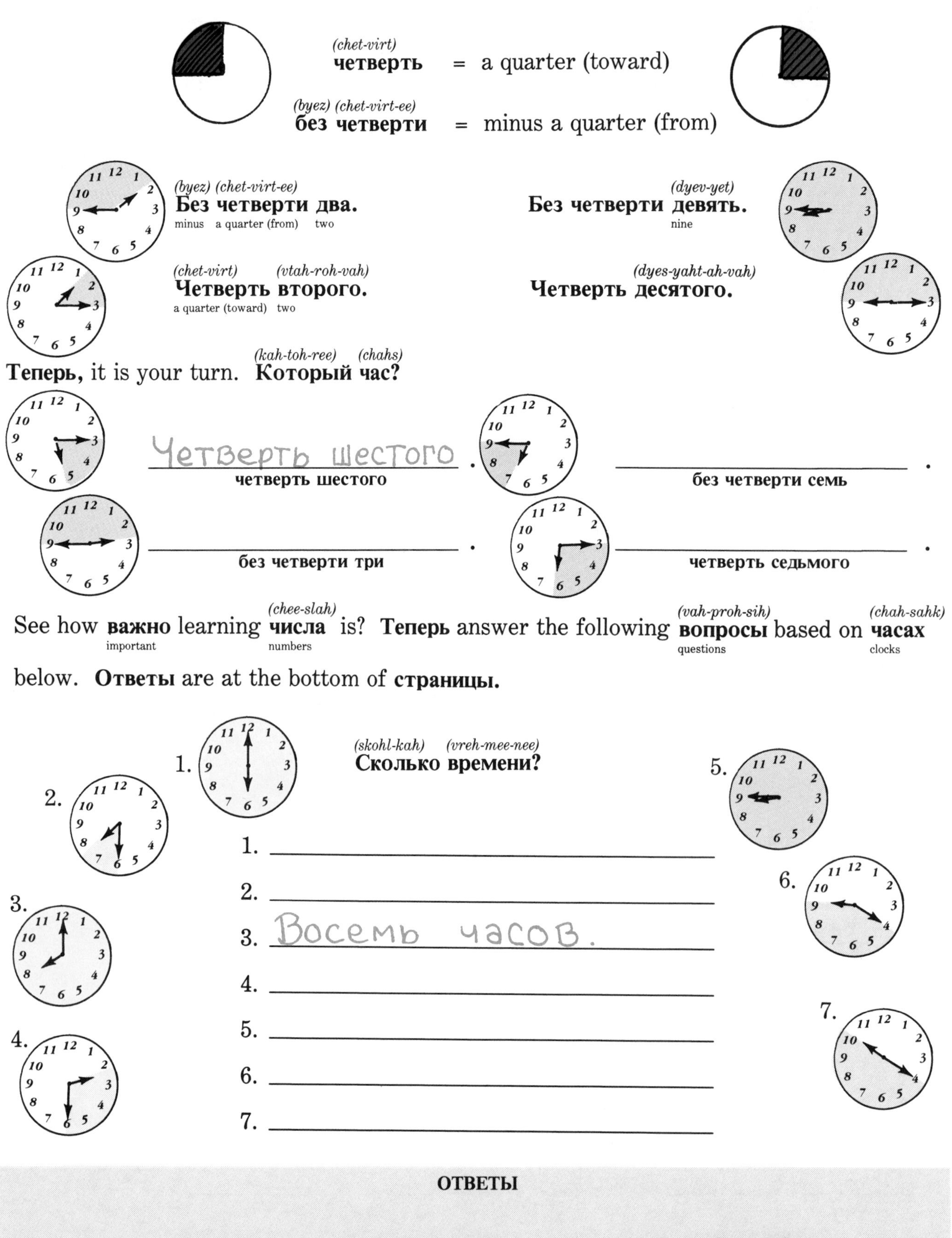

(chet-virt)
четверть = a quarter (toward)

(byez) (chet-virt-ee)
без четверти = minus a quarter (from)

(byez) (chet-virt-ee)
Без четверти два.
minus a quarter (from) two

(dyev-yet)
Без четверти девять.
nine

(chet-virt) (vtah-roh-vah)
Четверть второго.
a quarter (toward) two

(dyes-yaht-ah-vah)
Четверть десятого.

(kah-toh-ree) (chahs)
Теперь, it is your turn. **Который час?**

Четверть шестого.
четверть шестого

_______________________________.
без четверти семь

_______________________________.
без четверти три

_______________________________.
четверть седьмого

See how **важно** *(important)* learning **числа** *(chee-slah)* *(numbers)* is? **Теперь** answer the following **вопросы** *(vah-proh-sih)* *(questions)* based on **часах** *(chah-sahk)* *(clocks)* below. **Ответы** are at the bottom of **страницы.**

(skohl-kah) (vreh-mee-nee)
Сколько времени?

1. _______________________________
2. _______________________________
3. Восемь часов.
4. _______________________________
5. _______________________________
6. _______________________________
7. _______________________________

ОТВЕТЫ

1. Шесть часов.
2. Половина восьмого.
3. Восемь часов.
4. Половина третьего.
5. Без четверти девять.
6. Двадцать минут десятого.
7. Двадцать минут одиннадцатого.

When **вы** *(vwee)* answer a „**когда**" *(kahg-dah)* when question, say „**в**" *(vuh)* at before **вы** *(vwee)* give the time.

поезд 43 6:00

Когда придёт поезд? *(pree-dyoht)* comes *(poh-yezd)* train В шесть часов.

Теперь answer the following **вопросы** *(vah-proh-sih)* questions based on **часах** *(chah-sahk)* clocks **внизу.** *(vnee-zoo)* below. Be sure to practice saying each **вопрос** *(vah-prohs)* question out loud several times.

Когда *(kahg-dah)* **начинается** *(nah-chee-nah-yet-syah)* begins **концерт?** *(kohn-tsairt)* concert ______

Когда начинается *(nah-chee-nah-yet-syah)* begins **фильм?** *(feelm)* film В семь часов

Когда *(kahg-dah)* **придёт** *(pree-dyoht)* comes **автобус?** *(ahv-toh-boos)* bus ______

Когда придёт *(pree-dyoht)* comes **такси?** *(tahk-see)* ______

Когда открывается *(aht-krih-vah-yet-syah)* opens **ресторан?** *(res-tah-rahn)* restaurant ______

Когда закрывается *(zah-krih-vah-yet-syah)* closes **ресторан?** ______

В *(vuh)* at **восемь** *(voh-syem)* **часов утра,** *(oo-trah)* in morning **мы говорим** *(gah-vah-reem)* say **„Доброе** *(doh-brah-yeh)* good **утро,** *(oo-trah)* morning **Мария Николаевна."** *(nee-kah-lah-yev-nah)*

В восемь часов *(chah-sohv)* **вечера,** *(vyeh-cheh-rah)* in evening **мы говорим „Добрый** *(doh-brih)* **вечер,** *(vyeh-cher)* **Анна Петровна."** *(pee-trohv-nah)*

В час *(chahs)* one **дня,** *(den-yah)* in afternoon **мы** *(mwee)* **говорим „Добрый день,** *(dyen)* **Иван Николаевич"** *(nee-kah-lah-yev-eech)*

В десять *(dyes-yet)* ten **часов вечера,** in evening **мы говорим „Спокойной** *(spah-koy-noy)* good **ночи,** *(noh-chee)* night **Зина Ивановна."**

☐ **капитал** *(kah-pee-tahl)*.................... capital (money)
☐ **—капиталист** *(kah-pee-tah-leest)*............ capitalist
☐ **карамель** *(kah-rah-myel)*.................. caramel
☐ **класс** *(klahs)*.......................... class
☐ **классик** *(klahs-seek)*.................... classic

К

Remember:

What time is it?	=	*(kah-toh-ree)* **Который час?** *(vreh-mee-nee)* **Сколько времени?**

When	=	**Когда**

Can *(vwee)* **вы** pronounce **и** understand the following paragraph?

(poh-yezd) *(eez)* *(pree-dyoht)* *(chet-virt)*
Поезд (train) **из** (from) **Москвы придёт в четверть**
(shest-oh-vah) *(dvahd-tset)*
шестого. Теперь двадцать минут шестого.
(ah-pahz-dahl) *(see-vohd-nyah)* *(pree-dyoht)*
Поезд опоздал (late). **Сегодня** (today) **поезд придёт**
(vahs-moh-vah) *(zahv-trah)* *(pree-dyoht)*
в четверть восьмого. Завтра (tomorrow) **поезд придёт**
в четверть шестого.

(voht) **Вот** some more practice exercises. Answer *(vah-proh-sih)* **вопросы** based on the times given below.

(kah-toh-ree) *(chahs)*
Который час?

1. (10:30) ____________________
2. (6:30) Половина седьмого.
3. (6:15) ____________________
4. (10:45) ____________________
5. (5:45) ____________________
6. (7:20) ____________________
7. (3:10) ____________________
8. (4:05) ____________________
9. (8:30) ____________________
10. (4:00) ____________________

К

- ☐ **клоун** *(kloh-oon)*.......................... clown
- ☐ **коллекция** *(kahl-yekt-see-yah)*............. collection
- ☐ **командир** *(kah-mahn-deer)*.................. commander
- ☐ **комедия** *(kah-myeh-dee-yah)*................ comedy
- ☐ **комиссар** *(kah-mees-sar)*.................. commissar

Вот *(voht)* a quick quiz. Fill in the blanks **с** *(suh)* the correct **числами** *(chee-slah-mee)* numbers. **Ответы** *(aht-vyet-ih)* **внизу** *(vnee-zoo)* from.

1. **В** *(vuh)* **минуте** *(mee-noot-yeh)* minute (there are) ________ (?) **секунд** *(see-koond)* seconds.
2. **В часе** *(chahs-yeh)* hour ________ (?) **минут** minutes.
3. **В неделе** *(nee-dyel-yeh)* ___семь___ (?) **дней** *(dnay)* days.
4. **В месяце** *(myes-yets-yeh)* ________ (?) **дней** days.
5. **В году** *(gah-doo)* ________ **месяцев** *(myes-yet-syev)* months.
6. **В году** ________ **недели** *(nee-dyel-ee)* weeks.
7. **В году** ________ (?) **дней.**
8. **В феврале** ________ (?) **дней.**

If **вы** are traveling between large cities **в Советском Союзе, вы** will more than likely take **поезд** *(poh-yezd)* train. **Вы** may want to do as the **русские** *(roos-skee-yeh)* Russians do **и** carry your luggage on the train, rather than check it on board.

Вот *(voht)* a sample **страница из** *(eez)* **русского** *(roos-skah-vah)* **расписания** *(rah-spee-sah-nee-yah)* schedule **поездов** *(pah-yez-dohv)* of trains.

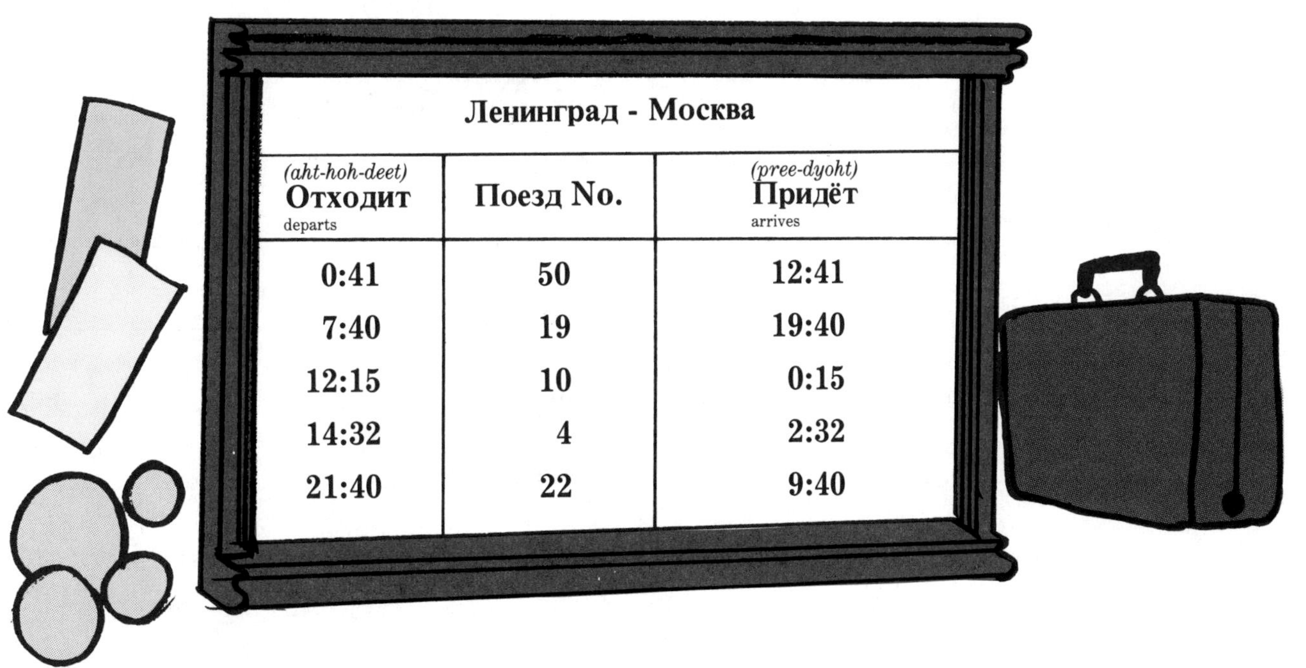

Ленинград - Москва		
Отходит *(aht-hoh-deet)* departs	**Поезд No.**	**Придёт** *(pree-dyoht)* arrives
0:41	50	12:41
7:40	19	19:40
12:15	10	0:15
14:32	4	2:32
21:40	22	9:40

ОТВЕТЫ

1. шестьдесят
2. шестьдесят
3. семь
4. тридцать
5. двенадцать
6. пятьдесят две
7. триста шестьдесят пять
8. двадцать восемь

Вот *(noh-vih-yeh)* **новые** (new) verbs for Step 12.

(gah-vah-reet) **говорить** = to say/speak | *(yest)* **есть** = to eat | *(peet)* **пить** = to drink

________________ есть ________________ ________________

(gah-vah-reet) **говорить** (to say)

Я ________________ *(doh-brah-yeh)* **„доброе утро."**

Он / Она ________________ *(doh-brih)* **„добрый** *(dyen)* **день."**

Мы говорим ________________ *(nyet)* **„нет."** (no)

Вы ________________ *(dah)* **„да."** (yes)

(ah-nee) **Они** ________________ *(spah-see-bah)* **„Спасибо."**

(yest) **есть** (to eat)

(yah) **Я** ем/ ________________ *(soop)* **суп.**

Он / Она ест/ ________________ *(borshch)* **борщ.**

Мы едим/ ________________ *(mnoh-gah)* **много.** (a lot)

Вы едите/ ________________ *(hlyeb)* **хлеб.** (bread)

Они едят/ ________________ *(rib-oo)* **рыбу.** (fish)

(peet) **пить** (to drink)

Я пью/ ________________ **молоко.** (milk)

Он / Она пьёт/ ________________ *(byel-lah-yeh)* **белое** (white) *(vee-noh)* **вино.**

(mwee) **Мы** пьём/ ________________ *(pee-vah)* **пиво.**

Вы пьёте/ ________________ *(stah-kahn)* **стакан** *(vah-dih)* **воды.**

Они пьют/ ________________ *(chy)* **чай.** (tea)

As **вы** have probably noticed, the sound of the Russian letter **„й"** varies greatly. Here are some examples.

(kar-teen-koy) **картинкой** picture	*(yev-ray-kah)* **еврейка** Jewish woman	*(moo-zay)* **музей** museum	*(chy)* **чай** tea	*(syeh-ree)* **серый** blue

К

- ☐ **коммунист** *(kahm-moo-neest)*............ communist ________________
- ☐ **компас** *(kohm-pahs)*............ compass ________________
- ☐ **композитор** *(kahm-pah-zee-tar)*............ composer ________________
- ☐ **конференция** *(kahn-fyair-yent-see-yah)*...... conference ________________
- ☐ **концерт** *(kohn-tsairt)*............ concert ________________

PLUS . . .

Your book includes a number of other innovative features. At the back of the book, you'll find seven pages of flash cards. Cut them out and flip through them at least once a day.

On pages 112 and 113, you'll find a beverage guide and a menu guide. Don't wait until your trip to use them. Clip out the menu guide and use it tonight at the dinner table. And use the beverage guide to practice ordering your favorite drinks.

By using the special features in this book, you will be speaking Russian before you know it.

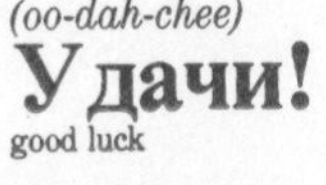

(hlyeb) **хлеб**	*(zhoor-nahl)* **журнал**	*(gryeb-yen)* **гребень**	*(roo-bahsh-kah)* **рубашка**
(chy) **чай**	*(gah-zyet-ah)* **газета**	*(pahl-toh)* **пальто**	*(peed-zhahk)* **пиджак**
(kohf-yeh) **кофе**	*(ahch-kee)* **очки**	*(plahshch)* **плащ**	*(bryoo-kee)* **брюки**
(krah-vaht) **кровать**	*(tee-lee-vee-zar)* **телевизор**	*(zohn-teek)* **зонтик**	*(plaht-yeh)* **платье**
(ah-dee-yah-lah) **одеяло**	*(kar-zee-nah)* **корзина**	*(pyair-chaht-kee)* **перчатки**	*(blooz-kah)* **блузка**
(pah-doosh-kah) **подушка**	*(pahs-port)* **паспорт**	*(shlah-pah)* **шляпа**	*(yoob-kah)* **юбка**
(boo-deel-neek) **будильник**	*(beel-yet)* **билет**	*(sah-poh-gee)* **сапоги**	*(sveet-yair)* **свитер**
(shkahf) **шкаф**	*(cheh-mah-dahn)* **чемодан**	*(too-flee)* **туфли**	*(leef-cheek)* **лифчик**
(oo-mih-vahl-neek) **умывальник**	*(soom-kah)* **сумка**	*(nah-skee)* **носки**	*(kohm-bee-naht-see-yah)* **комбинация**
(doosh) **душ**	*(boo-mahzh-neek)* **бумажник**	*(chool-kee)* **чулки**	*(troo-sih)* **трусы**
(too-ahl-yet) **туалет**	*(dyen-gee)* **деньги**	*(pee-zhah-mah)* **пижама**	*(may-kah)* **майка**
(zyair-kah-lah) **зеркало**	*(foh-toh-ahp-pah-raht)* **фотоаппарат**	*(nohch-nah-yah) (roo-bahsh-kah)* **ночная рубашка**	*(zahn-yah-tah)* **занято**
(pahl-ah-tyent-sah) **полотенца**	*(feelm)* **фильм**	*(koo-pahl-nee) (hah-laht)* **купальный халат**	*(eez-vee-neet-yeh)* **извините**
(kah-rahn-dahsh) **карандаш**	*(koo-pahl-nee) (kohst-yoom)* **купальный костюм**	*(bahsh-mah-kee)* **башмаки**	*(aht-krit-tah)* **открыто**
(rooch-kah) **пучка**	*(sahn-dahl-ee)* **сандалии**	*(kohst-yoom)* **костюм**	*(pree-yaht-nah-vah) (ahp-pyeh-tee-tah)* **приятного аппетита**
(boo-mah-gah) **бумага**	*(mwee-lah)* **мыло**	*(gahl-stook)* **галстук**	*(zah-krit-tah)* **закрыто**
(pees-moh) **письмо**	*(zoob-nah-yah) (shchoht-kah)* **зубная щётка**	*(plah-tohk)* **платок**	*(voh-dah)* **вода**
(aht-krit-kah) **открытка**	*(zoob-nah-yah) (pahs-tah)* **зубная паста**	*(yah) (ah-myeh-ree-kah-nyets)* **Я американец.**	
(mar-kah) **марка**	*(breet-vah)* **бритва**	*(yah) (hah-choo) (ee-zoo-chaht) (roos-skee)* **Я хочу изучать русский.**	
(kuh-nee-gah) **книга**	*(dyeh-zah-doh-rahnt)* **дезодорант**	*(men-yah) (zah-voot)* **Меня зовут ________.**	

STICKY LABELS

This book has over 150 special sticky labels for you to use as you learn new words. When you are introduced to a word, remove the corresponding label from these pages. Be sure to use each of these unique labels by adhering them to a picture, window, lamp, or whatever object it refers to. The sticky labels make learning to speak Russian much more fun and a lot easier than you ever expected.

For example, when you look in the mirror and see the label, say

(zyair-kah-lah)
„зеркало.“ ”

Don’t just say it once, say it again and again.

And once you label the refrigerator, you should never again open that door without saying

(hah-lah-deel-neek)
„холодильник.“

By using the sticky labels, you not only learn new words but friends and family learn along with you!

(kar-tee-nah) картина	(gah-stee-nah-yah) гостиная	(dyev-yet) 9 девять	(doh-brih) (dyen) добрый день
(pah-tah-lohk) потолок	(gah-rahzh) гараж	(dyes-yet) 10 десять	(doh-brih) (vyeh-cher) добрый вечер
(oog-ahl) угол	(pahd-vahl) подвал	(chyor-nee) чёрный	(spah-koy-nih) (noh-chee) спокойной ночи
(ahk-noh) окно	(ahv-tah-mah-beel) автомобиль	(zhyol-tee) жёлтый	(kahk) (dee-lah) Как дела?
(lahm-pah) лампа	(mah-tah-tsee-kul) мотоцикл	(see-nee) синий	(hah-lah-deel-neek) холодильник
(dee-vahn) диван	(sah-bah-kah) собака	(syeh-ree) серый	(plee-tah) плита
(stool) стул	(koht) кот	(kah-reech-nyeh-vwee) коричневый	(vee-noh) вино
(kahv-yor) ковёр	(sahd) сад	(roh-zah-vwee) розовый	(pee-vah) пиво
(stohl) стол	(poach-tah) почта	(byel-lee) белый	(mah-lah-koh) молоко
(dvyair) дверь	(pahch-toh-vee) (yahsh-chik) почтовый ящик	(krahs-nee) красный	(mah-slah) масло
(chah-sih) часы	(tsvet-ih) цветы	(zyel-yoh-nee) зелёный	(tar-yel-kah) тарелка
(zah-nahv-yes) занавес	(zvah-nohk) звонок	(ah-rahn-zheh-vwee) оранжевый	(sole) соль
(styen-ah) стена	(ah-deen) 1 один	(pah-nee-dyel-neek) понедельник	(pyeh-rets) перец
(teh-leh-fohn) телефон	(dvah) 2 два	(vtor-neek) вторник	(nohzh) нож
(dohm) дом	(tree) 3 три	(sree-dah) среда	(chahsh-kah) чашка
(kah-bee-nyet) кабинет	(cheh-tir-ee) 4 четыре	(chet-vyairg) четверг	(veel-kah) вилка
(vahn-nah-yah) ванная	(pyaht) 5 пять	(pyaht-neet-sah) пятница	(stah-kahn) стакан
(koohk-nyah) кухня	(shest) 6 шесть	(soo-boh-tah) суббота	(sahl-fyet-kah) салфетка
(spahl-nyah) спальня	(syem) 7 семь	(voh-skree-syen-yah) воскресенье	(lohzh-kah) ложка
(stah-loh-vah-yah) столовая	(voh-syem) 8 восемь	(doh-brah-yeh) (oo-trah) доброе утро	(shkahf) шкаф

(syev-yair) **Север** - (yoog) **Юг,** (vah-stohk) **Восток** - (zah-pahd) **Запад**
north - south, east - west

If (vwee) **вы** are looking at (kar-too) **карту** (map) **и вы** see the following **слова,** it should (nyeh) **не** (not) be too difficult to figure out (shtoh) **что** (what) (ah-nee) **они** (they) mean. Take an educated guess. **Ответы** (vnee-zoo) **внизу** (below).

(syev-yair-nah-yah) (dah-koh-tah) **Северная Дакота**	(yoozh-nah-yah) **Южная Дакота**	(zah-pahd-nee) (bair-leen) **Западный Берлин**
(ah-myeh-ree-kah) **Северная Америка**	**Южная Америка**	(zah-pahd-nah-yah) (gair-mah-nee-yah) **Западная Германия**
(kah-roh-lee-nah) **Северная Каролина**	**Южная Каролина**	(vah-stohch-nee) **Восточный Берлин**
(kah-reh-yah) **Северная Корея**	(ah-free-kah) **Южная Африка**	(vah-stohch-nah-yah) **Восточная Германия**

Do **вы** recognize **русское** (sloh-vah) **слово** for east in (vlah-dee-vah-stohk) **„Владивосток"?** It means "eastern domain." (vlah-dee-vah-stohk) **Владивосток** is the easternmost seaport in (es-es-es-air) **СССР.** It is also the terminus of the Trans-Siberian Railroad, 5700 miles west of (mahsk-vih) **Москвы** (Moscow).

(syev-yair) **север**	=	the north	____________
(yoog) **юг**	=	the south	____________
(vah-stohk) **восток**	=	the east	ВОСТОК
(zah-pahd) **запад**	=	the west	____________

(syev-yair-nee) **северный**	=	northern	____________
(yoozh-nee) **южный**	=	southern	ЮЖНЫЙ
(vah-stohch-nee) **восточный**	=	eastern	____________
(zah-pahd-nee) **западный**	=	western	____________

But what about more basic (oo-kah-zah-nee-yah) **указания** (directions) such as "left," "right," **и** "straight ahead"? Let's learn these **слова.**

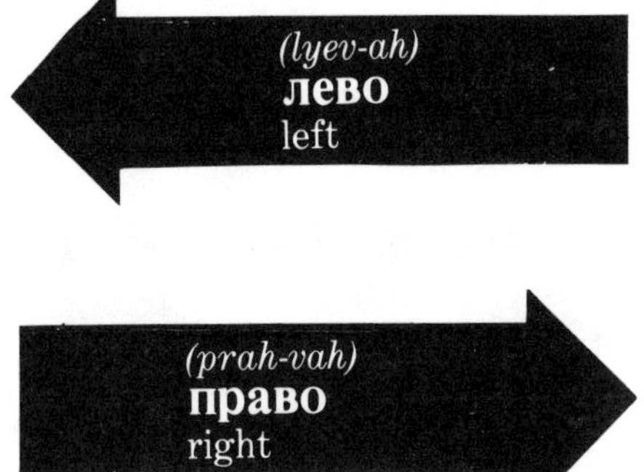

to the left	=	(nah-lyev-ah) **налево**
to the right	=	(nah-prah-vah) **направо**
straight ahead	=	(pryah-mah) **прямо**
on the corner	=	(nah) (oo-gloo) **на углу**

ОТВЕТЫ

North Dakota	South Dakota	West Berlin
North America	South America	West Germany
North Carolina	South Carolina	East Berlin
North Korea	South Africa	East Germany

Just as **по-английски** (in English), these (*cheh-tir-ee*) **четыре** (four) **слова** go a long way.

(*pah-zhahl-oos-tah*) **пожвлуйста**	=	please ______________
(*spah-see-bah*) **спасибо**	=	thank you спасибо, спасибо, спасибо
(*eez-vee-neet-yeh*) **извините**	=	excuse me ______________
(*pah-zhahl-oos-tah*) **пожалуйста**	=	you're welcome ______________

(*voht*) **Вот** (*dvah*) **два** (two) typical (*dee-ah-loh-gah*) **диалога** (dialogues/conversations) (*dil-yah*) **для** (for) someone who is trying to find something.

(*bahr-ees*) **Борис:** (*eez-vee-neet-yeh*) **Извините.** (excuse me) **Где** (*gah-stee-neet-sah*) **гостиница** (hotel) (*lyen-een-grahd*) **Ленинград?** (Leningrad)

(*lyen-ah*) **Лена:** (*prah-ee-dyoht-yeh*) **Пройдёте** (go) (*doh*) **до** (to) (*oo-leet-sih*) **улицы** (street) (*gairt-sen-ah*) **Герцена и** **там** (there) (*nah-prah-vah*) **направо.** (to the right) (*gah-stee-neet-sah*) **Гостиница** (*lyen-een-grahd*) **Ленинград** (*nah*) **на** (on) (*oo-gloo*) **углу.** (corner)

(*ahl-yeg*) **Олег:** (*eez-vee-neet-yeh*) **Извините.** (excuse me) **Где** (*moo-zay*) **Музей** (museum) (*tahl-stoh-vah*) **Толстого.** (Tolstoy)

(*ohl-gah*) **Ольга:** (*prah-ee-dyoht-yeh*) **Пройдёте** (go) (*nah-prah-vah*) **направо;** (to the right) (*pah-tohm*) **потом** (then) (*pryah-mah*) **прямо** (straight ahead) (*doh*) **до** (to) (*oo-leet-sih*) **улицы** (street) (*tahl-stoh-vah*) **Толстого.** (Tolstoy) **Там** (*nah-lyev-ah*) **налево,** (to the left) **и** (*moo-zay*) **музей** (*nah*) **на** (*oo-gloo*) **углу.**

Are **вы** lost? There is no need to be lost if (*vwee*) **вы** have learned the basic direction **слова.** Do not try to memorize these (*dee-ah-loh-gee*) **диалоги** (dialogues/conversations) because **вы** will never be looking for precisely these places. One day, **вы** might need to ask (*oo-kah-zah-nee-yeh*) **указание** (directions) to the (*bahl-shoy*) **Большой** (Bolshoi) (*tee-ah-ter*) **Театр,** (Theater) (*goom*) **ГУМ** (GUM Department Store) or (*kreml*) **Кремль.** (Kremlin) Learn the key direction **слова и** be sure **вы** can find your destination. **Вы** may want to buy a guidebook to start planning what places **вы** would like to visit. Practice asking (*oo-kah-zah-nee-yah*) **указания** (directions) to these special places. What if the person responding to your (*vah-prohs*) **вопрос** answers too quickly for **вы** to understand the entire reply? Look at the reply on the next **странице.** Practice saying…

- ☐ **коньяк** (*kohn-yahk*) .... cognac
- ☐ **корт** (*kort*) .... court (tennis)
- ☐ **кот** (*koht*) .... cat
- ☐ **краб** (*krahb*) .... crab
- ☐ **Куба** (*koo-bah*) .... Cuba

К ______________

	(yah)	(nyeh)	(pah-nee-mah-yoo)	(pah-zhahl-oos-tah)	(pahv-tah-reet-yeh)	(spah-see-bah)
Извините.	**Я**	**не**	**понимаю.**	**Пожалуйста**	**повторите.**	**Спасибо.**
excuse me	I	(do) not	understand	please	repeat	

Теперь say it again **и** again.

Извините. Я не понимаю. Пожалуйста повторите. Спасибо.

Да *(dah)* yes, it is difficult at first but don't give up! **Когда** *(kahg-dah)* when **указания** *(oo-kah-zah-nee-yah)* directions are repeated, **вы** will be able to understand if **вы** have learned the key **слова** for **указания** *(oo-kah-zah-nee-yah)*. Quiz yourself by filling in the blanks below **с** *(suh)* the correct **русскими** *(roos-skee-mee)* **словами** *(slah-vah-mee)* words.

Иван *(ee-vahn)*: **Извините** *(eez-vee-neet-yeh)*. **Где ресторан** *(res-tah-rahn)* restaurant **Садко** *(sahd-koh)*?

Таня: **Пройдёте** go ______________________ straight ahead **и у** *(oo)* at **музея** *(mooz-yah)*, **пройдёте**

направо ______________________ to the right. **У** *(oo)* by **гостиницы** *(gah-stee-neet-sih)* hotel **Космос** *(kohs-mahs)* **пройдёте**

______________________ to the left. **Ресторан Садко** *(sahd-koh)* ______________________ on the corner. **Удачи!** *(oo-dah-chee)* good luck

---

Вот четыре *(cheh-tir-ee)* **новых** *(noh-vihk)* new verbs. **Они** *(ah-nee)* they are different from the patterns **вы** have learned, so pay close attention. **Вы** will probably use these verbs more than any others.

я хочу *(yah)(hah-choo)* = I would like ______________________

мне нужно *(men-yeh) (noozh-nah)* = I need мне нужно ______________________

меня зовут *(men-yah) (zah-voot)* = my name is... ______________________

у меня есть *(oo) (men-yah) (yest)* = I have ______________________

- ☐ **лаборатория** *(lah-bah-rah-toh-ree-yah)*...... laboratory ______________________
- ☐ **лимон** *(lee-mohn)*........................ lemon ______________________
- ☐ **—лимонад** *(lee-mah-nahd)*................ lemonade **Л** ______________________
- ☐ **линия** *(lee-nee-yah)*...................... line ______________________
- ☐ **литература** *(lee-tyair-ah-too-rah)*.......... literature ______________________

As always, say each sentence out loud. Say each **и** every **слово** carefully, pronouncing each **русский** sound as well as **вы** can.

(yah) (hah-choo)
я хочу
I would like

Я хочу/ ____ *(stah-kahn)* **стакан** *(vee-nah)* **вина.**
glass of

Он хочет/ ____ **стакан** *(mah-lah-kah)* **молока.**
Она

(mwee) **Мы** хотим/ ____ **стакан** *(vah-dih)* **воды.**

Вы хотите/ ____ *(chahsh-koo)* **чашку** *(kohf-yeh)* **кофе.**
cup of

Они хотят/ ____ **чашку** *(chah-yah)* **чая.**
they

(men-yah) (zah-voot)
меня зовут…
my name is

(men-yah) **Меня** зовут/ ____ *(nah-tahl-yah)* **Наталья.**

(yee-voh) **Его** ____ **Олег/Ольга.**
(ee-yoh) **Её**

Нас зовут/ ____ *(bahr-ees)* **Борис и** *(lyen-ah)* **Лена.**
our name is

(vahs) **Вас** ____ *(ahn-tohn)* **Антон.**
your name is

(eehk) **Их** зовут/ ____ *(ahn-nah)* **Анна и** *(pyoh-ter)* **Пётр.**
their name is

(men-yeh) (noozh-nah)
мне нужно
I need

(men-yeh) **Мне** нужно/ ____ *(stah-kahn)* **стакан** *(lee-mah-nah-dah)* **лимонада.**

(ee-moo) **Ему** ____ **стакан молока.**
(yay) **Ей**

Нам нужно/ ____ *(chahsh-koo)* **чашку кофе.**

(vahm) **Вам** ____ **чашку** *(chah-yah)* **чая.**

(eem) **Им** нужно/ ____ **чашку** *(kah-kah-oh)* **какао.**
cocoa

(oo) (men-yah) (yest)
у меня есть
I have

(oo) **У** *(men-yah)* **меня** ____ *(pyaht)* **пять** *(kah-pyeh-eek)* **копеек.**

У *(nyeh-voh)* **него** есть/ ____ *(shest)* **шесть** *(roo-blay)* **рублей.**
У *(nyeh-yoh)* **неё**

У нас ____ *(dyes-yet)* **десять рублей.**

У *(vahs)* **вас** есть/ ____ *(dveh)* **две** *(kah-pay-kee)* **копейки.**

У *(neehk)* **них** ____ *(tree)* **три** *(roob-lyah)* **рубля.**

(tyep-yair) **Теперь** see if **вы** can translate the following thoughts **на русский.** *(aht-vyet-ih)* **Ответы** *(vnee-zoo)* **внизу.**
below

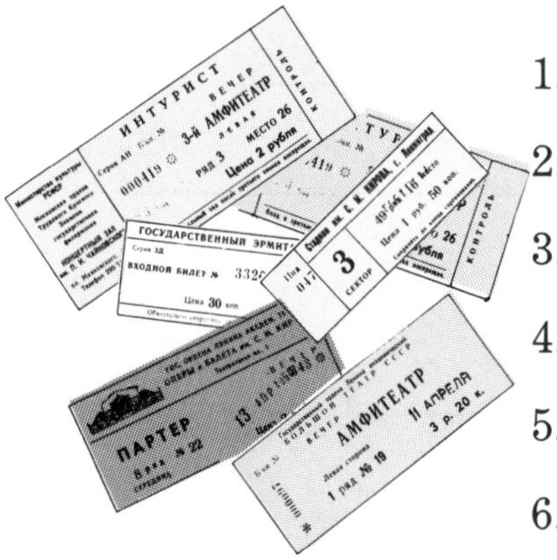

1. My name is …. ____
2. We would like a cup of coffee. ____
3. I have six rubles. У меня есть шесть рублей.
4. We need to buy a glass of lemonade. ____
5. I need a cup of tea. ____
6. We have five rubles. ____

ОТВЕТЫ

1. Мень зовут…
2. Мы хотим чашку кофе.
3. У меня есть шесть рублей.
4. Нам нужно купить стакан лимонада.
5. Мне нужно чашку чая.
6. У нас есть пять рублей.

(nah-vyair-hoo) **Наверху** - *(vnee-zoo)* **Внизу**
upstairs - downstairs/below

Before **вы** begin Step 14, review Step 8. *(tyep-yair)* **Теперь** let's learn *(bohl-shee)* **больше** (more) **слов.**

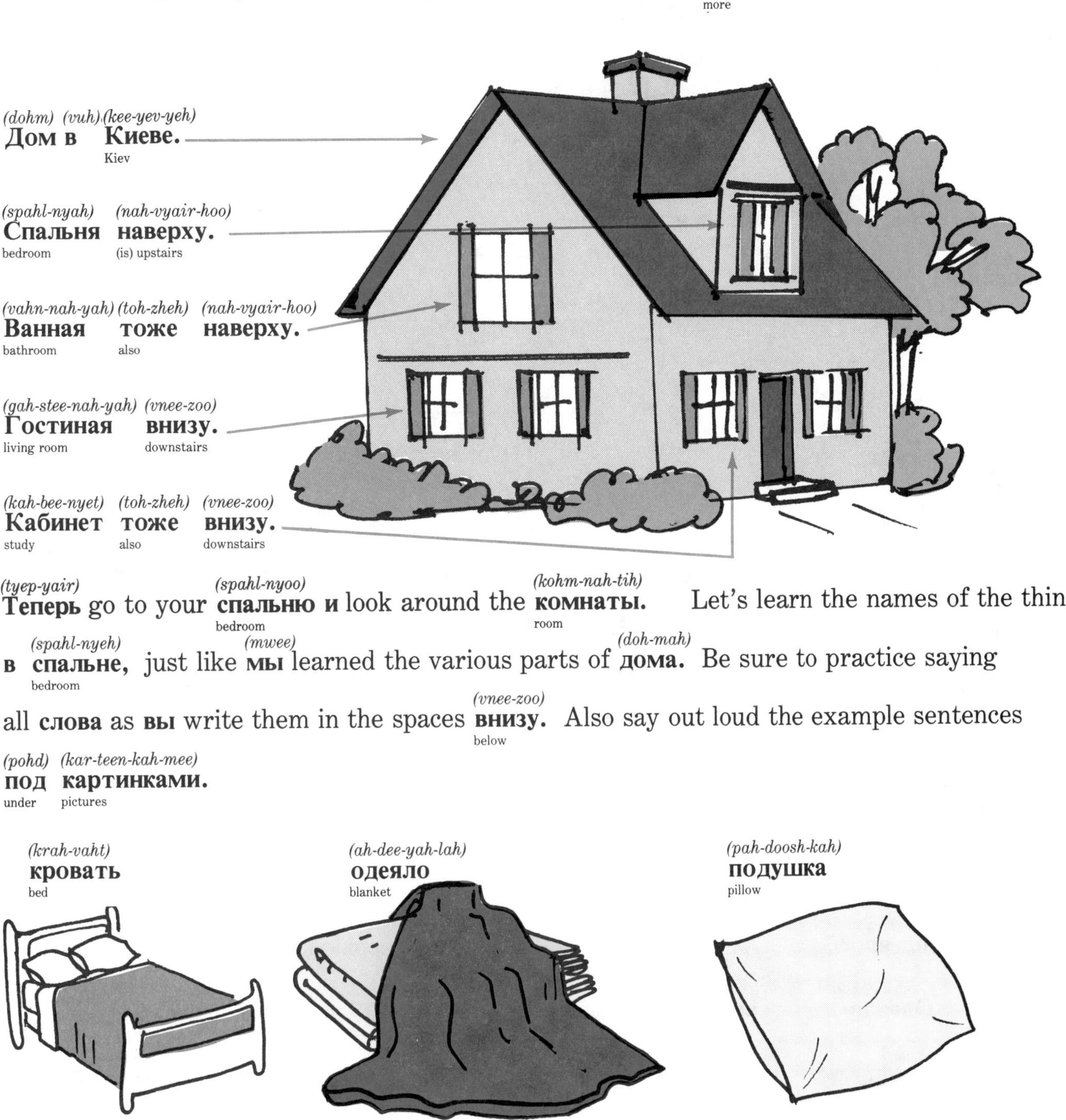

(dohm) (vuh) (kee-yev-yeh) **Дом в Киеве.** (Kiev)

(spahl-nyah) (nah-vyair-hoo) **Спальня наверху.** (bedroom (is) upstairs)

(vahn-nah-yah) (toh-zheh) (nah-vyair-hoo) **Ванная тоже наверху.** (bathroom also)

(gah-stee-nah-yah) (vnee-zoo) **Гостиная внизу.** (living room downstairs)

(kah-bee-nyet) (toh-zheh) (vnee-zoo) **Кабинет тоже внизу.** (study also downstairs)

(tyep-yair) **Теперь** go to your *(spahl-nyoo)* **спальню** (bedroom) **и** look around the *(kohm-nah-tih)* **комнаты** (room). Let's learn the names of the things **в** *(spahl-nyeh)* **спальне** (bedroom), just like *(mwee)* **мы** learned the various parts of *(doh-mah)* **дома.** Be sure to practice saying all **слова** as **вы** write them in the spaces *(vnee-zoo)* **внизу** (below). Also say out loud the example sentences *(pohd)* **под** (under) *(kar-teen-kah-mee)* **картинками** (pictures).

(krah-vaht) **кровать** — bed

(ah-dee-yah-lah) **одеяло** — blanket

(pah-doosh-kah) **подушка** — pillow

Кровать большая.

(krah-vaht) (bahl-shah-yah) **Кровать большая.** (bed (is) big)

(men-yeh) (noozh-nah) (ah-dee-yah-lah) **Мне нужно одеяло.** (I need)

(men-yeh) (noozh-nah) (pah-doosh-koo) **Мне нужно подушку.** (I need)

М

- ☐ **май** *(my)* . . . . May
- ☐ **март** *(mart)* . . . . March
- ☐ **масса** *(mahs-sah)* . . . . mass
- ☐ **мастер** *(mahs-tyair)* . . . . master
- ☐ **математика** *(mah-tyeh-mah-tee-kah)* . . . . mathematics

(boo-deel-neek)
будильник
alarm clock

(shkahf)
шкаф
wardrobe

(oo) (men-yah) (yest)
У меня есть *(boo-deel-neek)* **будильник.**
I have

(vuh)(spahl-nyeh)
Шкаф в спальне.
bedroom

Теперь, remove the next **пять** *(pyaht)* stickers **и** label these things **в** *(vuh)* your **спальне.** *(spahl-nyeh)*

(spahl-nyah) (gah-stee-neet-seh)
Спальня в гостинице
hotel

(spaht)
спать = to sleep, so a sleeping room.

Study the following **вопросы** *(vah-proh-sih)* (questions) **и** their **ответы** *(aht-vyet-ih)* based **на** *(nah)* (on) **картинке** *(kar-teen-kyeh)* (picture) to the left.

1. **Где** *(gdyeh)* **будильник?** *(boo-deel-neek)* (alarm clock)
   Будильник *(boo-deel-neek)* **на** *(nah)* (on) **столе.** *(stohl-yeh)* (table)
2. **Где одеяло?** *(ah-dee-yah-lah)* (blanket)
   Одеяло *(ah-dee-yah-lah)* **на** *(nah)* **кровати.** *(krah-vah-tee)* (bed)
3. **Где шкаф?** *(shkahf)*
   Шкаф *(shkahf)* **в** *(vuh)* **спальне.** *(spahl-nyeh)* (bedroom)
4. **Где подушка?** *(pah-doosh-kah)* (pillow)
   Подушка *(pah-doosh-kah)* **на** *(nah)* **кровати.** *(krah-vah-tee)*
5. **Где кровать?** *(krah-vaht)* (bed)
   Кровать *(krah-vaht)* **в спальне.** *(spahl-nyeh)*
6. **Кровать** *(krah-vaht)* (bed) **большая** *(bahl-shah-yah)* (big) **или** *(ee-lee)* **маленькая?** *(mah-lyen-kah-yah)* (small)
   Кровать *(krah-vaht)* **не** *(nyeh)* (not) **большая.** *(bahl-shah-yah)* (big)
   Кроват маленькая. *(mah-lyen-kah-yah)* (small)

- ☐ **материя** *(mah-tyair-ee-yah)* .... material
- ☐ **матч** *(mahtch)* .... match (game)
- ☐ **машина** *(mah-shen-nah)* .... machine (car)
- ☐ **медаль** *(myeh-dahl)* .... medal
- ☐ **медик** *(myeh-deek)* .... medic

M

Теперь answer **вопросы** *(vah-proh-sih)* questions based on **картинке** *(kar-teen-kyeh)* picture on **странице** 54.

Где будильник? *(boo-deel-neek)*

Где кровать? *(krah-vaht)*

Где ______________________ ______________________

Let's move **в** *(vuh)* into **ванную** *(vahn-noo-yoo)* bathroom **и** do the same thing.

умывальник *(oo-mih-vahl-neek)* washstand

душ *(doosh)* shower

туалет *(too-ahl-yet)* toilet

____

Зелёный *(zyel-yoh-nee)* green **умывальник** *(oo-mih-vahl-neek)* **в номере.** *(nohm-yair-yeh)* hotel room

____

Серый *(syeh-ree)* gray **душ** *(doosh)* **тоже** *(toh-zheh)* also **в номере.** *(nohm-yair-yeh)* hotel room

____

Белый *(byel-lee)* white **и зелёный** *(zyel-yoh-nee)* green **туалет тоже в номере.** *(nohm-yair-yeh)*

зеркало *(zyair-kah-lah)* mirror ______________________

полотенца *(pah-lah-tyent-sah)* towels полотенца

красное *(krahs-nah-yeh)* **полотенце** ______________________

коричневое *(kah-reech-nyeh-vah-yeh)* **полотенце** ______________________

оранжевое *(ah-rahn-zheh-vah-yeh)* **полотенце** ______________________

Не *(nyeh)* not forget to remove the next **семь** *(syem)* stickers **и** label these things in your **ванной.** *(vahn-noy)* bathroom

- ☐ **медицина** *(myeh-deet-see-nah)* .... medicine
- ☐ **мелодия** *(myeh-loh-dee-yah)* .... melody
- ☐ **металл** *(myeh-tahl)* .... metal
- ☐ **метод** *(myeh-tohd)* .... method
- ☐ **метро** *(myeh-troh)* .... metro

М ______________________

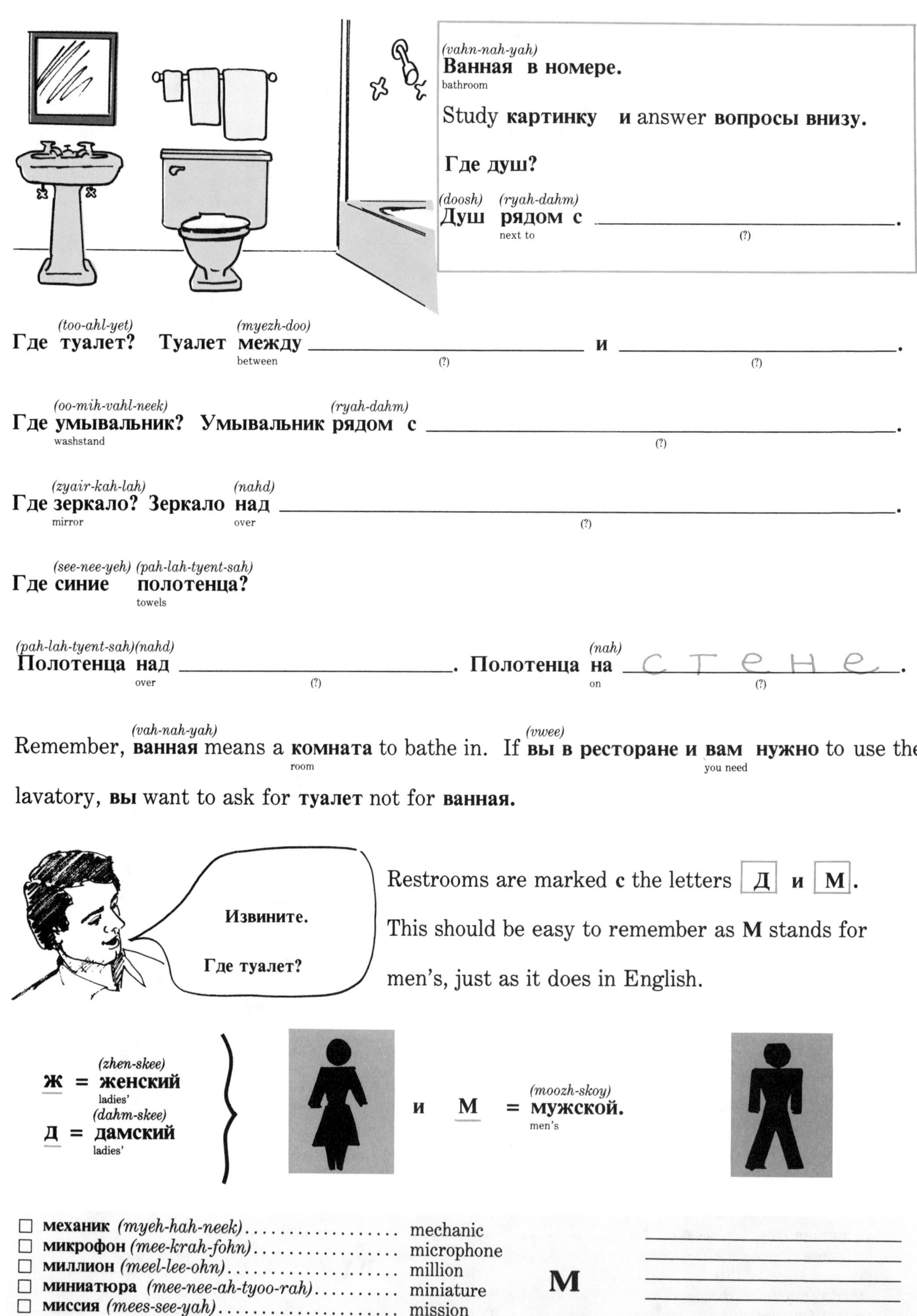

(vahn-nah-yah)
Ванная в номере.
bathroom

Study **картинку** и answer **вопросы внизу.**

Где душ?

(doosh) *(ryah-dahm)*
Душ рядом с ______________________.
next to (?)

(too-ahl-yet) *(myezh-doo)*
Где туалет? Туалет между ______________________ **и** ______________________.
between (?) (?)

(oo-mih-vahl-neek) *(ryah-dahm)*
Где умывальник? Умывальник рядом с ______________________.
washstand (?)

(zyair-kah-lah) *(nahd)*
Где зеркало? Зеркало над ______________________.
mirror over (?)

(see-nee-yeh) *(pah-lah-tyent-sah)*
Где синие полотенца?
towels

(pah-lah-tyent-sah)(nahd) *(nah)*
Полотенца над ______________________. **Полотенца на** стене.
over (?) on (?)

Remember, *(vah-nah-yah)* **ванная** means a **комната** (room) to bathe in. If *(vwee)* **вы в ресторане и вам нужно** (you need) to use the lavatory, **вы** want to ask for **туалет** not for **ванная.**

Restrooms are marked **с** the letters **Д** и **М**. This should be easy to remember as **М** stands for men's, just as it does in English.

Ж = *(zhen-skee)* **женский** (ladies')
Д = *(dahm-skee)* **дамский** (ladies')

и **М** = *(moozh-skoy)* **мужской.** (men's)

- ☐ **механик** *(myeh-hah-neek)*.................. mechanic
- ☐ **микрофон** *(mee-krah-fohn)*.................. microphone
- ☐ **миллион** *(meel-lee-ohn)*.................. million
- ☐ **миниатюра** *(mee-nee-ah-tyoo-rah)*.......... miniature
- ☐ **миссия** *(mees-see-yah)*.................. mission

М

Next stop — *(kah-bee-nyet)* **кабинет,** specifically *(stohl)* **стол** *(kah-bee-nyet-yeh)* **в кабинете.** *(shtoh)* **Что на столе?**
study — desk/table — study — what

Let's identify things that one normally finds **на столе** or strewn about **дома.**

(kah-rahn-dahsh)
карандаш
pencil

____

(rooch-kah)
ручка
pen

____

(boo-mah-gah)
бумага
paper

____

(pees-moh)
письмо
letter

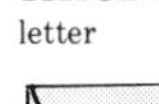

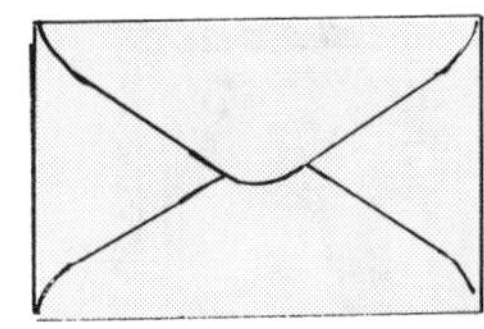

____

(aht-krit-kah)
открытка
postcard

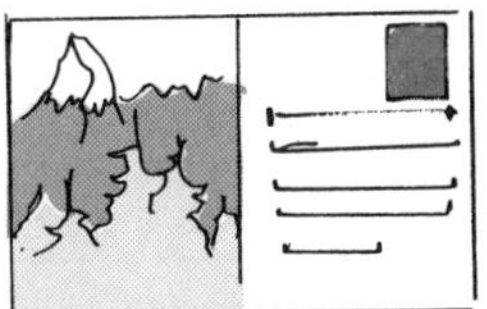

____

(mar-kah)
марка
stamp

____

(kuh-nee-gah)
книга
book

____

(zhoor-nahl)
журнал
magazine

____

(gah-zyet-ah)
газета
newspaper

____

(ahch-kee)
очки
eyeglasses

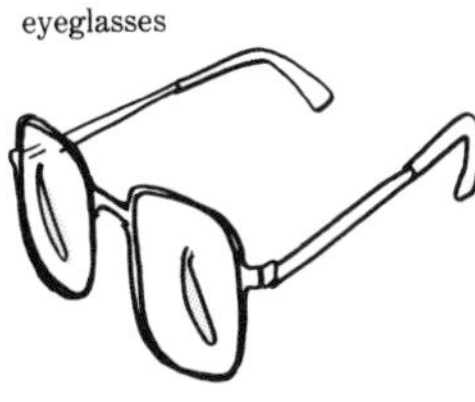

____

(tee-lee-vee-zar)
телевизор
television

____

(kar-zee-nah)
корзина
basket

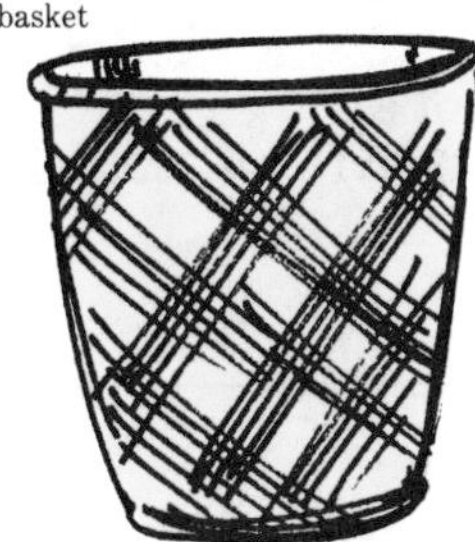

____

- ☐ **митинг** *(mee-teeng)*........................ meeting
- ☐ **модель** *(mah-dyel)*........................ model
- ☐ **момент** *(mah-myent)*........................ moment
- ☐ **мотор** *(mah-tor)*........................ motor
- ☐

М

____
____
____
____
____

Теперь label these things **в** **кабинете** *(kah-bee-nyet-yeh)* with your stickers. Do not forget to say these **слова** out loud whenever **вы** write them, **вы** see them **или вы** apply the stickers. **Теперь** identify the things **на картинке** **внизу** *(vnee-zoo)* by filling in each blank with the correct **русскими словами.**

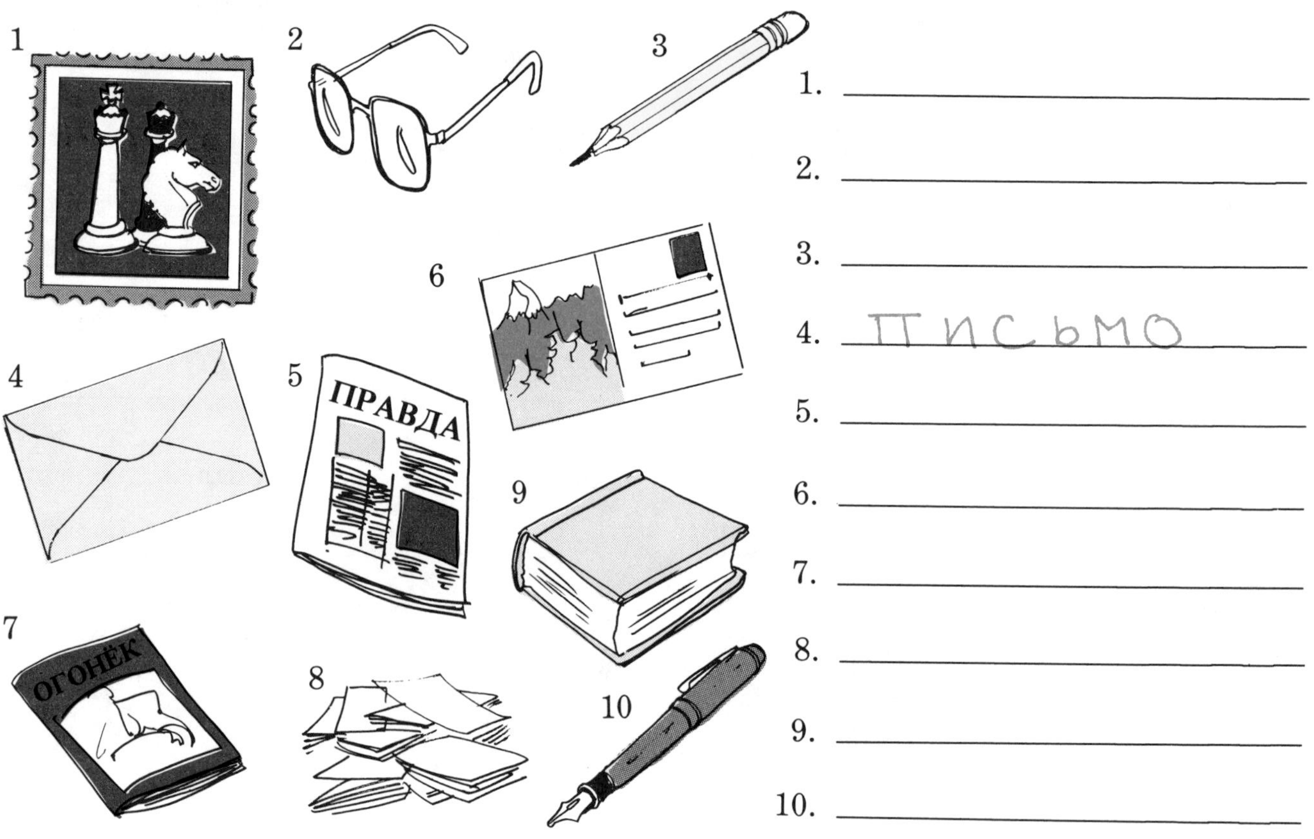

1. ____________
2. ____________
3. ____________
4. ____________
5. ____________
6. ____________
7. ____________
8. ____________
9. ____________
10. ____________

Вот четыре verbs.

(prah-dah-vaht) **продавать** = to sell	*(pah-sih-laht)* **посылать** = to send	*(spaht)* **спать** = to sleep	*(zvah-neet)* **звонить** = to phone
____________	____________	____________	____________

Теперь fill in the blanks on the next **странице** with the correct form of these verbs. Practice saying the sentences out loud many times. Don't get discouraged! Just look at how much **вы** have already learned **и** think ahead to **икра,** *(eek-rah)* (caviar) **балет** *(bahl-yet)* **и** adventure.

☐ **музей** *(moo-zay)*.......................... museum
☐ **музыка** *(moo-zih-kah)*.......................... music
☐ **нация** *(naht-see-yah)*.......................... nation
☐ **не** *(nyeh)*.......................... not, no
☐ **—несерьёзный** *(nyeh-syair-ohz-nee)*......... not serious

М

____
____
____
____
____

(prah-dah-vaht)
продавать
to sell

Я продаю/ ______ *(tsvet-ih)* **цветы.** flowers

Он/Она продаёт/ ______ *(frook-tih)* **фрукты.** fruit

Мы продаём/ ______ *(beel-yet-ih)* **билеты.**

Вы продаёте/ ______ *(mnoh-gah)* **много** many *(beel-yet-ahv)* **билетов.**

Они продают/ ______ *(aht-krit-kee)* **открытки.**

(pah-sih-laht)
посылать
to send

Я посылаю/ ______ *(pees-moh)* **письмо.** letter

Он/Она посылает/ ______ *(aht-krit-koo)* **открытку.**

Мы посылаем/ ______ *(kuh-nee-goo)* **книгу.**

Вы посылаете/ ______ *(cheh-tir-ee)* **четыре** *(aht-krit-kee)* **открытки.**

Они посылают/ ______ **три** *(pees-mah)* **письма.**

(spaht)
спать
to sleep

Я сплю/ ______ *(vuh)* **в** *(spahl-nyeh)* **спальне.** bedroom

Он/Она спит/ ______ **на** *(krah-vah-tee)* **кровати.**

Мы спим/ ______ **в гостинице.**

Вы спите/ ______ **в доме.**

Они спят/ ______ **под** under *(ah-dee-yah-lahm)* **одеялом.** blanket

(zvah-neet)
звонить
to phone

Я звоню/ ______ **в Ленинград.**

Он/Она звонит/ ______ **в** *(shah)* **США.** U.S.A.

Мы звоним/ ______ **в Канаду.**

Вы звоните/ ______ **в Англию.** England

Они звонят/ ______ **во Владивосток.**

The word *(nyeh)* **не** (not) is extremely useful **по-русски.** Add **не** before a verb **и вы** negate the sentence.

я посылаю письмо. = I send a letter.

я не посылаю письмо. = I do not send a letter.

Simple, isn't it? **Теперь, вы** negate the following sentences.

Я хочу стакан воды. ______

Мы звоним в Канаду. ______

Я понимаю по-русски. ______

Н

- ☐ **нейлон** *(nay-lohn)* .... nylon ______
- ☐ **нет!** *(nyet)* .... no! ______
- ☐ **никель** *(neek-yehl)* .... nickel ______
- ☐ **норма** *(nor-mah)* .... norm, standard ______
- ☐ **нос** *(nohs)* .... nose ______

Step 15

Теперь вы *(vwee)* know **как** *(kahk)* to count, **как** to ask **вопросы,** *(vah-proh-sih)* **как** to use verbs **с** *(suh)* the "plug-in" formula, **как** to make statements, **и как** to describe something, be it the location of **гостиница или цвет** *(tsvet)* [color] **дома** [of house]**.** Let's now take the basics that **вы** have learned **и** expand them in special areas that will be most helpful in your travels. What does everyone do on a holiday? Send **открытки,** *(aht-krit-kee)* of course! Let's learn exactly **как русское почтовое** *(poach-toh-vah-yeh)* [post] **отделение,** *(aht-dyel-yen-ee-yeh)* [office] commonly called **„почта,"** *(poach-tah)* works.

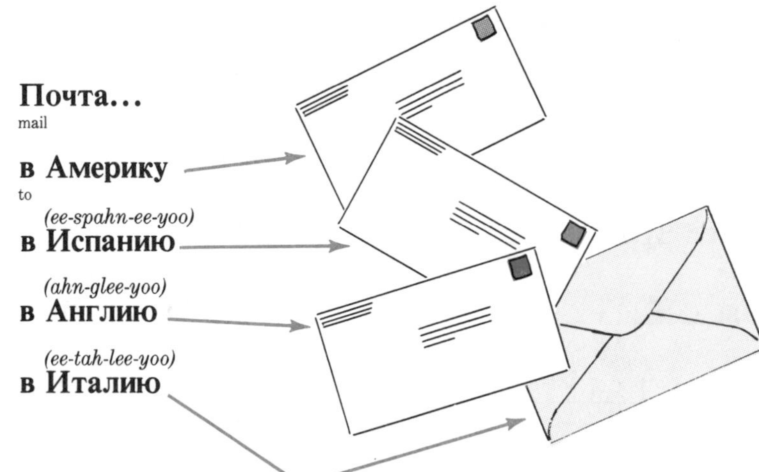

Почта is where **вы** need to go **в СССР** to buy **марки** *(mar-kee)* **и конверты,** *(kahn-vyair-tih)* [envelopes] mail a package, send a telegram or use **телефон. Вот** *(voht)* [here are] some necessary **слова для** *(dil-yah)* [for] **почты.** *(poach-tih)* [post office] Be sure to practice them out loud **и тогда** *(tahg-dah)* write **слова под** *(pohd)* [under] **картинкой.** *(kar-teen-koy)*

(kahn-vyairt) **конверт** — envelope

(aht-krit-kah) **открытка** — postcard

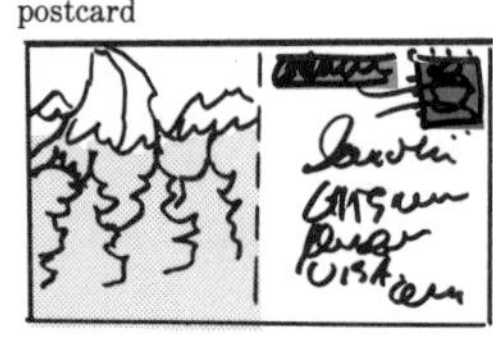

(mar-kah) **марка** — stamp

(teh-leh-grahm-mah) **телеграмма**

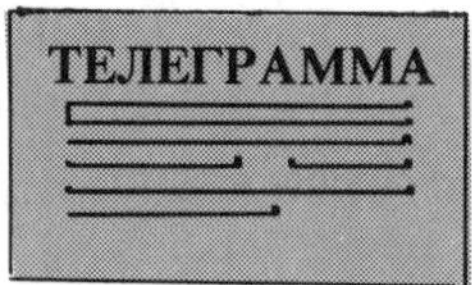

________ открытка ________ ________

- ☐ **Норвегия** *(nar-vyeh-gee-yah)*............... Norway
- ☐ —where they speak **по-норвежски** *(pah-nar-vyezh-skee)*
- ☐ **ноябрь** *(nah-yah-bair)*..................... November
- ☐ **октябрь** *(ahk-tyah-bair)*.................. October
- ☐ **олимпиада** *(ah-leem-pee-ah-dah)*............ Olympics

О

(pah-sil-kah)
посылка
package

(pahch-toh-vee) (yahsh-chik)
почтовый ящик
mailbox

(ah-vee-ah-poach-toy)
авиапочтой
by airmail

(ahk-noh)
окно
window

(teh-leh-fohn-ahv-tah-maht)
телефон-автомат
public telephone

(teh-leh-fohn)
телефон
telephone

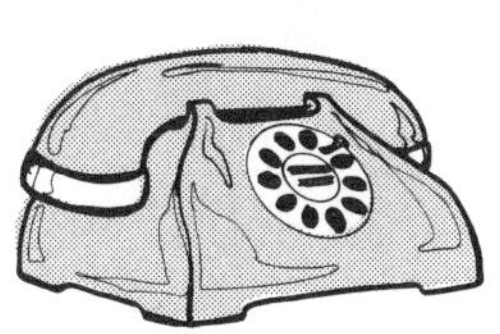

(poach-tah)
почта
post office

(pah-sil-kee) (pees-mah) (aht-krit-kee) (poach-tih)
Почта в СССР has everything. **Вы** send **посылки, письма и открытки с почты.**
packages letters postcards from

(nah) (teh-leh-grahm-moo) (aht-krit-ah)
Вы buy **марки на почте. Вы** can send **телеграмму с почты. Почта** is generally **открыта**
at telegram open

(suh) (tee) (chah-sohv) (oo-trah) (doh) (tee) (vyeh-cheh-rah) (poh) (soo-boh-tahm) (voh-skree-syen-yahm)
с 9-ти часов утра до 20-ти часов вечера. По субботам и воскресеньям,
from o'clock morning until evening on Saturdays Sundays

(zah-krit-ah) (vahm) (noozh-nah) (shah) (kah-nah-doo)
почта закрыта. If **вам нужно** to send **телеграмму в США или Канаду,** this can be done
closed you need telegram U.S.A.

(poach-too)
на почте. Let's go to **почту.** Okay. First step—enter **почту.**
at

(hah-roh-shee) (dee-ah-loh-gah) (slah-vah-mee)
The following is **хороший** sample **диалога.** Familiarize yourself **с** these **словами.** Don't wait until your holiday.
good dialogue

О

- ☐ **опера** *(oh-pyair-ih)*........................ opera
- ☐ **органист** *(ar-gah-neest)*.................... organist
- ☐ **оркестр** *(ar-kyes-ter)*...................... orchestra
- ☐ **офицер** *(ah-feet-syair)*..................... officer
- ☐ **официальный** *(ah-feet-see-ahl-nih)*........... official

Я хочу купить конверты для двух (2) писем в США и двух (2) открыток в Англию.

Авиапочтой?

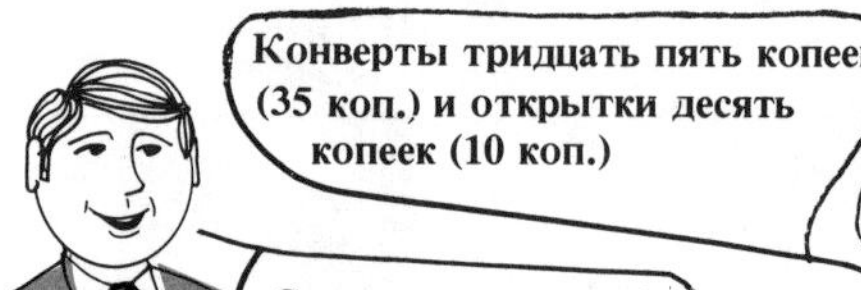

Конверты тридцать пять копеек (35 коп.) и открытки десять копеек (10 коп.)
Сколько это стоит?

Да, авиапочтой, пожалуйста. я хочу купить марки для двух писем в Одессу. Сколько это стоит?

Шесть копеек (6 коп.).
Да, хорошо.
Вот марки. Это один рубль и две копейки.

Next step—**вы** ask **вопросы** like those **внизу,** depending on what **вы** **хотите.** *(hah-teet-yeh)* would like

Где я могу купить марки? — *(mah-goo)* can, *(koo-peet)* buy, *(mar-kee)*; **я** = I

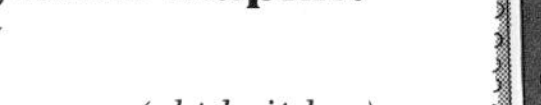

Где я могу купить открытку? *(aht-krit-koo)*

Где телефон?

Где почтовый ящик? *(pahch-toh-vee) (yahsh-chik)* mailbox

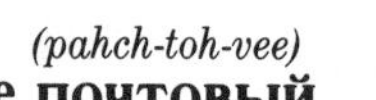

Где телефон-автомат? public telephone

Где я могу послать телеграмму? *(mah-goo)(pah-slaht)* send, *(teh-leh-grahm-moo)*

Где я могу послать посылку? *(pah-sil-koo)* package

Где я могу звонить в США? *(zvah-neet)* phone, *(shah)* U.S.A.

Сколько это стоит? *(stoy-eet)* costs

Где я могу звонить в Ялту? *(zvah-neet)* *(yahl-too)* Yalta

Повторяйте *(pahv-tah-ryah-eet-yeh)* repeat the above sentences many times.

Теперь, quiz yourself. See if **вы** can translate the following thoughts **на русский.**

Ответы are at the bottom of the next **страницы.**

1. Where is a public telephone? ____________________
2. Where can I phone? ____________________
3. Where can I phone to the U.S.A.? ____________________
4. Where can I phone to Leningrad? ____________________
5. Where is the post office? ____________________

П

- ☐ **павильон** *(pah-veel-yohn)* .... pavilion ____________
- ☐ **пакет** *(pah-kyet)* .... package ____________
- ☐ **Пакистан** *(pah-kee-stahn)* .... Pakistan ____________
- ☐ **Польша** *(pohl-shah)* .... Poland ____________
- ☐ **парад** *(pah-rahd)* .... parade ____________

6. Where can I buy stamps? ____________________

7. Airmail envelopes? ____________________

8. Where can I send a package? ____________________

9. Where can I send a telegram? ____________________

10. Where is window eight? ____________________

(voht)
Вот are more verbs.

(die-tee) **дайте** = give (me) *(pee-saht)* **писать** = to write *(pah-kah-zih-vaht)* **показывать** = to show *(plah-teet) (zah)* **платить за** = to pay for

____________ ____________ ____________ ____________

(die-tee)
дайте
give (me)

Дайте мне **пожалуйста,** *(pah-zhahl-oos-tah)* **счёт.** *(shyoht)* bill

____________ **пожалуйста, адрес.** *(ah-dres)* address

____________ **пожалуйста, сдачу.** *(sdah-choo)* change

Дайте мне **пожалуйста, меню.**

____________ **пожалуйста, билет.**

(pee-saht)
писать
to write

Я пишу/ ____________ **письмо.**

Он / **Она** пишет/ ____________ **много.** *(mnoh-gah)* a lot

Мы пишем/ ____________ **телеграмму.**

Вы пишете/ ____________ **адрес.** *(ah-dres)*

Они пишут/ ____________ **открытку.**

(pah-kah-zih-vaht)
показывать
to show

Я показываю/ ____________ **вам** *(vahm)* to you **книгу.**

Он / **Она** показывает/ ____________ **мне** *(men-yeh)* to me **Кремль.**

Мы показываем/ ____________ **вам** *(vahm)* to you **музей.** *(moo-zay)*

Вы показываете/ ____________ **мне** *(men-yeh)* to me **письмо.** letter

Они показывают/ ____________ **мне почту.**

(plah-teet) (zah)
платить за
to pay for

Я плачу за/ ____________ **счёт** *(shyoht)* bill **в ресторане.** *(res-tah-rahn-yeh)* restaurant

Он / **Она** платит за/ ____________ **счёт в гостиница.** *(gah-stee-neet-sah)*

Мы платим за/ ____________ **билеты** *(beel-yet-ih)* tickets **в театр.** *(tee-ah-ter)* theater

Вы платите за/ ____________ **билеты на балет.** *(bahl-yet)*

Они платят за/ ____________ **билеты на концерт.** *(kahn-tsairt)* concert

ОТВЕТЫ

1. Где телефон-автомат?
2. Где я могу позвонить?
3. Где я могу позвонить в США?
4. Где я могу позвонить в Ленинград?
5. Где почта?
6. Где я могу купить марки?
7. Конверты авиапочты?
8. Где я могу послать посылку?
9. Где я могу послать телеграмму?
10. Где окно восемь?

Step 16

Как Платить *(kahk) (plah-teet)* how to pay

Да, there are also **счёта** *(shyoh-tah)* bills to pay **в СССР. Вы** have just finished your delicious dinner **и вы хотите** *(hah-teet-yeh)* would like **счёт.** *(shyoht)* bill **Как вы можете** *(moh-zhet-yeh)* can **платить?** *(plah-teet)* pay **Вы** call for **официанта:** *(ah-feet-see-ahn-tah)* waiter **„Официант!"**

Извините. Дайте, пожалуйста, счёт.
Да, одну минуту, пожалуйста.

Официант *(ah-feet-see-ahnt)* waiter will normally reel off what **вы** have eaten, while writing rapidly. **Он** will then place **счёт на стол** *(shyoht) (stohl)* bill that looks something like the one **на картинке,** while saying something like

„Вот счёт. Восемь рублей, *(roo-blay)* **пожалуйста."** (Вот = here is)

Вы will pay **официанту** *(ah-feet-see-ahn-too)* **или** perhaps **вы** will pay **кассиру.** *(kahs-see-roo)* cashier Being a seasoned traveler, **вы** know that tipping as **мы** *(mwee)* know it **в США и Канаде нет** *(nyet)* is not a custom **в СССР.** Generally the service is included **в счёте.** *(shyoht-yeh)*

If **вы** are planning to dine out **в СССР, вы** should definitely make reservations. It can be very difficult to get into a popular **ресторан.** *(res-tah-rahn)* Nevertheless, the experience is well worth the trouble **вы** will go to to obtain a reservation. **И** remember, **вы** know enough **русский** to make a reservation.

П

- ☐ **парк** *(park)*.............................. park ____________
- ☐ **парламент** *(par-lah-myent)*.............. parliament ____________
- ☐ **партия** *(par-tee-yah)*..................... party ____________
- ☐ **паспорт** *(pahs-port)*....................... passport ____________
- ☐ **пассажир** *(pahs-sah-zheer)*............... passenger ____________

Remember these key **слова** when dining out **в СССР.**

(myen-yoo) **меню** menu	*(shyoht)* **счёт** bill	*(ah-feet-see-ahnt)* **официант** waiter
(kvee-tahn-tsee-yah) **квитанция** receipt	*(sdah-chah)* **сдача** change	*(ah-feet-see-ahnt-kah)* **официантка** waitress

Politeness is *(oh-chen)* **очень** *(vahzh-nah)* **важна в СССР. Вы** will feel more **как** (like) **русский** ((a) Russian) if **вы** practice **и** use these expressions.

(eez-vee-neet-yeh) **извините.** excuse me	*(pah-zhahl-oos-tah)* **пожалуйста** please	*(spah-see-bah)* **спасибо** thank you	*(pah-zhahl-oos-tah)* **пожалуцста** you're welcome

Вот a sample conversation involving paying *(shyoht)* **счёт когда** leaving **гостиницу.**

(zee-nah) Зина:	**Извините. Я хочу** *(ah-plah-teet)* **оплатить** (to pay) **счёт.**
(ahd-mee-nee-strah-tor) Администратор:	*(nohm-yair)* **Номер** (number), *(pah-zhahl-oos-tah)* **пожалуцста?**
Зина:	*(nohm-yair)* **Номер** (number) *(tree-stah)* **триста** *(dyes-yet)* **десять.**
Администратор:	**Спасибо.** *(ahd-noo)* **Одну минуту, пожалуйста.**
Администратор:	**Вот счёт.** *(so-rahk)* **Сорок пять** *(roo-blay)* **рублей, пожалуйста.**
Зина:	**Спасибо. (И Зина** hands him **пятьдесят рублей. Администратор** returns shortly **и** *(gah-vah-reet)* **говорит...)**
Администратор:	**Вот** *(vah-shah)* **ваша** (your) *(kvee-tahn-tsee-yah)* **квитанция** (receipt) **и** *(vah-shah)* **ваша** (your) *(sdah-chah)* **сдача** (change). **Спасибо и** *(doh)* **до** *(svee-dahn-ee-yah)* **свидания** (goodbye).

Simple, right? If **вы** have any problems **с** *(chee-slah-mee)* **числами** (numbers), just ask someone to write out *(chee-slah)* **числа,** so that **вы** can be sure you understand everything correctly.

Пожалуйста *(nah-pee-sheet-yeh)* **напишите** (write out) **числа. Спасибо.**

Let's take a break from *(dyen-yeg)* **денег и,** starting on the next **странице,** learn some *(noh-vih-yeh)* **новые** fun **слова.**

- ☐ **программа** *(prah-grah-mah)*............... program
- ☐ **позиция** *(pah-zeet-see-yah)*................ position
- ☐ **полиция** *(pah-leet-see-yah)*................ police
- ☐ **порт** *(port)*.............................. port
- ☐ **портрет** *(part-ryet)*...................... portrait

П __________

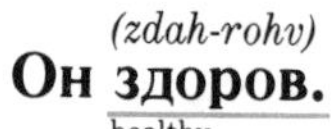

(zdah-rohv)
Он здоров.
healthy

(bohl-yen)
Он болен.
sick

(vah-dah) (gar-yah-chah-yah)
Вода горячая -
water hot

(grah-doo-sahv)
тридцать пять градусов.
degrees

(hah-lohd-nah-yah)
Вода холодная -
cold

пять градусов.

(zhen-shchee-nah) (vwee-soh-kah-yah)
Женщина высокая.
woman tall

(ryeb-yoh-nahk) (mah-lyen-kee)
Ребёнок маленький.
child small/short

(tohl-stah-yah)
Красная книга толстая.
thick

(tohn-kah-yah)
Зелёная книга тонкая.
green thin

(hah-rah-shoh)
Это хорошо.
good

(nyeh)
Это не хорошо.
not good

(ploh-hah)
Это плохо.
bad

(gah-vah-reet-yeh) (grohm-kah)
Вы говорите громко.
speak loudly

(gah-vah-reet) (tee-hah)
Он говорит тихо.
speaks softly

(lee-nee-yah) (kah-roht-kah-yah)
Красная линия короткая.
line short

(dleen-nah-yah)
Синяя линия длинная.
long

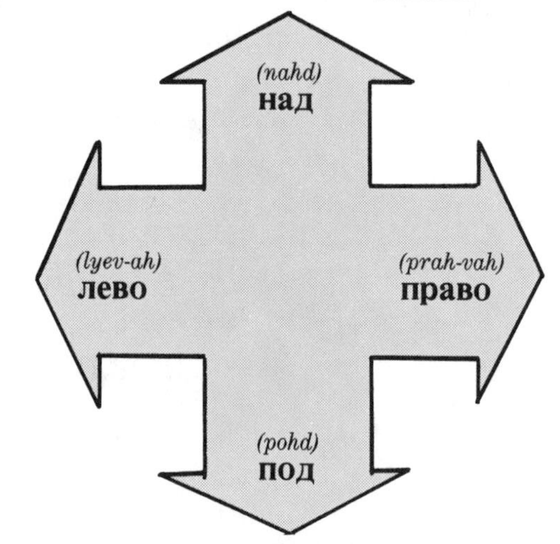

(kee-lah-myeh-trahv) (chahs)
20 километров в час

(myed-lyen-nah)
медленно
slow

200 километров в час

(bis-trah)
быстро
fast

- ☐ **прогресс** *(prahg-ryes)* .... progress
- ☐ **продукт** *(prah-dookt)* .... product
- ☐ **проект** *(prah-yekt)* .... project
- ☐ **профессия** *(prah-fyes-see-yah)* .... profession
- ☐ **профессор** *(prah-fyes-sar)* .... professor

П ________________

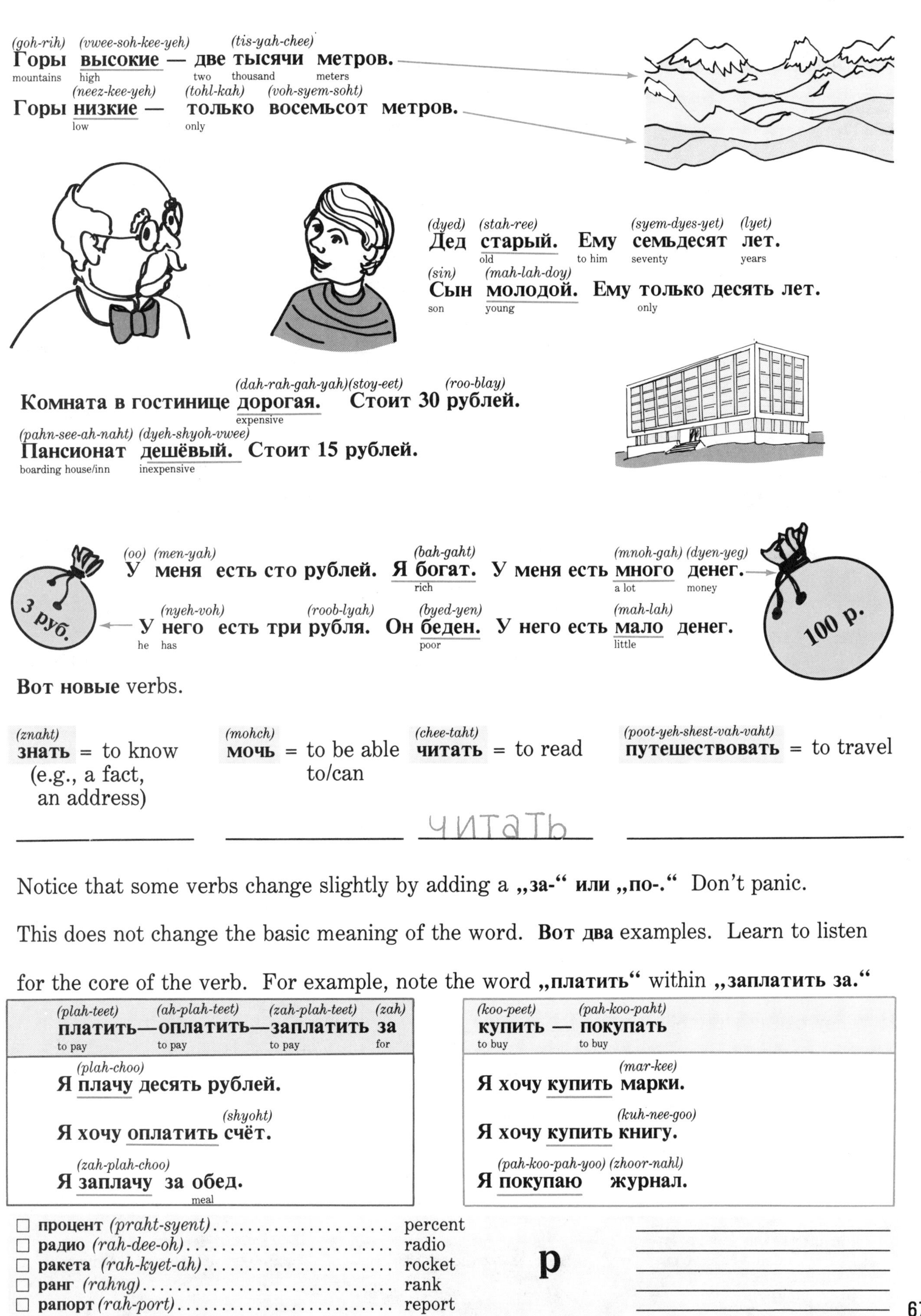

(goh-rih) (vwee-soh-kee-yeh) (tis-yah-chee)
Горы высокие — две тысячи метров.
mountains high two thousand meters

(neez-kee-yeh) (tohl-kah) (voh-syem-soht)
Горы низкие — только восемьсот метров.
low only

(dyed) (stah-ree) (syem-dyes-yet) (lyet)
Дед старый. Ему семьдесят лет.
old to him seventy years

(sin) (mah-lah-doy)
Сын молодой. Ему только десять лет.
son young only

(dah-rah-gah-yah)(stoy-eet) (roo-blay)
Комната в гостинице дорогая. Стоит 30 рублей.
expensive

(pahn-see-ah-naht) (dyeh-shyoh-vwee)
Пансионат дешёвый. Стоит 15 рублей.
boarding house/inn inexpensive

(oo) (men-yah) (bah-gaht) (mnoh-gah) (dyen-yeg)
У меня есть сто рублей. Я богат. У меня есть много денег.
rich a lot money

(nyeh-voh) (roob-lyah) (byed-yen) (mah-lah)
У него есть три рубля. Он беден. У него есть мало денег.
he has poor little

Вот новые verbs.

(znaht) **знать** = to know (e.g., a fact, an address) __________

(mohch) **мочь** = to be able to/can __________

(chee-taht) **читать** = to read читать

(poot-yeh-shest-vah-vaht) **путешествовать** = to travel __________

Notice that some verbs change slightly by adding a **„за-“ или „по-.“** Don't panic. This does not change the basic meaning of the word. **Вот два** examples. Learn to listen for the core of the verb. For example, note the word **„платить“** within **„заплатить за.“**

(plah-teet) (ah-plah-teet) (zah-plah-teet) (zah) **платить—оплатить—заплатить за** to pay to pay to pay for	*(koo-peet) (pah-koo-paht)* **купить — покупать** to buy to buy
(plah-choo) **Я плачу десять рублей.**	*(mar-kee)* **Я хочу купить марки.**
(shyoht) **Я хочу оплатить счёт.**	*(kuh-nee-goo)* **Я хочу купить книгу.**
(zah-plah-choo) **Я заплачу за обед.** meal	*(pah-koo-pah-yoo) (zhoor-nahl)* **Я покупаю журнал.**

р

- ☐ **процент** *(praht-syent)*.................... percent __________
- ☐ **радио** *(rah-dee-oh)*.................... radio __________
- ☐ **ракета** *(rah-kyet-ah)*.................... rocket __________
- ☐ **ранг** *(rahng)*.................... rank __________
- ☐ **рапорт** *(rah-port)*.................... report __________

Study the patterns **внизу** closely, as **вы** will use these verbs a lot.

(znaht)
знать
to know

Я знаю/ ________ *(vsyoh)* **всё.** (everything)

Он знает/ ________ *(ah-dres)* **адрес.** (address)
Она

Мы знаем/ ________ **как** (how) *(gah-vah-reet)* **говорить** (to speak) **по-русски.**

Вы знаете/ ________ *(nahz-vah-nee-yeh)* **название** (name) **гостиницы.**

Они знают/ ________ **название** *(res-tah-rah-nah)* **ресторана.**

(mohch)
мочь
to be able to/can

Я могу/ ________ *(gah-vah-reet)* **говорить** (speak) **по-русски.**

Он может/ ________ *(pah-nee-maht)* **понимать** (understand) **по-английски.**
Она

Мы можем/ ________ **понимать по-русски.**

Вы можете/ ________ **говорить по-английски.**

Они могут/ ________ **говорить по-русски** *(toh-zheh)* **тоже.** (also)

(chee-taht)
читать
to read

Я читаю/ ________ **книгу.**

Он читает/ ________ **журнал.** (magazine)
Она

Мы читаем/ ________ **меню.**

Вы читаете/ ________ **много.** (a lot)

Они читают/ ________ **газету.** (newspaper)

(poot-yeh-shest-vah-vaht)
путешествовать
to travel

Я путешествую/ ________ *(vuh)* **в** *(yahn-var-yeh)* **январе.** (January)

Он путешествует/ ________ *(zee-moy)* **зимой.** (in winter)
Она

Мы путешествуем/ ________ *(ee-yool-yeh)* **в июле.** (July)

Вы путешествуете/ ________ *(lyet-ahm)* **летом.** (in summer)

Они путешествуют/ ________ *(vees-noy)* **весной.** (in spring)

Вы *(mohzh-yet-yeh)* **можете** (can) translate the sentences **внизу на** (into) **русский? Ответы внизу.**

1. I can speak Russian. ________
2. They can pay the bill. ________
3. He needs to pay the bill. ________
4. We know the address. Мы знаем адрес.
5. She knows a lot. ________
6. We can read Russian. ________

ОТВЕТЫ

1. **Я могу говорить по-русски.**
2. **Они могут оплатить счёт.**
3. **Ему нужно оплатить счёт.**
4. **Мы знаем адрес.**
5. **Она знает много.**
6. **Мы можем читать по-русски.**

Теперь, draw **линию** *(lee-nee-yoo)* [lines] **между** *(myezh-doo)* [between] the opposites **внизу. Не** forget to say them out loud. Use **эти** *(et-tee)* **слова** every day to describe **вещи** *(vesh-chee)* **в доме** [home], **в школе** *(shkohl-yeh)* [school], at work, etc.

(vwee-soh-kah-yah) **высокая**
(lyev-ah) **лево**
(mah-lah-doy) **молодой**
(byed-yen) **беден**
(zdah-rohv) **здоров**
(dleen-nah-yah) **длинная**
(mnoh-gah) **много**
(hah-rah-shoh) **хорошо**
(tohl-stah-yah) **толстая**
(vwee-soh-kee-yeh) **высокие**
(gah-yah-chah-yah) **горячая**
(pohd) **под**
(myed-lyen-nah) **медленно**
(dah-rah-gah-yah) **дорогая**
(tee-hah) **тихо**
(nahd) **над**
(neez-kee-yeh) **низкие**
(kah-roht-kah-yah) **короткая**
(grohm-kah) **громко**
(tohn-kah-yah) **тонкая**
(dyeh-shoh-vwee) **дешёвый**
(mah-lah) **мало**
(bohl-yen) **болен**
(stah-ree) **старый**
(bis-trah) **быстро**
(prah-vah) **право**
(hah-lohd-nah-yah) **холодная**
(bah-gaht) **богат**
(ploh-hah) **плохо**
(mah-lyen-kee) **маленький**

Теперь вы знаете что [that] **„большой"** means "large" **по-русски.** Haven't **вы** heard of the world-famous **„Большой Театр"?** In addition to being one of the world's foremost ballet companies, it is also **старейший** *(star-yeh-shee)* [oldest] **московский театр.** It is a must to see **когда вы** are **в Москве.** If **вы** travel **в Ленинград, тогда** [then] visit **театр оперы** *(oh-pyair-ih)* [(of) opera] **и балета** called **С.М. Кирова** *(kee-rah-vah)* [Kirov].

☐ **револьвер** *(ryeh-vohl-vyair)* . . . . revolver
☐ **революция** *(ryeh-vahl-yoot-see-yah)* . . . . revolution
☐ **регистрация** *(ryeh-geest-raht-see-yah)* . . . . . . registration
☐ **рекорд** *(ryeh-kord)* . . . . record
☐ **религия** *(ryeh-lee-gee-yah)* . . . . religion

р

Step 17

(poot-yeh-shest-vah-vaht)
Путешествовать
to travel

(vchee-rah) (lyen-een-grahd-yeh)
Вчера в Ленинграде!
yesterday

(see-vohd-nyah) (nohv-gah-rahd-yeh)
Сегодня в Новгороде!
today

(zahv-trah) (smahl-yensk-yeh)
Завтра в Смоленске!

If you know a few key **слова,** traveling can be easy, clean **и** *(oh-chen)* **очень** (very) efficient **в СССР.** **В Советском Союзе** *(pyaht-nod-tset)* **пятнадцать** republics. **СССР** is 6,000 miles wide which is equivalent to the distance *(myezh-doo)* **между** (between) California **и** France, **и** it has *(ah-deen-nud-tset)* **одиннадцать** time zones. This can make traveling **в СССР** a major undertaking.

Иван (Ivan) *(yed-yet)* **едет** (goes) **на машине.**

Борис *(lee-teet)* **летит** (flies) **на** *(sah-mahl-yoht-yeh)* **самолёте** (airplane)**.**

(ee-ree-nah) **Ирина едет на** *(mah-tah-tsee-kul-yeh)* **мотоцикле** (motorcycle)**.**

Нина едет на *(poh-yezd-yeh)* **поезде** (train)**.**

Зина едет на *(myeh-troh)* **метро** (subway)**.**

(veek-tor) **Виктор едет на автобусе.**

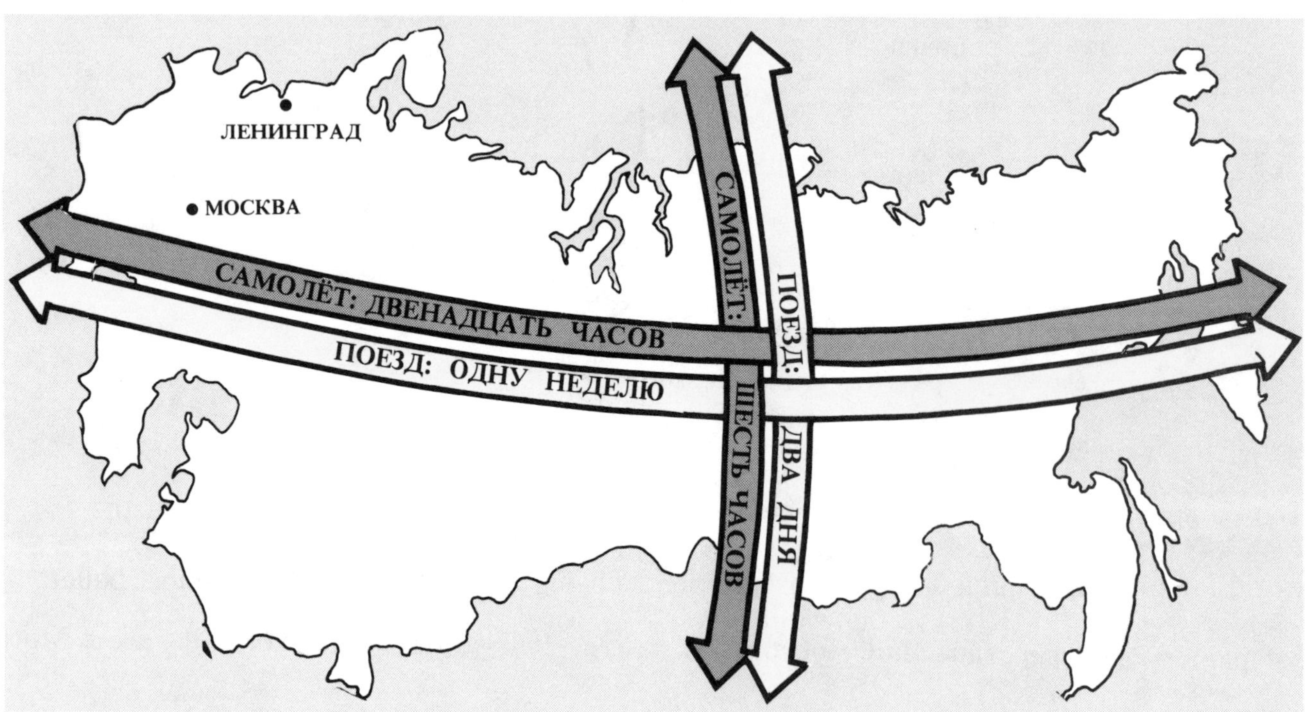

Вы (do you) *(vee-deet-yeh)* **видите** (see) **карту** (map) *(nah-vyair-hoo)* **наверху? Это СССР.** *(yek-haht)* **Ехать** (to go) **с** (from) *(syev-yair-ah)* **севера** (north) **на** (to) *(yoog)* **юг** (south)**,** *(zah-nee-mah-yet)* **занимает** (it takes) **шесть часов на самолёте, и два** *(den-yah)* **дня** (days) **на поезде. Это не плохо** (bad)**.**

- ☐ **салат** *(sah-laht)* .... salad
- ☐ **самовар** *(sah-mah-var)* .... samovar
- ☐ **сезон** *(syeh-zone)* .... season
- ☐ **секунда** *(syek-oon-dah)* .... second
- ☐ **семинар** *(syem-ee-nar)* .... seminar

с

Русские *(loob-yaht)* **любят** (love) *(poot-yeh-shest-vah-vaht)* **путешествовать,** so **это** *(nyeh)* **не** surprise to find **много слов** revolving around the concept of travel which is exactly what **вы** *(hah-teet-yeh)* **хотите** (want) to do. Practice saying the following **слова** many times. **Вы** will see them *(chah-stah)* **часто.** (often)

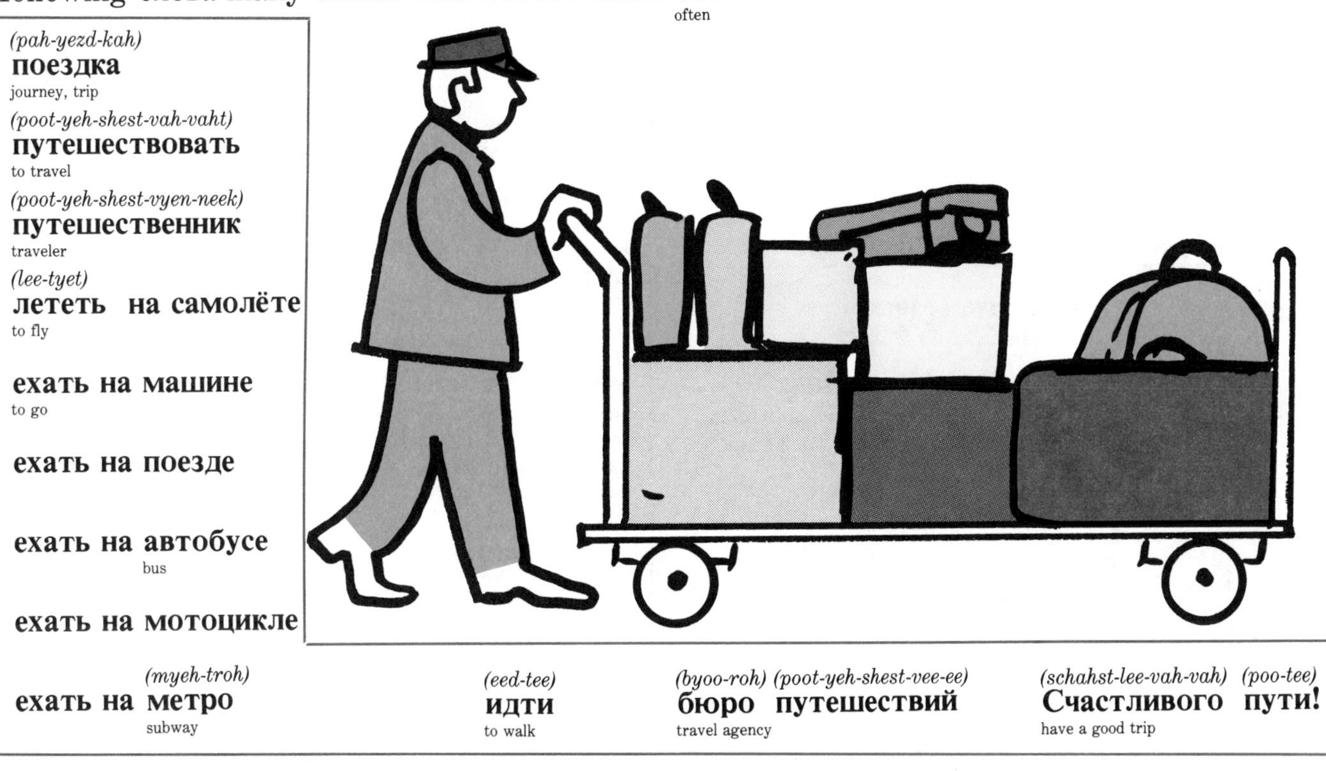

(pah-yezd-kah) **поездка** — journey, trip

(poot-yeh-shest-vah-vaht) **путешествовать** — to travel

(poot-yeh-shest-vyen-neek) **путешественник** — traveler

(lee-tyet) **лететь** (to fly) **на самолёте**

ехать (to go) **на машине**

ехать на поезде

ехать на автобусе (bus)

ехать на мотоцикле

ехать на *(myeh-troh)* **метро** (subway)

(eed-tee) **идти** — to walk

(byoo-roh) **бюро** *(poot-yeh-shest-vee-ee)* **путешествий** — travel agency

(schahst-lee-vah-vah) **Счастливого** *(poo-tee)* **пути!** — have a good trip

(vnee-zoo) **Внизу** some basic signs which *(vahm)* **вам** *(noozh-nah)* **нужно** *(znaht)* **знать** (to know). Most of these **слов** come from the verbs, *(vhah-deet)* **входить** = to enter **и** *(vwee-hah-deet)* **выходить** = to go out/to exit.

(vhohd) **вход** (entrance) ____________________

(glahv-nee) **главный** (main) **вход** (entrance) ____________________

(vhoh-dah) **входа нет** (do not enter) входа нет

(vwee-hahd) **выход** (exit) ____________________

(zah-pahs-noy) **запасной** (emergency) **выход** (exit) ____________________

(oht) **от** *(syeb-yah)* **себя** (push (doors)) ____________________

(kuh) **к** *(syeb-yeh)* **себе** (pull (doors)) ____________________

ВХОД

ВЫХОД

ОТ СЕБЯ

К СЕБЕ

☐ **сигара** *(see-gah-rah)* .... cigar ____________________
☐ **сигарета** *(see-gah-ryet-ah)* .... cigarette ____________________
☐ **симфония** *(seem-foh-nee-yah)* .... symphony **с** ____________________
☐ **советский** *(sah-vyet-skee)* .... Soviet ____________________
☐ **стадион** *(stah-dee-ohn)* .... stadium ____________________

(yek-haht) *(vahzh-nee)* *(dil-yah)* *(too-rees-tah)*
„Ехать" is **очень важный** verb **для** (for) **туриста.** If **вы** choose **ехать на машине, вот** a few key **слов.**

(shohs-syeh)
шоссе (main road) шоссе, шоссе ____

(dah-roh-gah)
дорога в Ленинград (road) ____

(oo-leet-sah)
улица (street) ____

(mah-shen-nah)(nah-prah-kaht)
машина напрокат (rental car) ____

(byoo-roh) *(prah-kah-tah)*
бюро проката (car rental agency) ____

(ahv-tah-stahnt-see-yah)
автостанция (service station) ____

Вот четыре очень important opposites.

Ленинград - Москва		
(aht-hoh-deet) **Отходит** departs	**Поезд No.**	*(pree-dyoht)* **Придёт** arrives
0:41	50	12:41
7:40	19	19:40
12:15	10	0:15
14:32	4	2:32
21:40	22	9:40

(pree-yezd)
приезд (arrival) ____

(aht-prahv-lyen-ee-yeh)
отправление (departure) ____

(ee-nah-strahn-nee)
иностранный (foreign) ____

(myest-nee)
местный (domestic/internal) местный ____

Let's learn the basic travel verbs. Follow the same pattern **вы** have in previous steps.

(lee-tyet)
лететь = to fly

лететь ____

(prah-veet)
править = to drive

____

(zah-kah-zih-vaht)
заказывать = to reserve/order

____

(pree-yez-zhaht)
приезжать = to arrive

____

(oo-yez-zhaht)
уезжать = to leave

____

(dyeh-laht)
делать = to make

____

(ah-pahz-dih-vaht)
опаздывать = to be late

____

(dyeh-laht) (pyair-yeh-sahd-koo)
делать пересадку = to make a transfer

____

(oo-klah-dih-vaht)
укладывать = to pack

____

(pree-hah-deet)
приходить = to arrive (trains, buses, ships)

____

(aht-hah-deet)
отходить = to depart (trains, buses, ships)

____

Т

- ☐ **старт** *(start)*............................ start ____
- ☐ **студент** *(stoo-dyent)*...................... student ____
- ☐ **суп** *(soup)*............................. soup ____
- ☐ **табак** *(tah-bahk)*......................... tobacco ____
- ☐ **такси** *(tahk-see)*......................... taxi ____

С these verbs, вы are ready for any trip anywhere. Вы should have no problem с these verbs, just remember the basic "plug-in" formula вы have already learned. Use that knowledge to translate the following thoughts **на русский** (into). **Ответы внизу.**

1. I fly to the Soviet Union. ______________________________
2. I make a transfer in Moscow. ______________________________
3. He arrives in Yalta. ______________________________
4. We leave tomorrow. ______________________________
5. We reserve tickets to Kiev. ______________________________
6. They drive to Novgorod. ______________________________
7. Where is the train to Odessa? ______________________________
8. How can I fly to the Soviet Union? On British Airways or Aeroflot? ______________________________

____

Вот some **новые** *(noh-vih-yeh)* **слова для** *(dil-yah)* **поездки.** *(pah-yezd-kee)* As always, write out **слова и** practice the sample sentences out loud.

(plaht-for-mah)
платформа
platform

____

Извините. Где платформа номер два?

(vahk-zahl)
вокзал
train station

вокзал

Извините. Где вокзал?

(air-oh-drohm)
аэродром
airport

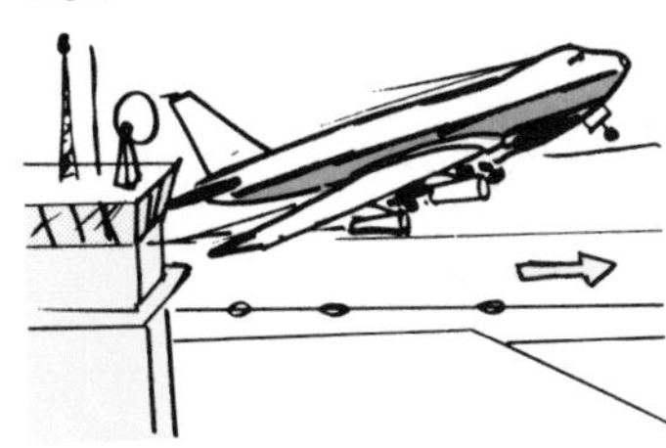

____

Извините. Где аэродром?

ответы

1. Я лечу в СССР.
2. Я делаю пересадку в Москве.
3. Он приезжает в Ялту.
4. Мы уезжаем завтра.
5. Мы заказываем билеты в Киев.
6. Они правят в Новгород.
7. Где поезд в Одессу?
8. Как я могу лететь в СССР? Британской Авиалинией или Аэрофлотом?

(bahnk)
банк
bank

____

Извините. Где банк?

(byoo-roh) (nah-hoh-dahk)
бюро находок
office for lost-and-found

____

Извините. Где бюро находок?

(rah-spee-sah-nee-yeh)
расписание поездов
timetable

Ленинград - Москва		
(aht-hah-deet) Отходит departs	Поезд No.	*(pree-dyoht)* Придёт arrives
0:41	50	12:41
7:40	19	19:40
12:15	10	0:15
14:32	4	2:32
21:40	22	9:40

____

Извините. Где расписание поездов?

(zahn-yah-tah)
занято _______________
occupied

(svah-bohd-nah)
свободно _______________
free

(vah-gohn)
вагон _______________
compartment/wagon

(myes-tah)
место место, место, место
seat/place

(et-tah)
Это место занято? _______________

Это место свободно? _______________

(et-tut) (vah-gohn) (zahn-yaht)
Этот вагон занят? _______________
this

(svah-bohd-yen)
Этот вагон свободен? _______________

Practice writing out the following **вопросы.** It will help you **позже.** *(pohzh-yeh)* later

Извините. Где туалет? _______________

(vah-gohn-res-tah-rahn)
Извините. Где вагон-ресторан? _______________
dining compartment

(zahl) (ah-zhee-dahn-ee-yah)
Где зал ожидания? Где зал ожидания?
waiting room

Где окно номер восемь? _______________
window

(mohzh-nah) (koo-reet)
Можно курить? _______________
is it possible to smoke

НЕ КУРИТЬ! _______________
no smoking

- ☐ **театр** *(tee-ah-ter)*........................ theater
- ☐ **телевизор** *(teh-leh-vee-zor)*................ television
- ☐ **телеграмма** *(teh-leh-grahm-mah)*.......... telegram
- ☐ **телескоп** *(tel-leh-skope)*.................. telescope
- ☐ **телефон** *(teh-leh-fohn)*.................... telephone

Т

Increase your travel **слова** by writing out **слова внизу и** practicing the sample sentences out loud. Practice asking „**где**" questions.

(vuh)
в ______________________
to
Где поезд в Москву?

(poot)
путь ______________________
line/route
Где путь номер семь?

(kah-myair-ah)(hrahn-yen-ee-yah)
камера хранения ______________________
left-luggage office
Где...?

(nah-seelsh-cheek)
носильщик ______________________
porter
Где носильщик?

(vreh-mee-nee)
времени ______________________
time
У меня мало времени.

(sprah-vahch-nah-yeh)(byoo-roh)
справочное бюро ______________________
information bureau
Где...?

(tah-mohzh-nyah)
таможня ______________________
customs
Где таможня?

(kahs-sah)
касса ______________________
tickets/cashier
Где касса?

Practice these **слова** every day. **Вы** will be surprised **как часто** *(chahs-tah)* [often] **вы** will use them.

Вы можете *(mohzh-yet-yeh)* [can] **прочитать** *(prah-chee-taht)* [read] the following paragraph?

Вы теперь в самолёте *(sah-mahl-yoht-yeh)* **и вы летите** *(lee-teet-yeh)* [fly] **в СССР. У** *(oo)* [you] **вас** *(vahs)* [have] **есть деньги** *(dyen-gee)* (you do, don't you?), **билеты, паспорт** *(pahs-port)* [passport], **виза** *(vee-zah)* [visa] **и чемодан** *(cheh-mah-dahn)* [suitcases]. **Теперь вы турист** *(too-reest)*. **Вы приедете** *(pree-yed-yet-yeh)* [arrive] **завтра в пять часов в СССР. Счастливого** *(schahst-lee-vah-vah)* **пути!** *(poo-tee)*

В СССР, there are **два** main types of **поезда. Пригородные** *(pree-gah-rahd-nee-yeh)* [suburban] **поезда,** called „**электрички,**" *(el-ek-treech-kee)* provide the main transportation from **пригородов** *(pree-gah-rah-dahv)* [suburbs] to **центра** *(tsen-trah)* [center] **города** *(goh-rah-dah)* [(of) city]. **Междугородные** *(myezh-doo-gah-rohd-nee-yeh)* [inter-city/long distance] **поезда** travel longer distances, **между** *(myezh-doo)* [between] **городами** *(gah-rah-dah-mee)* [cities]. If **вы путешествуете** *(poot-yeh-shest-voo-yet-yeh)* [travel] **из** [from] **Москвы в Ленинград, или из Москвы во Владивосток, вы** may want to catch **скорый** *(skor-ee)* [express] **поезд** that travels faster **и** makes no intermediate stops.

Some **поезда** have **вагоны-рестораны и** some **поезда** have **спальные** *(spahl-nee-yeh)* [sleeping] **вагоны** [wagons]. All this will be indicated on your **расписание,** *(rah-spee-sah-nee-yeh)* [timetable] but remember **вы знаете** *(znah-yet-yeh)* [know] **как** to ask things like this.

Practice your possible **вопросы** combinations by writing out the following samples.

Где спальный *(spahl-nee)* [sleeping] **вагон?** [compartment/wagon] ______________________

Где буфет? *(boof-yet)* [snack car] ______________________

Т

- ☐ **теннис** *(tyen-nees)*........................ tennis ______________
- ☐ **три** *(tree)*........................ three ______________
- ☐ **томат** *(tah-maht)*........................ tomato ______________
- ☐ **тост** *(toast)*........................ toast ______________
- ☐ **турист** *(toor-eest)*........................ tourist ______________

What about inquiring about the price of (beel-yet-tohv) **билетов?** tickets **Вы** (mohzh-yet-yeh) **можете** can ask **вопросы.**

(beel-yet)
Сколько стоит билет в Ленинград? ______________________________

(ahd-nohm)(nah-prahv-lyen-ee-ee) **В одном направлении** one-way ______________________ (too-dah) **туда** there **и** (ahb-raht-nah) **обратно** and back ______________________

(ah-des-soo)
Сколько стоит билет в Одессу? ______________________________

(mahsk-voo)
Сколько стоит билет в Москву? ______________________________

(ahb-raht-nah)
Туда и обратно? Туда и обратно?

What about times of (aht-prahv-lyen-ee-yah) **отправления** departures **и** (pree-bit-ee-yah) **прибытия?** arrivals **Вы** (toh-zheh) **тоже можете** ask these **вопросы.**

(kahg-dah) **Когда** when **я** (mah-goo) **могу** can (yek-haht) **ехать** go **на поезде в** (tahsh-kyent) **Ташкент?** ______________________________

Когда я могу (lee-tyet) **лететь на** (sah-mahl-yoht-yeh) **самолёте в Москву?** ______________________________

Когда я могу лететь на самолёте (voh) **во** (vlah-dee-vah-stohk) **Владивосток?** ______________________________

Когда (pree-dyoht) **придёт** arrives **поезд из** from (ree-gee) **Риги?** Riga ______________________________

Когда придёт поезд из (bah-koo) **Баку?** Baku ______________________________

Вы have just arrived **в СССР. Вы теперь на** at (vahk-zahl-yeh) **вокзале. Вы** (hah-teet-yeh) **хотите** want **ехать** to go **в Ленинград?** (kee-yev) **В Киев?** Kiev **В Москву?** Well, tell that to the person at **окна** window selling **билеты.**

(hah-choo) **Я хочу** (pah-yek-haht) **поехать в** (nohv-gah-rahd) **Новгород.** ______________________________

Я хочу поехать в (yahl-too) **Ялту.** Yalta Я хочу поехать в Ялту.

Я хочу поехать в (ah-des-soo) **Одессу.** Odessa ______________________________

Когда я (mah-goo) **могу ехать на поезде в Одессу?** ______________________________

Сколько стоит билет в Одессу? ______________________________

Я хочу купить билет в Одессу. ______________________________

(ahb-raht-nah)
Туда и обратно? ______________________________

(men-yeh) **Мне** I need (noozh-nah) **нужно** (sdyeh-laht) **сделать** to make (pyair-yeh-sahd-koo) **пересадку?** a transfer ______________________ (spah-see-bah) **Спасибо.** ______________________

С this practice, **вы** are off **и** running. These travel **слова** will make your holiday twice as enjoyable **и** at least three times as easy. Review these **новые слова** by doing the crossword puzzle (nah) **на странице** 77. Practice drilling yourself on this Step by selecting other locations **и** asking your own **вопросы** about **поездах,** *(poh-yez-dahk)* **автобусах** *(ahv-toh-boo-sahk)* **или самолётах** *(sah-mahl-yoh-tahk)* that go there. Select **новые слова из** *(eez)* from **словаря** *(slah-var-yah)* dictionary **и** practice asking questions that begin **с**

ГДЕ **КОГДА** **СКОЛЬКО** **КАК ЧАСТО** **или** making statements like

Я хочу поехать в Смоленск.
Я хочу купить билет.

ACROSS

1. to arrive
2. station
3. platform
4. excuse me
5. main road
6. compartment/wagon
7. to eat
8. one
9. thank-you
10. arrival
11. eastern
12. cat
13. customs
14. under
15. fast
16. domestic/internal
17. to order/reserve
18. street
19. bank
20. motorcycle

DOWN

3. traveler
8. departure
14. to drink
16. menu
21. restaurant
22. to go/to ride
23. or
24. tomorrow
25. over
26. schedule
27. airport
28. left
29. mail/post office
30. to open
31. porter
32. give!
33. taxi
34. toilet

ACROSS

1. приезжать
2. станция
3. платформа
4. извините
5. шоссе
6. вагон
7. есть
8. один
9. спасибо
10. приезд
11. восточный
12. кот
13. таможня
14. под
15. быстро
16. местный
17. заказывать
18. улица
19. банк
20. мотоцикл

DOWN

3. путешественник
8. отправление
14. пить
16. меню
21. ресторан
22. ехать
23. или
24. завтра
25. над
26. расписание
27. аэродром
28. лево
29. почта
30. открывать
31. носильщик
32. дайте
33. такси
34. туалет

Step 18

(myen-yoo) **Меню** (menu)

Вы теперь в СССР и у (oo) (you have) **вас** (vahs) **есть номер. Вы голодны** (gah-lohd-nih) (hungry)**. Вы хотите** (hah-teet-yeh) **есть** (yest) (to eat)**. Где хороший** (hah-roh-shee) (good) **ресторан** (res-tah-rahn)**?** First of all, there are different types of places to eat. Let's learn them.

(res-tah-rahn) **ресторан**	= the most expensive and fancy of **русских** restaurants— frequently a dinner-and-dance establishment
(stah-loh-vah-yah) **столовая**	= generally self-service, similar to a cafeteria **или** canteen
(boof-yet) **буфет**	= a snack bar generally found in **гостиницах,** theaters, **музеях** (moo-zay-yahk) **и** stations
(bar) **бар**	= exactly that, a place **где** drinks are served
(kahf-yeh) **кафе**	= similar to a restaurant serving meals through the evening

There are some **рестораны** whose names are indicative of the foods they serve.

(shahsh-leech-nah-yah) **шашлычная**	= where they serve **шашлык** (shahsh-leek) (shashlik, kebabs)
(pee-rohzh-kah-vah-yah) **пирожковая**	= **где** they serve **пирожки** (pee-rohzh-kee) (pastries, small cakes)
(bleen-nah-yah) **блинная**	= **где** they serve **блины** (blee-nee) (pancakes)
(pyel-myen-nah-yah) **пельменная**	= **где они** serve **пельмени** (pyel-myen-ee) (pelmeni, dumplings)
(zah-koo-sahch-nah-yah) **закусочная**	= **где они** serve **закуски** (zah-koo-skee) (snacks)

Try them all. Experiment. **Теперь вы** have found **хороший** (hah-roh-shee) **ресторан** (res-tah-rahn)**. Вы входите** (vhoh-deet-yeh) (enter) **в ресторан и находите** (nah-hoh-deet-yeh) (find) **место** (myes-tah) (seat)**.** Sharing **столы** (stoh-lih) (tables) **с** others is a common **и очень** (oh-chen) (very) pleasant **обычай** (ah-bih-chay) (custom) **в СССР.** If **вы видите** (vee-deet-yeh) (see) a vacant **стул,** (stool) (chair) just be sure to ask

Извините. Это место занято? (zahn-yah-tah) (occupied)

If **вам** (vahm) **нужно** (noozh-nah) (you need) **меню,** catch the attention of **официант** (ah-feet-see-ahnt) (waiter) **и** say

Официант! Дайте (die-tee) **мне меню, пожалуйста** (pah-zhahl-oos-tah)**.**

- ☐ **февраль** *(fyev-rahl)*........................ February
- ☐ **фильм** *(feelm)*............................ film
- ☐ **фотограф** *(fah-toh-grahf)*.................. photographer
- ☐ **Франция** *(frahn-tsee-yah)*.................. France
- ☐ —where they speak **по-французски** *(pah-frahn-tsoo-skee)*

ф

В СССР, there are **три** main meals to enjoy every day, plus (kohf-yeh) **кофе и** perhaps pastry (dil-yah) **для** (for) the tired traveler late in (den-yohm) **днём** (afternoon).

(zahv-trahk) **завтрак**	=	breakfast ...	**в СССР** can mean much more than **чай или кофе, хлеб, масло, и** jam. It may include ham **и** (yight-sah) **яйца,** (eggs) (seer) **сыр** (cheese) **или** (sah-see-skee) **сосиски** (sausages). Check serving times before **вы** retire for the night.
(ah-byed) **обед**	=	mid-day meal ...	generally served from 14:00 to 16:00. For most people, this is the main meal of the day.
(oo-zheen) **ужин**	=	evening meal ...	generally served from 19:00 to 22:30; frequently, after 22:30, only cold meals are served.

If **вы** look around you **в русском ресторане, вы** will see that some **русские** (ah-bih-chah-ee) **обычаи** (customs) are different from ours. (hlyeb) **Хлеб** (bread) may be set directly on the tablecloth, elbows are often rested (nah) **на столе и** please (nyeh) **не** forget to mop up your (soh-oos) **соус** (sauce) **с** your (hlyeb-ahm) **хлебом.** Before beginning your (ah-byed) **обед,** be sure to wish those sharing your table (pree-yaht-nah-vah) (ahp-peh-tee-tah) **„Приятного аппетита.“** (enjoy your meal) If your **официант** asks if **вы** enjoyed your (ah-byed) **обед,** a smile **и** a **„Да, спасибо,“** will tell him that **вы** did.

Теперь, it may be breakfast time at home, (noh) **но** (but) **вы в СССР и** it is 20:00. Most **русские** (res-tah-rah-nih) **рестораны** post **меню** outside **или** inside. Ask to see **меню** before being seated so **вы** (znah-yet-yeh) **знаете** (know) what type of (ah-byed-ih) **обеды** (meals) **и** (tsyen-ih) **цены** (prices) **вы** will encounter inside. Most **рестораны** offer a special meal of the day. This is a complete (ah-byed) **обед** (meal) at a fair (tsyen-yeh) **цене** (price). Be forewarned that frequently all items **в меню** are **не** available. So have a second **и** third choice in mind.

In addition, there are the following main categories **в меню.**

- ☐ **фрукт** *(frookt)*.......... fruit
- ☐ **футбол** *(foot-bohl)*.......... soccer, football
- ☐ **царь** *(tsar)*.......... czar, tsar
- ☐ **цирк** *(tseerk)*.......... circus
- ☐ **Чили** *(chee-lee)*.......... Chile

Ц ____________________ ____________________ ____________________

Ч ____________________ ____________________

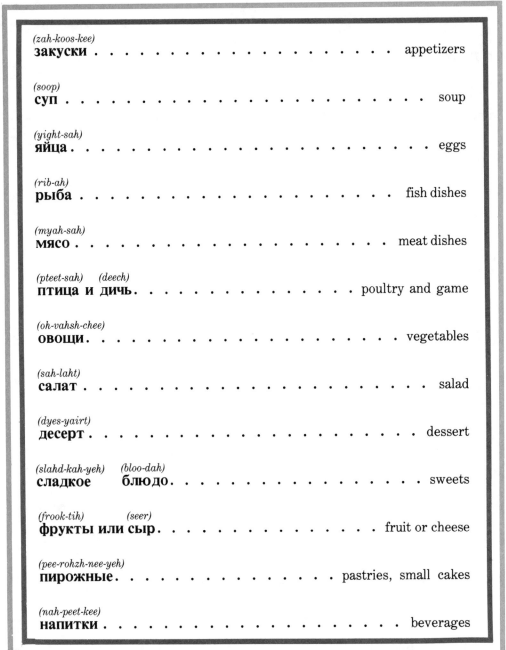

(zah-koos-kee)
закуски . . . . appetizers

(soop)
суп . . . . soup

(yight-sah)
яйца . . . . eggs

(rib-ah)
рыба . . . . fish dishes

(myah-sah)
мясо . . . . meat dishes

(pteet-sah) *(deech)*
птица и дичь . . . . poultry and game

(oh-vahsh-chee)
овощи . . . . vegetables

(sah-laht)
салат . . . . salad

(dyes-yairt)
десерт . . . . dessert

(slahd-kah-yeh) *(bloo-dah)*
сладкое блюдо . . . . sweets

(frook-tih) *(seer)*
фрукты или сыр . . . . fruit or cheese

(pee-rohzh-nee-yeh)
пирожные . . . . pastries, small cakes

(nah-peet-kee)
напитки . . . . beverages

Most **рестораны** have standard **меню.** Don't expect to get a separate wine list—it is usually printed on **меню.** Service can be slow, so be prepared to wait between courses. **Теперь** for a preview of delights to come... At the back of this *(kuh-nee-gee)* **книги, вы** will find a sample **русское меню.** Read **меню** *(see-vohd-nyah)* **сегодня** (today) **и** learn **новые слова! Когда вы** are ready to leave for **СССР** cut out **меню,** fold it **и** carry it in your pocket, wallet **или** purse. **Не** study **меню** until after **вы** have eaten **или вы** will be **очень** hungry.

Ш

- ☐ **шарф** *(sharf)*. . . . . scarf
- ☐ **Швеция** *(shvet-see-yah)*. . . . . Sweden
- ☐ —where they speak **по-шведски** *(pah-shved-skee)*
- ☐ **штат** *(shtaht)*. . . . . state
- ☐ **шторм** *(shtorm)*. . . . . storm

In addition, learning the following should help you to identify what kind of meat **или** poultry **вы хотите** *(hah-teet-yeh)* **заказывать** *(zah-kah-zih-vaht)* (to order) **и как** it will be prepared.

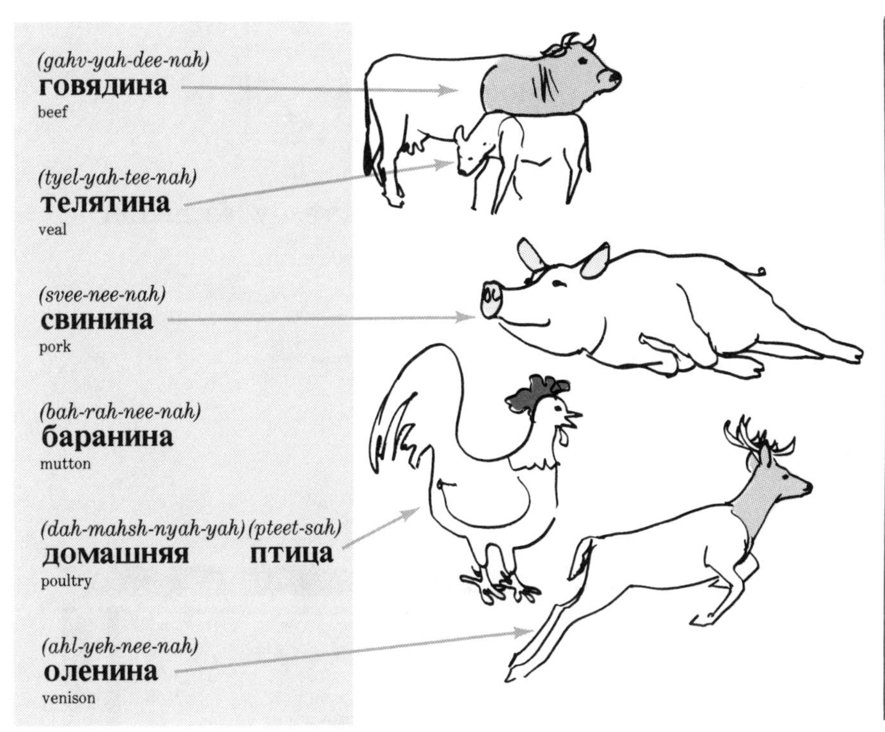

(aht-var-noh-yeh) **отварное** = boiled

(zhar-yen-ah-yeh) **жареное** = roasted/fried

(toosh-yoh-nah-yeh) **тушёное** = stewed

(zahp-yeh-chen-nah-yeh) **запеченное** = baked

(nah-too-rahl-nee) **натуральный** = grilled

(far-shee-roh-vah-nee) **фаршированый** = stuffed

Вы will also get **овощи** *(oh-vahsh-chee)* (vegetables) with your **обедом** *(ahb-yed-ahm)* (meal) **и** perhaps **салат.** One day at an open-air **рынке** *(rin-kyeh)* (market) will teach you **названия** *(nahz-vah-nee-yah)* (names) for all the different kinds of **овощей** *(ah-vahsh-chay)* **и фруктов,** *(frook-tahv)* (fruit) plus it will be a delightful experience for you. **Вы можете** *(mohzh-yet-yeh)* always consult your menu guide at the back of **книги** *(kuh-nee-gee)* if **вы** forget the correct **название. Теперь вы** have decided what **вы хотите** *(hah-teet-yeh)* (would like) **есть** *(yest)* (to eat) **и официант** *(ah-feet-see-ahnt)* arrives.

Э

- ☐ **экватор** *(ek-vah-tar)*. . . . . equator ____________
- ☐ **экзамен** *(ek-zah-myen)*. exam ____________
- ☐ **экономика** *(ek-ah-noh-mee-kah)*. . . . . economics ____________
- ☐ **экспресс** *(ek-spres)*. . . . . express ____________
- ☐ **эра** *(air-ah)*. . . . . era ____________

Не forget to treat yourself to **русским десертом.** You would not want to miss out on trying the following **десерт.**

(kees-yel) **кисель** jello-type dessert	*(mah-roh-zhen-ah-yeh)* **мороженое** ice cream
(pee-rohg) **пирог** tart	*(roh-mah-vah-yah) (bah-bah)* **ромовая баба** cake steeped in rum

After completing your *(ah-byed)* **обед,** call *(ah-feet-see-ahn-tah)* **официанта и** pay just as **вы** have already learned in Step 16:

(die-tee) *(pah-zhahl-oos-tah)*
Дайте счёт, пожалуйста.

Внизу is a sample **меню** to help you prepare for your holiday.

РЕСТОРАН „ЛЕНИНГРАД“

ОБЕДЕННОЕ МЕНЮ

ХОЛОДНЫЕ ЗАКУСКИ

Икра (caviar)............................**руб. 5-85**
Салат мясной (meat salad).................... **1-35**
Салат с крабами (crab salad)................. **1-10**
Осетрина (sturgeon)......................... **1-10**

СУПЫ

Борщ украинский.............................. **-45**
Щи (cabbage soup)............................ **-51**
Грибной суп (mushroom soup).................. **-56**
Уха (fish soup)............................... **-61**

САЛАТЫ

Салат из помидоров (tomato salad)............ **-52**
Салат из огурцов (cucumber salad)............ **-49**
Салат из капусты с яблоками (cabbage-and-apple salad).. **-59**

ГОРЯЧИЕ БЛЮДА

Бефстроганов (beef Stroganoff)................**3-77**
Котлеты „Ленинградские“ (lamb chops).........**2-60**
Судак в белом вине (perch in white wine)........**2-85**
Осетрина жареная с помидорами (fried sturgeon with tomatoes)..............................**2-91**
Курица жареная с грибами (fried chicken with mushrooms)...............................**2-65**

СЛАДКИИ БЛЮДА

Компот из свежих абрикос (compote of fresh apricots)................................... **-65**
Лимонный мусс (lemon mousse)................. **-85**
Мороженое из ягод (berry ice cream)............ **-95**
Кисель с мороженым (jello with ice cream)....... **-85**

НАПИТКИ

Чай (tea)...................................... **-20**
Кофе (coffee)................................... **-22**
Белое вино (white wine)........................ **-90**
Красное вино (red wine)........................ **-90**
Пиво (beer)..................................... **-85**
Молоко (milk).................................. **-50**
Лимонад (lemonade)............................. **-45**

Ресторан работает с 9 час. до 23 час. 30

- ☐ **эскалатор** *(es-kah-lah-tor)*................. escalator
- ☐ **январь** *(yahn-var)*........................ January
- ☐ **Япония** *(yah-pohn-ee-yah)*................. Japan
- ☐ —where they speak **по-японски** *(pah-yah-pohn-skee)*
- ☐ **яхта** *(yahk-tah)*.......................... yacht

Я

(zahv-trahk)
Завтрак is a little different because it can vary from a light continental breakfast to a
breakfast

hearty breakfast of eggs **или** cold cuts **или** vegetables. **Внизу** is a sample of what **вы**

(mohzh-yet-yeh) *(oo-trahm)*
можете expect to greet you **утром.**
in morning

СТОЛОВАЯ „ОКТЯБРЬСКАЯ“

Доброе Утро!

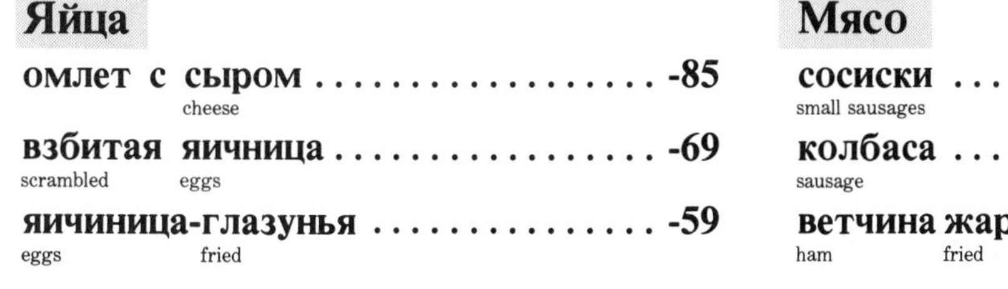

Яйца

омлет с сыром . . . . **-85**
cheese

взбитая яичница . . . . **-69**
scrambled eggs

яичиница-глазунья . . . . **-59**
eggs fried

Мясо

сосиски . . . . **-90**
small sausages

колбаса . . . . **-89**
sausage

ветчина жареная . . . . **-93**
ham fried

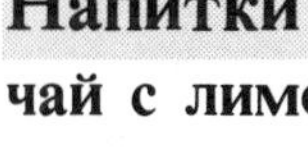

Напитки

чай с лимоном . . . . **-20**

чай с вареньем . . . . **-20**

кофе чёрный . . . . **-20**

кофе с молоком . . . . **-20**

апельсиновый сок . . . . **-30**
orange juice

какао . . . . **-20**

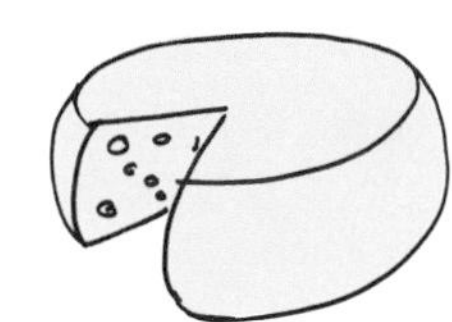

И...

сыр . . . . **-35**
cheese

пирожные . . . . **-28**

булочки . . . . **-15**
rolls

масло . . . . **-03**

варенье . . . . **-02**

блинчики с вареньем . . . . **-85**

Вот a few special greetings **по-русски.**

- ☐ **С Рождеством Христовым!** *(rahzh-dyest-vohm hrees-toh-vim)* . . . . Merry Christmas!
- ☐ **С Новым Годом!** *(noh-vim goh-dahm)* . . . . Happy New Year!
- ☐ **С Днём Рождения!** *(den-yohm rahzh-dyen-ee-yah)* . . . . Happy Birthday!
- ☐ **Поздравления!** *(pahz-drahv-lyen-ee-yah)* . . . . Congratulations!

Step 19

What is different about *(teh-leh-fohn-yeh)* **телефоне в СССР?** Well, **вы** never notice such things until **вы** want to use them. Be warned **теперь** that *(teh-leh-foh-nih)* **телефоны в СССР** are much less numerous than **в** *(shah)* **США или в Канаде.** Nevertheless, **телефон** allows you to call *(drooz-yahm)* **друзьям** (friends), reserve *(beel-yet-ih)* **билеты в** *(tee-ah-ter)* **театр,** *(bahl-yet)* **на балет и** *(kohn-tsairt)* **концерт,** make emergency calls, check on the hours of a *(moo-zyeh-yah)* **музея,** rent *(mah-shen-oo)* **машину** (car) **и** all those other things which *(nahm)* **нам** *(noozh-nah)* **нужно** (we need) **сделать** (to do) on a daily basis. It also gives you a certain amount of freedom **когда вы** *(mohzh-yet-yeh)* **можете** *(panz-vah-neet)* **позвонить** (phone) on your own.

Having **телефон в гостинице не** as common **в СССР** as **в США.** That means that *(vahm)* **вам** *(noozh-nah)* **нужно** *(znaht)* **знать** (to know) **как** to find **телефон:** **на** *(poach-teh)* **почте,** *(nah)* **на** *(oo-leet-seh)* **улице** (street), **в** *(bar-yeh)* **баре** (bar) **и** in the lobby of **гостиницы.**

Вот русский телефон-автомат.

So far, so good. **Теперь,** let's read the instructions for using **телефон.** This is one of those moments when you realize,

Я не в США.
Я не в Канаде.
Я не в Англии.

So let's learn how to operate **телефон.**

(een-strook-tsee-ee)
Инструкции look complicated but actually are not—some of these **слова вы** should be able
instructions

(een-strook-tsee-ee)
to recognize already. Let's learn the others. **Вот как инструкции** might go.

ТЕЛЕФОН-АВТОМАТ

1. Pick up the receiver.
2. Drop **две копейки** into the slot.
3. Wait for the dial tone **и** dial **номер.**

These are free telephone calls:

Бесплатно Вызываются

(pah-zhar-nah-yah) (ah-hrah-nah) **Пожарная охрана** (fire)	01	
Скорая помощь (emergency medical help)	03	
(mee-leet-see-yah) **Милиция** (police)	02	
Служба газа (heating gas service)	04	

(ahn-glee-skee) **Английский**		*(roos-skee)* **Русский**	*(ahn-glee-skee)* **Английский**		*(roos-skee)* **Русский**
telephone	=	*(teh-leh-fohn)* **телефон**	public telephone booth	=	**телефон-автомат**
to telephone	=	*(pahz-vah-neet)* **позвонить**	telephone book	=	*(teh-leh-fohn-nah-yah)* **телефонная книга**
operator	=	*(teh-leh-fahn-eest)* **телефонист**	telephone conversation	=	*(rahz-gah-vor)* **разговор по телефону**

Вы не можете звонить other cities from **телефон-автомат.** To call another city
can

(poach-too)
вам нужно идти на почту или звонить телефонисту из гостиницы.
you need · to go · operator

На почте tell **телефонисту „Мне нужно позвонить в США.“** Do not be surprised if **вы** have to pay for your call in advance. Sometimes it is even necessary to order your call a day in advance.

(troob-koo) (ahl-loh)
When answering **телефон, вы** pick up **трубку и** say, **Алло. Это** ________________.
receiver · your name

(voht)
When saying goodbye, you say **„До свиданья“** or **„До завтра.“** **Вот** some sample
until tomorrow

(dee-ah-loh-gee) (teh-leh-foh-noo)
диалоги по телефону. Write them in the blanks **внизу.**
dialogues

(yah) (pahz-vah-neet) (mahs-kohv-skee) (oo-nee-vyair-see-tyet)
Я хочу позвонить в Московский Университет. ________________
to call · Moscow · university

(hah-choo) (chee-kah-goh)
Я хочу позвонить в Чикаго. ________________
to call · Chicago

(bah-ree-soo) (nohv-gah-rahd-yeh)
Я хочу позвонить Борису в Новгороде. ________________
Boris · Novgorod

(eh-lyen-yeh) (bah-koo)
Я хочу позвонить Елене в Баку. ________________
Baku

(air-oh-floht) (air-ah-port)
Я хочу позвонить в Аэрофлот в Аэропорт. ________________

(lohn-dahn)
Я хочу позвонить в Лондон. ________________

Где телефон-автомат? Где телефон-автомат?
public telephone

Где телефонная книга? ________________
book

(moy) (nohm-yair)
Мой номер 344-21-89. ________________
my

(vahsh) (pah-zhahl-oos-tah)
Ваш номер телефона, пожалуйста? ________________
your · number · telephone

(ahk-tyah-ber-skah-yah)
Номер телефона гостиницы „Октябрьская,“ пожалуйста? ________________
of hotel

Вот another possible **диалог.** Pay close attention to **слова и как** they are used.

(ee-vahn) (ee-vah-nah-veech) (pah-gah-vah-reet) (ahn-noy)
Иван: **Алло. Это Иван Иванович. Я хочу поговорить с Анной Петровной.**
to speak

(syek-ryair-tar) (lee-nee-yah) (zahn-yah-tah)
Секретарь: **Одну минуту, пожалуйста. Извините, но линия занята.**
one, line, busy

(pahv-tah-reet-yeh) (mah-lah)
Иван: **Повторите, пожалуйста. Я мало говорю по-русски.**
repeat, a little

(myed-lyen-nah)
Говорите медленно.
speak, slowly

Секретарь: **Извините, но линия занята.**

Иван: **Ох. Спасибо. До свиданья.**

И still another possibility...

(kaht-yah) (noozh-yen) (pee-troh-veech-ah)
Катя: **Мне нужен номер телефона доктора Петровича в Иркутске, пожалуйста.**

(teh-leh-fahn-eest) (nohm-yair)
Телефонист: **Номер 254-43-96.**

Катя: **Повторите номер, пожалуйста.**

Телефонист: **Номер 254-43-96.**

Катя: **Большое спасибо. До свиданья.**

Телефонист: **Пожалуйста. До свиданья.**

(myed-lyen-nah)
Вы теперь ready to use any **телефон в СССР.** Just take it **медленно и** speak clearly.
slowly

(mohzh-yet-yeh)
Не forget that **вы можете** ask...
can

(skohl-kah) (stoy-eet) (pahz-vah-neet) (ree-goo)
Сколько стоит позвонить в Ригу?
to call, Riga

____

(shah)
Сколько стоит позвонить в США?
U.S.A.

____

(kee-yev)
Сколько стоит позвонить в Киев?
Kiev

____

Сколько стоит позвонить в Англию?

____

(vahm) (myel-ahch)
Remember that **вам нужна мелочь для телефона.**
you need, change

Step 20

An excellent means of transportation **в СССР** is **метро** *(myeh-troh)* (subway). Both **в Ленинграде и в Москве, метро** is an extensive system with express lines to the suburbs. **Трамвай** *(trahm-vy)* (streetcar/trolley) is also a good means of transportation, plus **вы можете** see your surroundings **на трамвае** *(trahm-vah-yeh)*.

Какие *(kahk-ee-yeh)* (what kind of) **слова** (words) **нужны** *(noozh-nih)* (necessary) **для** a traveler **на** (on) **метро** *(myeh-troh)* (subway), **на автобусе, на трамвае** *(trahm-vah-yeh)* **или в такси?**

Let's learn them by practicing them aloud **и** then by writing them in the blanks below.

метро *(myeh-troh)*	**трамвай** *(trahm-vy)*	**автобус** *(ahv-toh-boos)*
метро, метро ____	____	____

остановка *(ahs-tah-nohv-kah)* = stop ____

остановка автобуса *(ahv-toh-boo-sah)* = bus stop ____

линия *(lee-nee-yah)* = line ____

касса *(kahs-sah)* = ticket machine касса, касса, касса ____

остановка трамвая *(trahm-vah-yah)* = trolley stop ____

станция *(stahnt-see-yah)* **метро** = metro station ____

Let's also review the "transportation" verbs at this point. Yes, both **„уезжать"** *(oo-yez-zhaht)* and **„уходить"** *(oo-hah-deet)* can mean "to leave." Don't worry about it, just be aware of it.

уезжать *(oo-yez-zhaht)* = to leave (by vehicle)

____

уходить *(oo-hah-deet)* = to leave (on foot)

____

приезжать *(pree-yez-zhaht)* = to arrive

____

приходить *(pree-hah-deet)* = to arrive

____

Maps displaying the various **линии** *(lee-nee-ee)* lines **и остановки** *(ahs-tah-nohv-kee)* stops are generally posted inside **станции** *(stahnt-see-ee)* **метро.** Almost every **карта Москвы и Ленинграда** has **метро** map included. **Линии** are color-coded to facilitate reading. **Метро в Москве** has over 50 **станций** *(stahnt-see-ee)* **и** is famous for its elaborate stations with mosaics, chandeliers, paintings **и** sculptures. To enter **метро, вам нужно** to drop **пять** *(pyaht)* **копеек** into the turnstile at **входа.** *(vhoh-dah)* entrance **Вам нужно** a five-kopeck coin which is commonly called **„пятак.“** Other than having foreign words, the Russian **метро** functions just like **метро в США, в Канаде или в Англии.** Locate your destination, select the correct line **и** hop on board. See **карту внизу.**

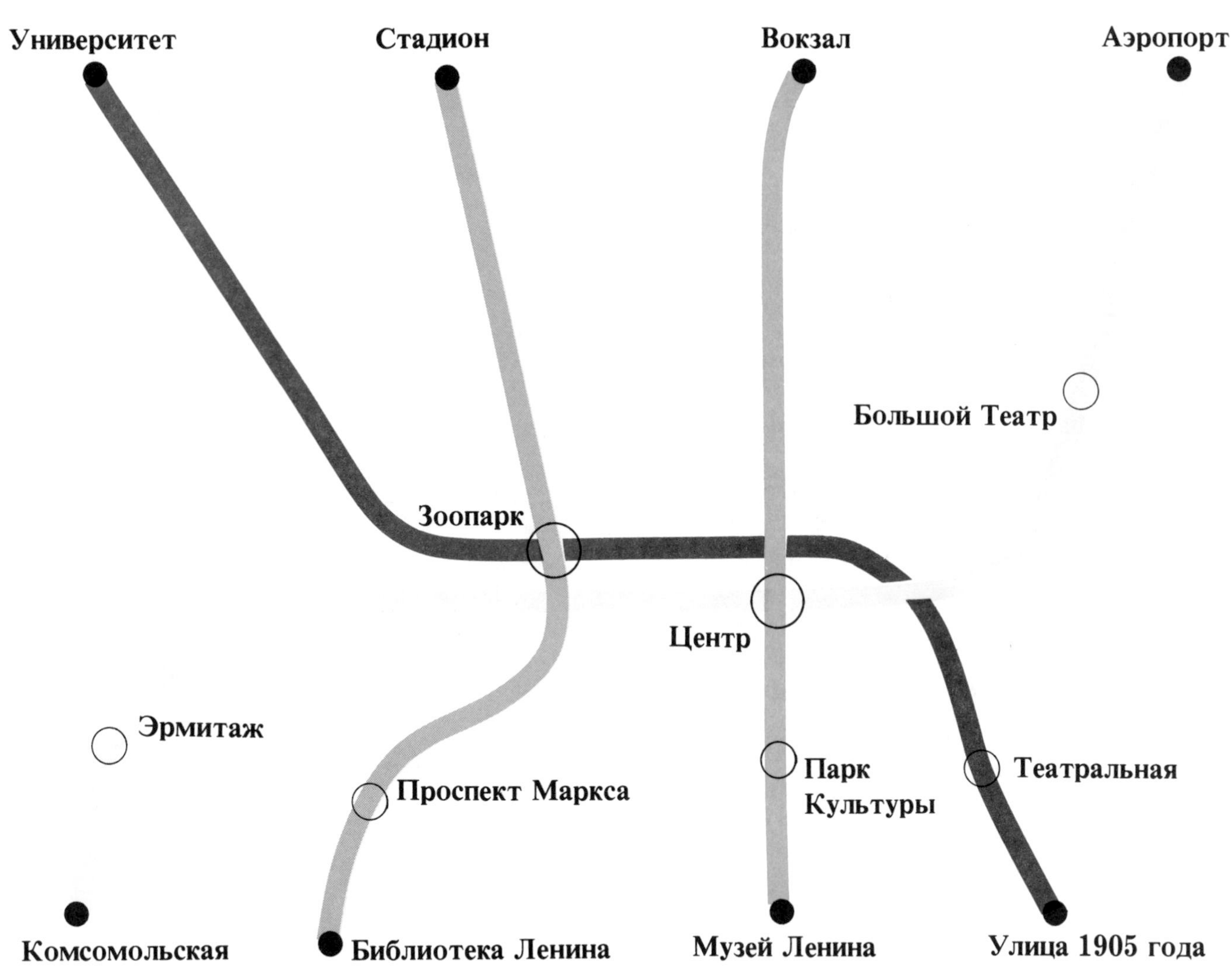

The same basic set of **слова и вопросы** will see you through traveling **на метро, на автобусе, на трамвае, на машине и** even **на поезде.**

Naturally, the first **вопрос** is **„где.“**

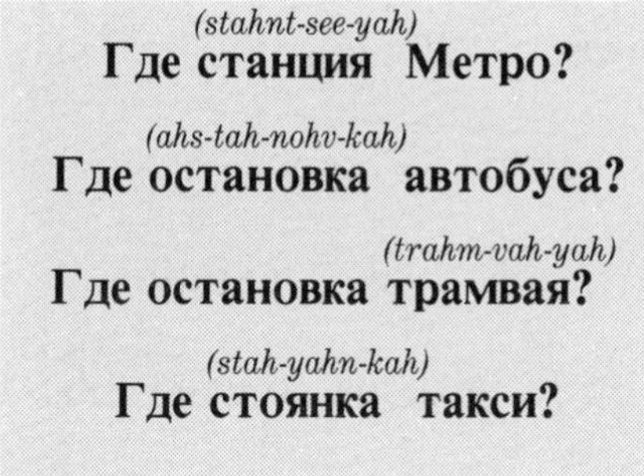

(stahnt-see-yah)
Где станция Метро?

(ahs-tah-nohv-kah)
Где остановка автобуса?

(trahm-vah-yah)
Где остановка трамвая?

(stah-yahn-kah)
Где стоянка такси?

Practice the following basic **вопросы** out loud **и** then write them in the blanks below.

1. **Где станция** *(stahnt-see-yah)* **Метро?** ____________________

   Где остановка автобуса? ____________________

   Где стоянка такси? Где стоянка такси?

2. **Как** (how) **часто** *(chahs-tah)* (often) **ходит** *(hoh-deet)* (goes) **автобус номер 36?** ____________________

   Как часто ходит трамвай *(trahm-vy)* **номер 20?** ____________________

   Как часто ходит поезд *(poh-yezd)* (train)**?** ____________________

3. **Когда** *(kahg-dah)* **отходит** *(aht-hoh-deet)* (leaves) **автобус номер восемь?** ____________________

   Когда отходит трамвай номер три? ____________________

   Когда отходит поезд в центр *(tsen-ter)* (city center)**?** ____________________

4. **Идёт** *(ee-dyoht)* **автобус до Большого Театра?** ____________________

   Идёт трамвай до Зоопарка? ____________________

   Идёт поезд до Гостиницы Метрополь? ____________________

5. **Сколько стоит билет на Метро?** ____________________

   Сколько стоит билет на автобус? ____________________

   Сколько стоит билет на поезд? Сколько стоит билет на поезд?

   Сколько стоит билет на трамвай? ____________________

Теперь that **вы** have gotten into the swing of things, practice the following patterns aloud substituting **„автобус“** for **„метро“** and so on.

1. Где я могу (mah-goo, can) купить (buy) билет на Метро? На автобус? На поезд?

2. Когда отходит (aht-hoh-deet, leaves) поезд в Университет (oo-nee-vyair-see-tyet, university)? В Гостиницу Ленинград? В Аэропорт?

   В Зоопарк? В Центр (tsen-ter, city center)? В Театр? В Музей (moo-zay) Ленина?

3. Где станция (stahnt-see-yah) метро „Проспект Маркса“?

   Где станция метро „Библиотека Ленина“?

   Где остановка (ahs-tah-nohv-kah) автобуса номер 17?

   Где остановка трамвая номер 11?

   Где станция метро „Университет“?

   Где станция метро „Аэропорт“?

   Где остановка автобуса восемь?

   Где станция метро „Вокзал“?

Read the following very typical conversation **и** write it in the blanks **направо.**

Которая (kah-tor-ah-yah, which) **линия для** (dil-yah) **университета** (oo-nee-vyair-see-tyet-ah)**?** ____________________

Красная (krahs-nah-yah, red) **линия до университета.** ____________________

Как часто (chahs-tah, how often)**?** ____________________

Каждые (kahzh-dih-yeh, every) **пять минут.** Каждые пять минут.

Мне (men-yeh, do I) **нужно** (noozh-nah, need) **сделать** (sdyeh-laht, to make) **пересадку** (pyair-yeh-sahd-koo, transfer)**?** ____________________

Да, у зоопарка вам (vahm, you) **нужно** (need) **сделать** (sdyeh-laht) **пересадку** (pyair-yeh-sahd-koo)**.** ____________________

Сколько (skohl-kah, how much) **времени** (vreh-mee-nee, time) **занимает** (takes) **до университета?** ____________________

Двадцать минут. ____________________

Сколько стоит билет до университета? ____________________

Пять копеек (kah-pyeh-eek)**.** ____________________

Вы можете translate the following thoughts **на русский? Ответы внизу.**

1. Where is the subway station? ____________________
2. What does a ticket cost to the university? ____________________
3. How often goes the bus to the airport? ____________________
4. Where can I buy a ticket for the subway? ____________________
5. Where is the bus stop? ____________________
6. Where is the exit? ____________________
7. Do I need to transfer?____________________
8. Where do I need to transfer? ____________________

Here are **три** more verbs.

(stee-raht)
стирать = to wash/clean (clothes)

(tyair-yaht)
терять = to lose

(zah-nee-mah-yet)
занимает = it takes

стирать ____________________ ____________________

Вы знаете the basic "plug-in" formula, so translate the following thoughts **с** these new verbs. **Ответы тоже внизу.**

1. I wash the jacket. ____________________
2. You wash the clothes.____________________
3. It takes 20 minutes to go to the Kremlin. ____________________
4. By car it takes three hours to Odessa.____________________

ОТВЕТЫ

1. **Где станция Метро?**
2. **Сколько стоит билет до университета?**
3. **Как часто ходит автобус в аэропорт?**
4. **Где я могу купить билет на Метро?**
5. **Где остановка автобуса?**
6. **Где выход?**
7. **Мне нужно сделать пересадку?**
8. **Где мне нужно сделать пересадку?**

---

1. **Я стираю жакет.**
2. **Вы стираете одежду.**
3. **Занимает двадцать минут доехать до Кремля.**
4. **На машине занимает три часа до Одессы.**

(prah-dah-vaht) Продавать и *(pah-koo-paht)* Покупать
to sell / to buy

Shopping abroad is exciting. The simple everyday task of buying *(lee-ter)* **литр** (liter) *(mah-lah-kah)* **молока** (milk) **или** *(yah-blah-kah)* **яблоко** (apple) becomes a challenge that *(vwee)* **вы** should **теперь** be able to meet quickly **и** easily. Of course, **вы** will purchase *(soov-yen-ee-rih)* **сувениры** (souvenirs)**, марки и открытки,** but *(nyeh)* **не** forget those many other *(vesh-chee)* **вещи** (things) ranging from shoelaces to **аспирина** that **вы** might need unexpectedly. **Вы** *(znah-yet-yeh)* **знаете** (do you know) the difference *(myezh-doo)* **между** (between) *(kuh-neezh-nim)* **книжным** (book) *(mah-gah-zee-nahm)* **магазином** (store) **и почтой? Нет.** Let's learn about the different *(aht-dyel-ahk)* **отделах** (shops) **и магазинах** (stores) **в СССР. Внизу карта** of a section of **Москвы.**

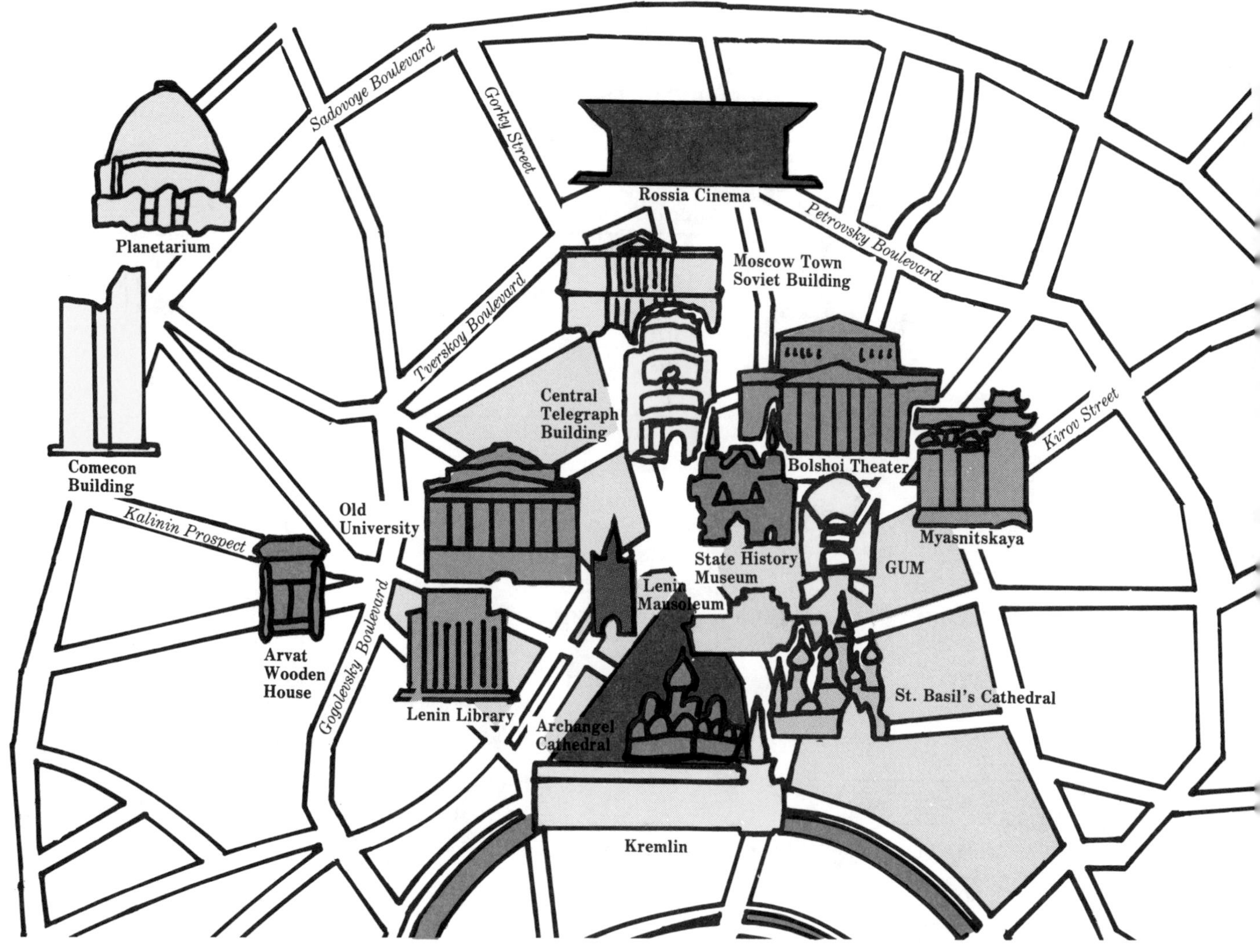

На (on) the following **странице,** there are all types of *(mah-gah-zeen)* **магазин вы** might find **в СССР.** Be sure to fill in the blanks *(kar-teen-kah-mee)* **под** (under) **картинками с** *(nahz-vah-nee-yah-mee)* **названиями** (names) **магазинов.**

(boo-lahch-nah-yah)
булочная, bakery **где**
можно one can **купить** *(koo-peet)* buy **хлеб** *(hlyeb)* bread

(myahs-noy) *(mah-gah-zeen)*
мясной butcher **магазин,** shop **где**
можно купить *(mohzh-nah)* **мясо** *(myah-sah)* meat

(prahch-yech-nah-yah)
прачечная, laundry **где**
можно стирать *(stee-raht)* wash **одежду** *(ah-dyezh-doo)* clothes

(kahf-yeh)
кафе, cafe **где**
можно пить *(peet)* drink **кофе**

(skahb-yah-noy) *(mah-gah-zeen)*
скобяной hardware **магазин,** store **где**
можно купить батарею *(bah-tar-yeh-yoo)* battery

(ahp-tyek-ah)
аптека, pharmacy **где**
можно купить аспирин *(ahs-pee-reen)* aspirin

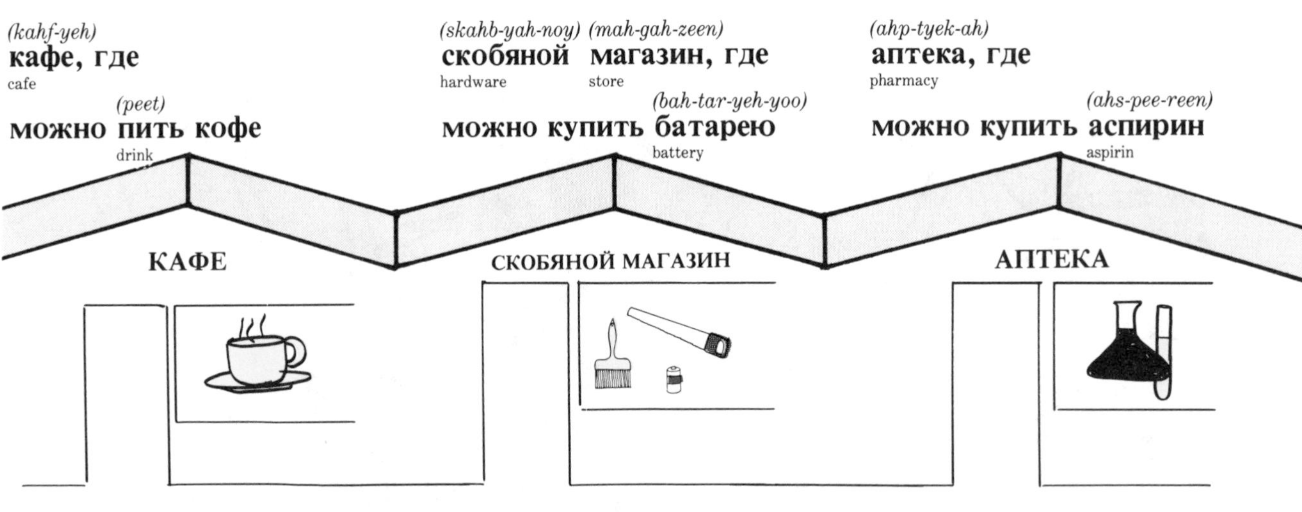

(tsveh-tohch-nih)
цветочный flower **магазин,** shop
где можно купить
(tsvet-ih)
цветы

(tah-bahch-nih)
табачный tobacco **магазин,** store
где можно купить
табак и сигареты *(see-gar-yet-tih)* cigarettes

(kahn-deet-yair-skah-yah)
кондитерская, candy store **где**
можно купить конфеты *(kahn-fyet-tih)* candy
и шоколад *(shah-kah-lahd)* chocolate

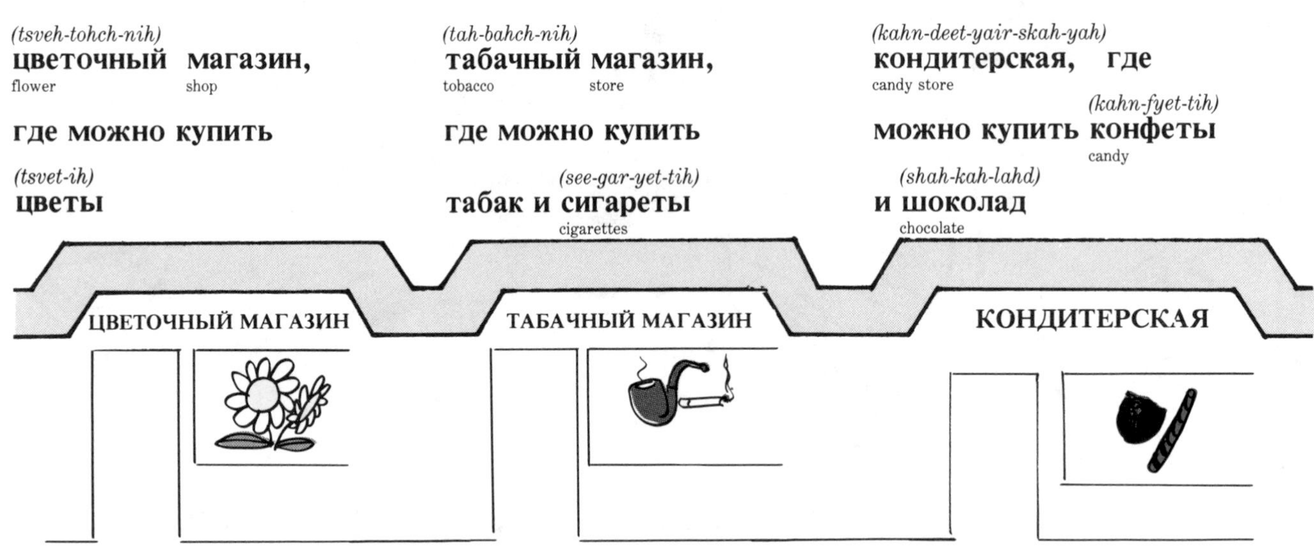

(mah-lohch-nah-yah)
молочная, **где**
dairy
(mah-lah-koh)
можно купить молоко
milk

(bool-lahch-nah-yah)
булочная, **где**
pastry shop
(mohzh-nah) *(pryah-nee-kee)*
можно купить пряники
pastries

(ah-vahsh-chnoy) *(mah-gah-zeen)*
овощной магазин, где
greengrocer's
(oh-vahsh-chee)
можно купить овощи
vegetables

(stah-yahn-kah)
стоянка, **где**
parking lot
(stah-veet)
можно ставить
park/put
(mah-shen-oo)
машину
car

(pah-reek-mahk-yairs-kah-yah)
парикмахерская,
hairdresser
(stree-goot)
где стригут
cut
(voh-lah-sih)
волосы
hair

(ah-tyel-yeh)
ателье, **где**
tailor
(part-noy) *(shyoht)*
портной шьёт
tailor sews
(ah-dyezh-doo)
одежду
clothes

(poach-tah)
почта, где
post office
можно купить
марки

(aht-dyel-yen-yeh) *(mee-leet-see)*
отделение милиции,
police station
(ny-tee)
где можно найти
find
(mee-leet-see-yoo)
милицию
police

(bahnk)
банк, **где**
bank
(ahb-myen-yaht)
можно обменять
exchange
(dyen-gee)
деньги
money

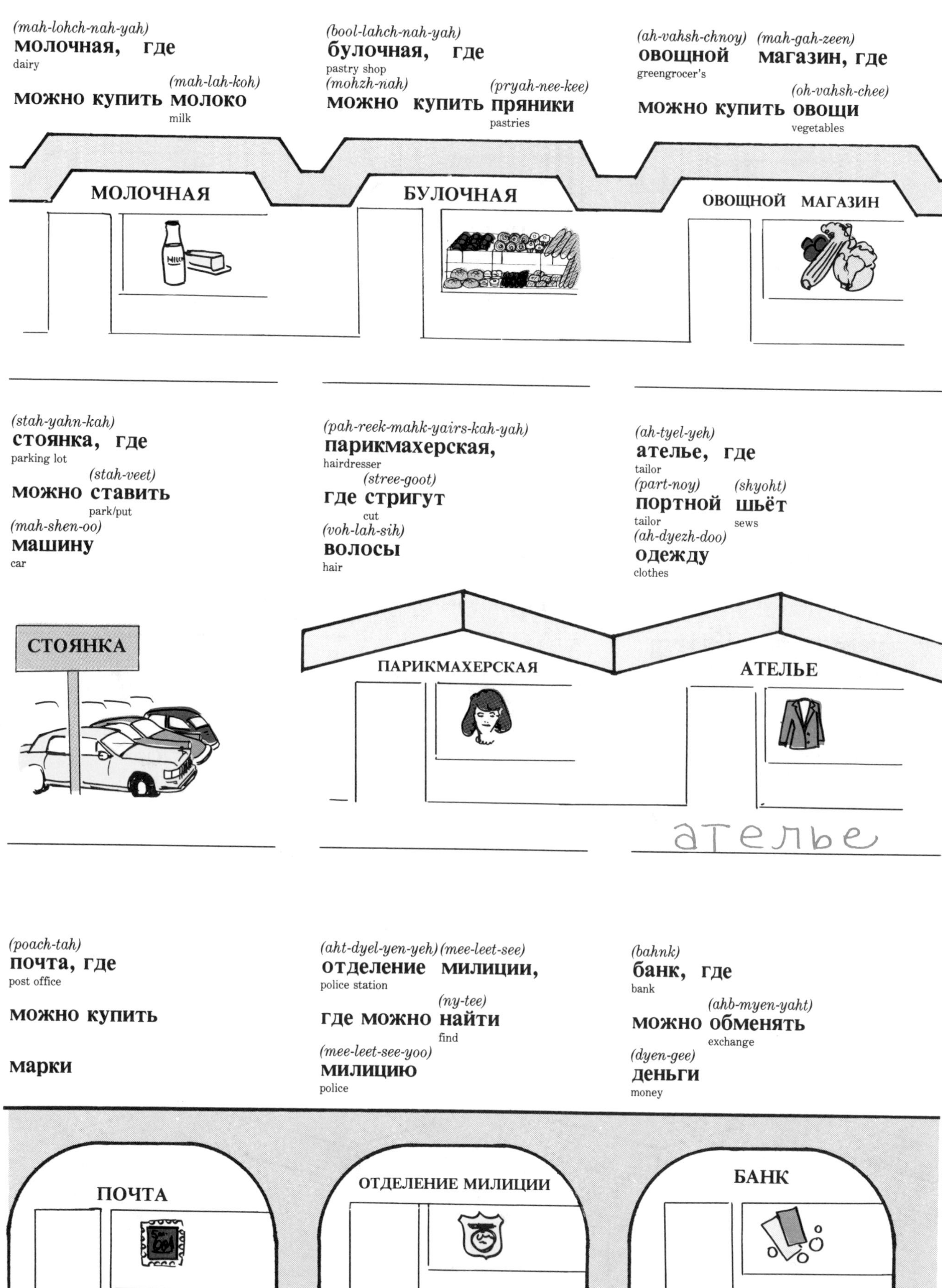

(prahd-mahg)
продмаг, где
food store
(myah-sah)
можно купить мясо,
meat
(frook-tih) *(mah-lah-koh)*
фрукты и молоко

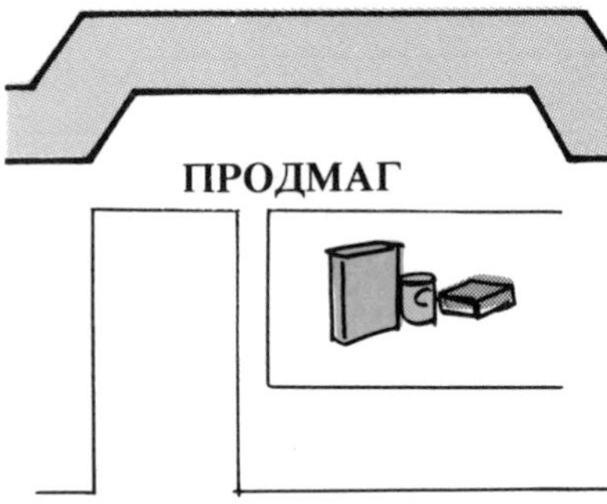

ПРОДМАГ

(gah-strah-nohm)
гастроном, где
delicatessen
можно купить
(kahl-bah-soo)
колбасу
sausage

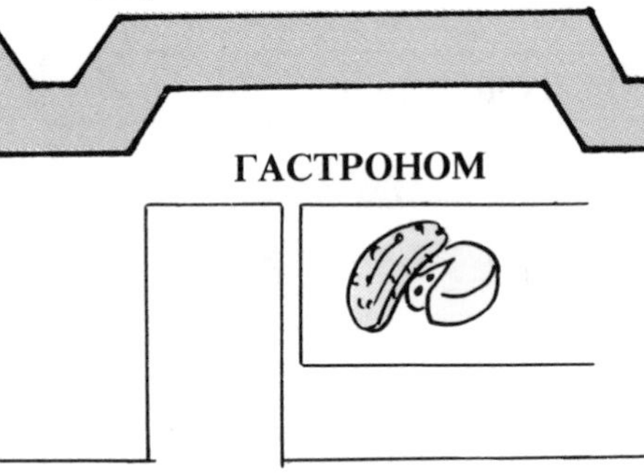

ГАСТРОНОМ

(bair-yohz-kah)
„Берёзка," где
specialty store
(vwee) *(moh-zhet-yeh)*
вы можете купить
(mah-trohsh-kee) *(yahn-tar)*
матрёшки и янтарь
Russian dolls amber

БЕРЁЗКА

(kee-noh)
кино, где
cinema
(pahs-maht-rairt)
можно посмотреть
see
(feelm)
фильм
film

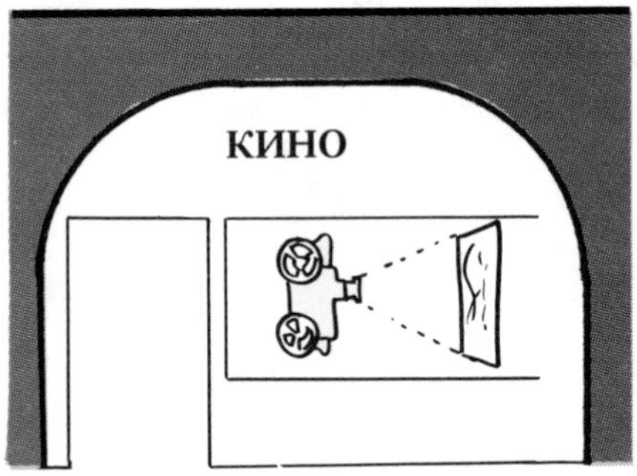

КИНО

КИНО, КИНО

(kee-ohsk)
киоск, где
newsstand
можно купить
(gah-zyet-ih) *(zhoor-nahl-ih)*
газеты и журналы

КИОСК

(heem-cheest-kah)
химчистка, где
dry cleaner's
(cheest-yaht) *(ah-dyezh-doo)*
чистят одежду
clean clothes
(hee-mee-ches-kee)
химически
chemically

ХИМЧИСТКА

(kahnt-stah-vah-rih)
канцтовары, где
stationery store
(rooch-kee)
можно купить ручки,
pens
(boo-mah-goo) *(kah-rahn-dah-shee)*
бумагу и карандаши
paper pencils

КАНЦТОВАРЫ

(kuh-neezh-nee)
книжный магазин,
bookstore
где можно купить
(kuh-nee-gee)
книги
books

КНИЖНЫЙ МАГАЗИН

(oo-nee-vyair-mahg)
универмаг, где
department store
(vsyoh)
можно купить всё
everything

(see Step 22)

УНИВЕРМАГ

(rin-ahk)
рынок, где
market

можно купить

фрукты и овощи

____

(foh-toh-mah-gah-zeen)
фотомагазин,
camera supplies

где можно купить

(foh-toh-plohn-kee)
фотоплёнки
film

фотомагазин

(byen-zah-kah-lohn-kah)
бензоколонка,
service station

где можно купить

(byen-zeen)
бензин
gas/petrol

____

(byoo-roh) (poot-yeh-shest-vee)
бюро путешествий
travel agency

где можно купить

(sah-mahl-yoht)
билеты на самолёт

(chah-sih)
часы, где

можно купить

часы

(rib-nee) (rin-ahk)
рыбный рынок,
fish market

где можно

(rib-oo)
купить рыбу

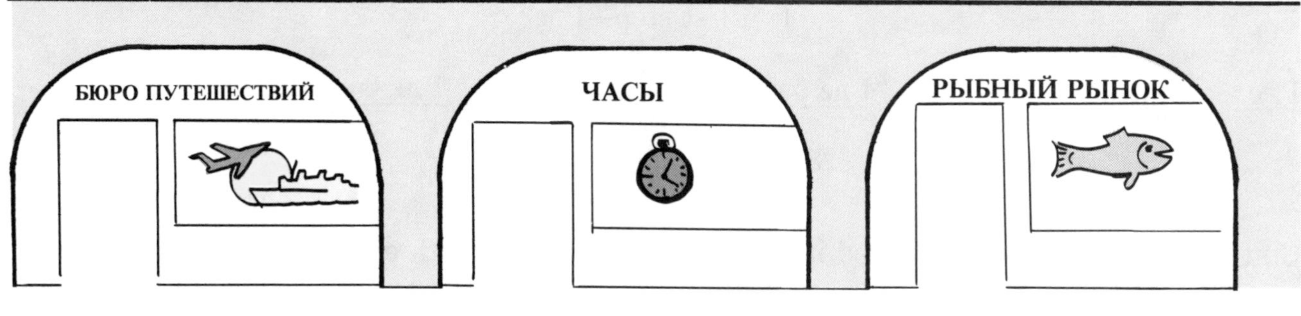

______________________________ ______________________________ ______________________________

Магазины are generally *(aht-krih-tih)* **открыты** (open) **с 8-ми до 20-ти часов.** *(den-yohm)* **Днём с 13-ти до 14-ти магазины** *(zah-krih-tih)* **закрыты** (closed) for lunch. To make one stop for food, go to a *(gah-strah-nohm)* **„гастроном.“** Within this store **вы** will find many small *(aht-dyel-ih)* **отделы:** (shops) *(hlyeb-nee)* **хлебный,** *(kahn-deet-yair-skee)* **кондитерский,** *(mah-lohch-nee)* **молочный,** *(myahs-noy)* **мясной** *(frook-toh-vee)* **и фруктовый. В гастрономе вы не можете купить овощей. Овощи** are sold **на рынках** (markets)**.**

Is there anything else which **вы** will want to know about Russian stores? **Да.** Look at **картинку на** next **странице.**

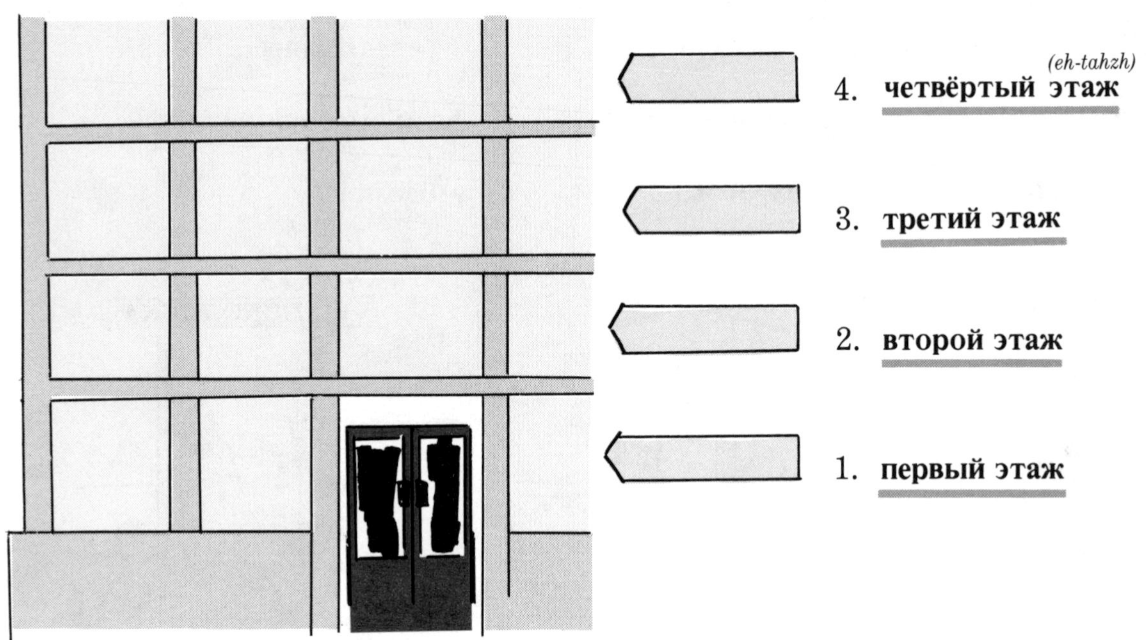

While **в Москве вы** will probably want to visit **ГУМ,** *(goom)* short for **„Государственный** *(gah-soo-darst-vyen-nee)* **Универсальный** *(oo-nee-vyair-sahl-nee)* **Магазин.“ ГУМ** sells everything **от чемоданов до телевизоров.**

Теперь вы know the names for **русских магазинов,** let's practice shopping.

1. First step—**Где?**

Где молочная? **Где банк?** **Где кино?**

Go through **магазины** introduced in this Step **и** ask, **„где“** with each **магазине.**

Где булочная? *(boo-lahch-nah-yah)*

Где прачечная? *(prahch-yech-nah-yah)*

Где кафе?

Где аптека? *(ahp-tyek-ah)*

II. Next step—tell them what **вы** are looking for, need **или хотите!**

1) **Мне нужно...** ______________________

2) **У вас есть...?** ______________________
do you have

3) **Я хочу...** ______________________

(men-yeh) (kah-rahn-dahsh)
Мне нужно купить карандаш.

(oo) (vahs) (yest)
У вас есть карандаш?
do you have

Я хочу купить карандаш.

(kee-loh) (yah-blahk)
Мне нужно кило яблок?
kilo apples

У вас есть кило яблок?
apples

Я хочу купить кило яблок.

Go through the glossary at the end of **этой** (et-toy, this) **книги и** select **двадцать слов.** (dvahd-tset) Drill the above patterns **с этими** (et-tee-mee, these) **двадцатью словами.** Don't cheat. Drill them **сегодня.** (see-vohd-nyah) **Теперь,** take **двадцать** (dvahd-tset) more **слов из** your glossary **и** do the same.

III. Next step—find out сколько это стоит.

(skohl-kah) (et-tah) (stoy-eet)

Сколько это стоит? ____________________________

Сколько стоит карандаш?

(aht-krit-kah)
Сколько стоит открытка?

Сколько стоит марка?

Сколько стоит карта?
map

Сколько стоит кило яблок?

(ah-pyel-see-nahv)
Сколько стоит кило апельсинов ?
oranges

(myah-sah)
Сколько стоит кило мяса?
meat

(chahsh-kah)
Сколько стоит чашка чая?
cup tea

Using these same **слова** that **вы** selected above, drill **эти** (these) **вопросы тоже.**

IV. If вы не знаете где to find something, вы можете спросить

(znah-yet-yeh, know) (sprah-seet, ask)

(mah-goo)
Где я могу купить аспирин?

(ahch-kee)
Где я могу купить очки?

Once **вы** find what **вы** would like, **говорите,** (gah-vah-reet-yeh, say)

Я хочу это, пожалуйста.

Или if **вы** would not like it,

(et-tah-vah)
Я не хочу этого, спасибо.
that

Теперь, вы are all set to shop for anything!

Step 22

(oo-nee-vyair-sahl-nee) *(mah-gah-zeen)*
Универсальный Магазин
department store

At this point, **вы** should just about be ready for your **поездки** (trip) **в СССР.** **Вы** have gone shopping for those last-minute odds 'n ends. Most likely, the store directory at your local *(oo-nee-vyair-sahl-nee)* **универсальный** (department) **магазин** (store) did not look like the one **внизу.** **Вы** already know **много слов и вы можете** guess at **много** others. **Вы знаете что** *(zhen-shchee-nah)* **„женщина“** is Russian for "woman" so if **вам нужно** something for a woman, **вы** would probably look **на** *(vtah-rohm)* **втором** (second) *(eh-tahzh-yeh)* **этаже,** (floor) wouldn't you?

7. этаж	Булочная Кафе Спиртные напитки	Вино Фрукты Овоши Мясо	Дичь Домашняя птица Мороженая
6. этаж	Кровати Полотно Зеркала	Мебель Лампы Ковры	Картины Электроприборы
5. этаж	Посуда Хрусталь Фарфор	Ножевые изделия Кухонные приборы	Ключи Керамика
4. этаж	Книги Телевизоры Игрушки Радио	Табак Газеты Журналы Ресторан	Детская мебель Музыкальные инструменты Писчебумажный отдел Пластинки
3. этаж	Косметика Бельё Платки	Детский отдел Детские туфли Купальные костюмы	Антикварные вещи Фотографические аппараты
2. этаж	Женская одежда Женские шляпы Женские туфли	Мужская одежда Мужские шляпы Мужские туфли	Носки Пояса Зонтики
1. этаж	Духи Конфеты Часы Перчатки	Кожаные вещи Ювелирные изделия Рабочие инструменты Спортивные принадлежности	Запчасти автомобиля Принадлежности туалета Карты

Let's start a checklist **для поездки** (trip). Besides *(ah-dyezh-dih)* **одежды, что вам нужно?**

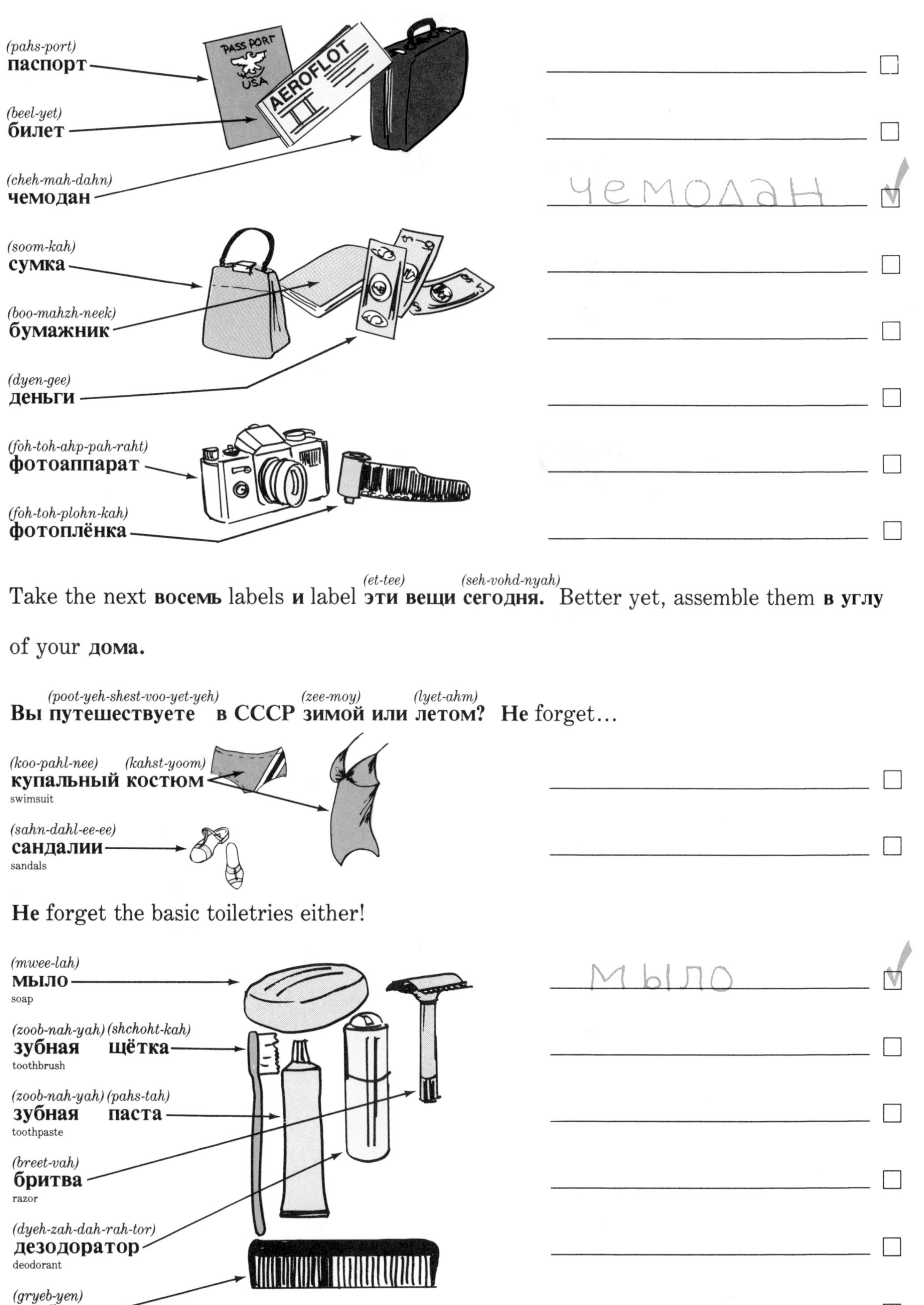

(pahs-port)
паспорт

(beel-yet)
билет

(cheh-mah-dahn)
чемодан — чемодан ✓

(soom-kah)
сумка

(boo-mahzh-neek)
бумажник

(dyen-gee)
деньги

(foh-toh-ahp-pah-raht)
фотоаппарат

(foh-toh-plohn-kah)
фотоплёнка

Take the next **восемь** labels **и** label **эти** *(et-tee)* **вещи сегодня** *(seh-vohd-nyah)*. Better yet, assemble them **в углу** of your **дома.**

Вы путешествуете *(poot-yeh-shest-voo-yet-yeh)* **в СССР зимой** *(zee-moy)* **или летом** *(lyet-ahm)*? **Не** forget...

(koo-pahl-nee) (kahst-yoom)
купальный костюм
swimsuit

(sahn-dahl-ee-ee)
сандалии
sandals

Не forget the basic toiletries either!

(mwee-lah)
мыло — мыло ✓
soap

(zoob-nah-yah) (shchoht-kah)
зубная щётка
toothbrush

(zoob-nah-yah) (pahs-tah)
зубная паста
toothpaste

(breet-vah)
бритва
razor

(dyeh-zah-dah-rah-tor)
дезодоратор
deodorant

(gryeb-yen)
гребень
comb

For the rest of **вещи** let's start with the outside layers **и** work our way in.

(pahl-toh)
пальто — overcoat ☐

(plahshch)
плащ — raincoat ☐

(zohn-teek)
зонтик — umbrella ☐

(pyair-chaht-kee)
перчатки — gloves ☐

(shlah-pah)
шляпа — hat ☐

(sah-pah-gee)
сапоги — boots ☐

(too-flee)
туфли — shoes ☐

(nahs-kee)
носки — socks НОСКИ ☐

(chool-kee)
чулки — stockings ☐

Take the next **пятнадцать** labels **и** label **эти** *(et-tee)* [these] **вещи.** Check **и** make sure that **они чистые** *(chees-tih-yeh)* [clean] **и** ready **для поездки** *(pah-yezd-kee)* [trip]. Be sure to do the same **с** the rest of **вещами** *(vesh-chah-mee)* that **вы** pack. Check them off on this list as **вы** organize them. From now on, **у** *(oo)* [you] **вас** *(vahs)* [have] **„зубная паста"** *(zoob-nah-yah) (pahs-tah)* **и не** "toothpaste."

(pee-zhah-mah)
пижама ☐

(nahch-nah-yah)(roo-bahsh-kah)
ночная рубашка ☐

(koo-pahl-nee) (hah-laht)
купальный халат — bathrobe ☐

(bahsh-mah-kee)
башмаки — slippers ☐

Купальный *(koo-pahl-nee)* **халат** *(hah-laht)* **и башмаки** *(bahsh-mah-kee)* **могут** *(moh-goot)* [can] double **для вас** *(vahs)* [you] **на** [at] **пляже** *(plyah-zheh)* [beach].

Having assembled **эти вещи, вы** *(et-tee)* (these) are ready **поехать** *(pah-yek-haht)* (to go). However, being human means occasionally forgetting something. Look again **в универсальный магазин** *(oo-nee-vyair-sahl-nee)* directory.

На каком этаже можно найти...
(kah-kohm) (eh-tahzh-yeh) (ny-tee)
which floor can one find

(moozh-skoo-yoo) (ah-dyezh-doo)
мужскую одежду? — **На** втором **этаже.** *(eh-tahzh-yeh)*

(zhen-skoo-yoo)
женскую одежду? (women's clothing) — **На** ______________ **этаже.**

книги? — **На** ______________ **этаже.**

(byel-yoh)
бельё? (lingerie) — **На** ______________ **этаже.**

(hroos-tahl)
хрусталь? На ______________ **этаже.**
crystal

(doo-hee)
духи? На ______________ **этаже.**
perfume

(ee-groosh-kee)
игрушки? На ______________ **этаже.**

Теперь, just remember your basic **вопросы.** (pahv-tah-reet-yeh) **Повторите** (repeat) (dee-ah-lohg) **диалог внизу** out loud **и** then by filling in the blanks.

Где можно (ny-tee) **найти** (zhyen-skee-yeh) **женские** (bryoo-kee) **брюки?** ______________
can one find women's trousers

В женской одежде. ______________
clothing

(ah-dyezh-dah)
Где женская одежда? ______________

(vtah-rohm)
На втором этаже. На втором этаже.
second

Где можно (ny-tee) **найти** (mih-lah) **мыло и зубную пасту?** ______________
find soap

(pyair-vahm)
На первом этаже. ______________

Also, **не** forget (sprah-seet) **спросить...**
to ask

(leeft)
Где лифт? ______________
elevator

(lyest-neet-sah)
Где лестница? ______________
stair

(es-kah-lah-tar)
Где эскалатор? ______________
escalator

Whether (vahm) **вам** (you) **нужно** (need) **купить** (zhyen-skee-yeh) **женские** (bryoo-kee) **брюки или** (moozh-skoo-yoo) **мужскую** (roo-bahsh-koo) **рубашку,** the necessary **слова** the same. **Где брюки? Где блузка?**

(kah-tor-ee) (rahz-myair)
Который размер?
what size

____

(too-fel)
Который размер туфель?
size shoes

____

(hah-rah-shoh) (see-deet)
Хорошо сидит.
well it fits

Хорошо сидит.

(ploh-hah) (see-deet)
Плохо сидит
badly it fits

____

Я хочу купить это.

____

Сколько это стоит?

____

(vsyoh)
Это всё, большое спасибо.
that's all

____

Clothing Sizes: 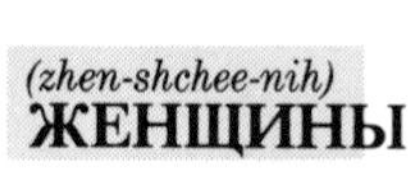
(zhen-shchee-nih) **ЖЕНЩИНЫ**

Блузки, Свитеры

American/British	32	34	36	38	40	42	44
Russian	40	42	44	46	48	50	52

Одежда

American	8	10	12	14	16	18
British	30	32	34	36	38	40
Russian	36	38	40	42	44	46

Туфли

American	5	5½	6	6½	7	7½	8	8½	9
Continental	35	35	36	37	37	38	38½	39	40

Clothing Sizes: *(moozh-chee-nih)* **МУЖЧИНЫ**

Туфли

American/British	7	7½	8	8½	9	9½	10	10½	11	11½
Russian	41	42	42	43	43	44	44	44	45	45

Одежда

American/British	34	36	38	40	42	44	46	48
Russian	44	46	48	50	52	54	56	58

Рубашки

American/British	14	14½	15	15½	16	16½	17	17½
Russian	36	37	38	40	41	42	43	44

Теперь вы are ready **поехать** *(pah-yek-haht)* (to go). **Вы знаете** *(znah-yet-yeh)* **всё** *(vsyoh)* (everything) that you need. The next Step gives you a quick review of the Russian alphabet **и** pronunciation **и** then **вы** are off to **аэродром** *(air-oh-drohm)*.

(oo-dah-chee) (schahst-lee-vah-vah) (poo-tee)
Удачи! Счастливого пути!
have a good trip

(Continued from page 2)

(sport) **спорт** ________ sport	*(teh-leh-fohn)* **телефон** ________ telephone	*(tseerk)* **цирк** ________ circus
(chee-slah) **числа** числа numbers	*(shkoh-lah)* **школа** ________ school	*(borshch)* **борщ** ________ Russian soup/borsch
(et-tah) **это** ________ this/that	*(myen-yoo)* **меню** ________ menu	*(vahn-nah-yah)* **ванная** ________ bathroom

There are also four special letters in Russian:

(ee/ih) **ы** ________	*(chah-sih)* **часы** ________ clock	*(sin)* **сын** ________ son
(varies) **й** ________	*(moo-zay)* **музей** ________ museum	*(zee-moy)* **зимой** ________ in winter

ь = *soft sign*
ъ = *hard sign*

These two letters do not have a sound. They act as word dividers and affect the preceding letter. So do not try to pronounce them. Here are some examples:

(skohl-kah) **сколько** ________ how much	*(spahl-nyah)* **спальня** ________ bedroom	*(shest)* **шесть** ________ six

Ы Щ Ж Й Г Д Ф Э

(ahl-fah-veet)
Алфавит

Here is the entire Russian alphabet in alphabetical order for quick reference. To make learning the alphabet more fun, practice these new letters and sounds with the examples given, which are Russian names. A black underline indicates a man's name and a red underline is for a woman's. Once you are finished here, turn to page one and practice saying the geographical locations indicated on the map.

Russian letter	English sound	Example	*Write it here*
а	ah	**Анна** *(ahn-nah)*	________
б	b	**Борис** *(bahr-ees)*	________
в	v	**Вадим** *(vah-deem)*	________
г	g (or v)	**Глеб** *(gleb)*	Глеб
д	d	**Дмитрий** *(dmee-tree)*	________
е *(varies)*	eh *(as in let)*	**Елена** *(eh-lyen-ah)*	________
	yeh *(as in yet)*		
ё	yoh	**Пётр** *(pyoh-ter)*	________
ж	zh	**Жанна** *(zhahn-nah)*	________
з	z	**Зина** *(zee-nah)*	________
и	ee	**Никита** *(nee-kee-tah)*	________

й *(varies)*	oy/ay/i/ee	**Майя** *(my-yah)*	____________
к	k	**Катя** *(kaht-yah)*	____________
л	l	**Лариса** *(lah-ree-sah)*	____________
м	m	**Максим** *(mahk-seem)*	____________
н	n	**Николай** *(nee-kah-lie)*	____________
о *(varies)*	oh	**Ольга** *(ohl-gah)*	Ольга
	ah	**Полина** *(pah-lee-nah)*	____________
п	p	**Паша** *(pah-shah)*	____________
р	r	**Рина** *(ree-nah)*	____________
с	s	**Сергей** *(syair-gay)*	____________
т	t	**Татьяна** *(taht-yah-nah)*	____________
у	oo	**Эдуард** *(ed-oo-ard)*	____________
ф	f	**Софья** *(sohf-yah)*	____________
х	h (or hk)	**Михаил** *(mee-hah-eel)*	____________
ц	ts	**Царёв** *(tsar-yohv)*	____________
ч	ch	**Вячеслав** *(vyah-cheh-slahv)*	____________
ш	sh	**Саша** *(sah-shah)*	____________
щ *(varies)*	shch/sht/sh	**Щукин** *(shchoo-keen)*	____________
ъ	no sound/called a hard sign		____________
ы *(varies)*	ee/ih	**Рыбаков** *(rih-bah-kahv)*	____________
ь	no sound/called a soft sign		____________
э *(varies)*	eh/air	**Элла** *(el-lah)*	____________
ю	yoo	**Юрий** *(yoor-ee)*	____________
я	yah	**Юлия** *(yool-ee-yah)*	____________

By now you should have a reasonable grasp on the Russian alphabet. Letters can change their pronunciation depending upon whether they are stressed or unstressed. Take the letter **о.** It is pronounced *"oh"* when stressed and *"ah"* otherwise. Now that isn't so difficult, is it?

Sometimes the phonetics may seem to contradict your pronunciation guide. Don't panic! The easiest and best possible phonetics have been chosen for each individual word. Pronounce the phonetics just as you see them. Don't over-analyze them. Try to speak with a Russian accent and, above all, enjoy yourself!

GLOSSARY

А

абрикос ... apricot
август ... August
авиапочта ... airmail
авиация ... aviation
Австралия ... Australia
автобиография ... autobiography
автобус ... bus
автограф ... autograph
автомат ... automat
автомобиль ... car
автор ... author
автостанция ... service station
агент ... agent
адвокат ... advocate, lawyer
адрес ... address
Азия ... Asia
академия ... academy
аккуратный ... fastidious, neat
акробат ... acrobat
акт ... act
актёр ... actor
акцент ... accent
алгебра ... algebra
алкоголь ... alcohol
алло ... hello
Америка ... America
Англия ... England
по-английски ... in English
анекдот ... anecdote, joke
антенна ... antenna
антибиотики ... antibiotics
апельсин ... orange (fruit)
аппетит ... appetite
апрель ... April
аптека ... drugstore
арена ... arena
арест ... arrest
армия ... army
аспирин ... aspirin
астронавт ... astronaut
ателье ... tailor's
атлет ... athlete
аэродром, аэропорт ... airport

Б

бабушка ... grandmother
багаж ... baggage
базар ... bazaar
бал ... ball (dance)
балалайка ... balalaika
балерина ... ballerina
балет ... ballet
балкон ... balcony
банан ... banana
банк ... bank
бар ... bar (restaurant)
баранина ... mutton
баржа ... barge
барьер ... barrier
бас ... bass (voice)
баскетбол ... basketball
батарея ... battery
башмаки ... slippers
беден ... poor
без ... minus, without
белый ... white
бензин ... gas/petrol
„Берёзка“ ... specialty store
билет ... ticket
бинокль ... binoculars
бланк ... blank (form)
богат ... rich
бокс ... boxing
болен ... sick
большой ... big, large
больше ... more
бомба ... bomb
борщ ... borsch (beet soup)
брат ... brother
брать ... to take
бритва ... razor
бронза ... bronze
брюнет ... brunette (male)
будет ... will be
будильник ... alarm clock
булочная ... bakery, pastry shop
бульвар ... boulevard
бумага ... paper
бумажник ... wallet
бюро ... bureau, office
был ... was
быстро ... fast

В

в ... in
важно ... important
ваза ... vase
вальс ... waltz
вам нужно ... you need
ванная ... bathroom
ваша ... your
веранда ... veranda
весной ... in spring
ветрено ... windy
вечер ... evening
вещи ... things
видеть ... to see
вилка ... fork
вино ... wine
витамин ... vitamin
внизу ... downstairs/below
вода ... water
водка ... vodka
вокзал ... train station
волейбол ... volleyball
вопрос ... question
восемь ... eight
восемнадцать ... eighteen
восемьдесят ... eighty
восемьсот ... 800
воскресенье ... Sunday
восток ... east
восточный ... eastern
вот ... here is
врач ... doctor
время ... time
Сколько времени? ... what time is it?
всё ... everything
вторник ... Tuesday
второй этаж ... second floor
вход ... entrance
входа нет ... do not enter
входить ... to enter
вчера ... yesterday
вы ... you
высокая ... high/tall
выход ... exit
выходить ... to go out, to exit

Г

газ ... natural gas
газета ... gazette, newspaper
газетчик ... newspaper man
галерея ... gallery
гараж ... garage
гастроном ... delicatessen, grocery store
где ... where
география ... geography
геология ... geology
геолог ... geologist
геометрия ... geometry
гид ... guide
гимнастика ... gymnastics
гитара ... guitar
говорить ... to speak/say
говядина ... beef
год ... year
голоден ... hungry
горы ... mountains
горячая ... hot
гостиная ... living room
гостиница ... hotel/inn
градусы ... degrees
грамм ... gram
гранит ... granite
гребень ... comb
громко ... loudly
группа ... group
гусь ... goose

Д

да ... yes
дайте мне ... give me
дама ... dame, lady, woman
дата ... date
два, две ... two
двадцать ... twenty
двенадцать ... twelve
дверь ... door
девять ... nine
девятнадцать ... nineteen
девяносто ... ninety
дед ... grandfather

дезодоратор . . . . deodorant
декабре . . . . December
делать . . . . to do/make
я делаю . . . . I do/make
делать пересадку . . . . . . to make a transfer
делегат . . . . delegate
день . . . . day
деньги . . . . money
десять . . . . ten
десяти . . . . ten from
детей, дети . . . . children
дешёвая . . . . inexpemsive
джин . . . . gin
джаз . . . . jazz
диагноз . . . . diagnosis
диаграмма . . . . diagram, blueprint
диалоги . . . . dialogues/conversations
диван . . . . divan, couch
дизель . . . . diesel
диплом . . . . diploma
дипломат . . . . diplomat
директор . . . . director
дискуссия . . . . discussion
длинная . . . . long
для . . . . for
до . . . . until
доброе утро . . . . good morning
добрый вечер . . . . good evening
добрый день . . . . good day, good afternoon
до свидания . . . . goodbye
дождь . . . . raining
доктор . . . . doctor
документ . . . . document
доллар . . . . dollar
дом . . . . house
домашняя птица . . . . poultry
дорога . . . . road
дорогая . . . . expensive
дочь . . . . daughter
драма . . . . drama
друзья . . . . friends
душ . . . . shower
дядя . . . . uncle

Е

еврей . . . . Jewish man
еврейка . . . . Jewish woman
есть . . . . to eat
ехать . . . . to go

Ж

жакет . . . . woman's jacket
жареное . . . . roasted, fried
жарко . . . . hot
ждать . . . . to wait for
желе . . . . jelly
женщина . . . . woman
женщины . . . . women
жёлтый . . . . yellow
жить . . . . to live/reside
журнал . . . . journal, magazine

З

за . . . . behind
завтра . . . . tomorrow
завтрак . . . . breakfast
заказывать . . . . to order/reserve
закрыто . . . . closed
занавес . . . . curtain
занята . . . . busy
запад . . . . west
западный . . . . western
запеченное . . . . baked
звонок . . . . doorbell
здесь . . . . here
здоров . . . . healthy
зелёный . . . . green
зеркало . . . . mirror
зимой . . . . in winter
знать . . . . to know
зовут . . . . is called
меня зовут . . . . I am called/my name is
зона . . . . zone
зонтик . . . . umbrella
зоопарк . . . . zoo
зубная паста . . . . toothpaste
зубная щётка . . . . toothbrush

И

и . . . . and
идти . . . . to go (on foot)
я еду . . . . I go
он/она идёт . . . . he/she goes
из . . . . out of/from
извините . . . . excuse me
изучать . . . . to learn
я изучаю . . . . I learn
икра . . . . caviar
или . . . . or
имена . . . . names
импортный . . . . imported
имя . . . . name
Индия . . . . India
индустриальный . . . . industrial
инженер . . . . engineer
иностранный . . . . foreign
инспектор . . . . inspector
институт . . . . institute
инструктор . . . . instructor
инструкции . . . . instructions
инструмент . . . . instrument
интеллигент . . . . intellectual
интервью . . . . interview
интерес . . . . interest
интернациональный . . . . international
информация . . . . information
искать . . . . to look for
я ищу . . . . I look for
Исландия . . . . Iceland
Ислания . . . . Spain
по-испански . . . . in Spanish
история . . . . history
Италия . . . . Italy
по-итальянски . . . . in Italian
июль . . . . July
июнь . . . . June

К

к себе . . . . pull (the doors)
кабина . . . . cabin, booth
кабинет . . . . study
каждые . . . . every
как . . . . how
Как дела? . How are things?/How are you?
какая, какие . . . . what kind of
какао . . . . cocoa
календарь . . . . calendar
камера . . . . camera
Канада . . . . Canada
канал . . . . canal
канарейка . . . . canary
кандидат . . . . candidate
канцтовары . . . . stationery store
капитал . . . . capital (money)
карандаш . . . . pencil
карта . . . . map
картина, картинка . . . . picture
касса . . . . ticket machine
кассир . . . . cashier
католик . . . . Catholic man
католичка . . . . Catholic woman
километр . . . . kilometer
кило . . . . kilo
кино . . . . cinema
киоск . . . . newsstand
класс . . . . class
классик . . . . classic
клоун . . . . clown
книга . . . . book
книжный магазин . . . . bookstore
ковёр . . . . carpet
когда . . . . when
колбаса . . . . sausage
коллекция . . . . collection
комедия . . . . comedy
компас . . . . compass
композитор . . . . composer
коньяк . . . . cognac
конференция . . . . conference
комната . . . . room
конверт . . . . envelope
концерт . . . . concert
копейки, копеек . . . . kopecks
корзина . . . . basket
коричневый . . . . brown
короткая . . . . short
кот . . . . cat
которая . . . . which
кофе . . . . coffee
краб . . . . crab
красивый . . . . pretty
красный . . . . red
Кремль . . . . Kremlin
кровать . . . . bed
кто . . . . who
Куба . . . . Cuba
купальный костюм . . . . swimsuit
купальный халат . . . . bathrobe
купить . . . . to buy
кухня . . . . kitchen

Л

лаборатория . . . . laboratory
лампа . . . . lamp
лево . . . . left
налево . . . . to the left
Ленинград . . . . Leningrad
лет . . . . years
лететь . . . . to fly
я лечу . . . . I fly
летом . . . . in summer
лимон . . . . lemon
лимонад . . . . lemonade
линия . . . . line
литература . . . . literature
литр . . . . liter
ложка . . . . spoon
любить . . . . to love
люди . . . . people

М

магазин . . . . store
май . . . . May
маленькая . . . . small
мало . . . . little
марка . . . . stamp
март . . . . March
масло . . . . butter
масса . . . . mass
мастер . . . . master
мать . . . . mother
математика . . . . mathematics
материя . . . . material
матрёшки . . . . Russian dolls
матч . . . . match (game)
машина . . . . machine (car)
машина напрокат . . . . rental car
медаль . . . . medal
медь . . . . copper coins

медик . . . . . medic
медицина . . . . . medicine
медленно . . . . . slow, slowly
между . . . . . between
мелодия . . . . . melody
мелочь . . . . . change (coins)
меню . . . . . menu
местный . . . . . domestic, internal
месяцы . . . . . months
металл . . . . . metal
метод . . . . . method
метро . . . . . metro, subway
механик . . . . . mechanic
микрофон . . . . . microphone
милиция . . . . . police
миллион . . . . . million
миниатюра . . . . . miniature
минут . . . . . minutes
миссия . . . . . mission
митинг . . . . . meeting
много . . . . . a lot, many
модель . . . . . model
мой . . . . . my
молодой . . . . . young
молоко . . . . . milk
молочная . . . . . dairy
момент . . . . . moment
монеты . . . . . coins
Москва . . . . . Moscow
мотор . . . . . motor
мотоцикл . . . . . motorcycle
мочь . . . . . to be able to/can
мужчина . . . . . man
  мужчины . . . . . men
музей . . . . . museum
музыка . . . . . music
мусульманин . . . . . Moslem man
мусульманка . . . . . Moslem woman
мы . . . . . we
мыло . . . . . soap
мясо . . . . . meat
мяч . . . . . ball

Н

на . . . . . on, into
наверху . . . . . upstairs
над . . . . . over
название . . . . . name
налево . . . . . to the left
напишите . . . . . write out
направо . . . . . to the right
например . . . . . for example
натуральный . . . . . grilled
нация . . . . . nation
начинается . . . . . begins
не . . . . . not, no
недел . . . . . week
нейлон . . . . . nylon
несерьёзный . . . . . not serious
нет . . . . . no
низкая . . . . . low
никель . . . . . nickel
новые . . . . . new
нож . . . . . knife
ноль . . . . . zero
номер . . . . . number
номере . . . . . hotel room
норма . . . . . norm, standard
нормальная . . . . . normal
нос . . . . . nose
носки . . . . . socks
ночь . . . . . night
ночная рубашка . . . . . nightshirt
ноябрь . . . . . November
нужно . . . . . need
  мне нужно . . . . . I need
нужны . . . . . necessary

О

обменять . . . . . exchange
обед . . . . . meal, dinner
овощи . . . . . vegetables
овощной . . . . . greengrocer's
одежда . . . . . clothes
один . . . . . one
одиннадцать . . . . . eleven
одеяло . . . . . blanket
окно . . . . . window
октябрь . . . . . October
оленина . . . . . venison
олимпиада . . . . . Olympics
он . . . . . he
она . . . . . she
они . . . . . they
опаздывать . . . . . to be late
оранжевый . . . . . orange (color)
органист . . . . . organist
опера . . . . . opera
оркестр . . . . . orchestra
оплатить . . . . . to pay
опоздал . . . . . late
осенью . . . . . in autumn
остановка . . . . . stop
  остановка автобуса . . . . . bus stop
  остановка трамвая . . . . . trolley stop
отварное . . . . . boiled
ответы . . . . . answers
отделение милиции . . . . . police station
отделы . . . . . shops, departments
отель . . . . . hotel
отец . . . . . father
открытка . . . . . postcard
открыто . . . . . open
отправление . . . . . departure
от себя . . . . . push (the doors)
отходить . . . to depart (trains, buses, ships)
офицер . . . . . officer
официальный . . . . . official
официант . . . . . waiter
официантка . . . . . waitress
очень . . . . . very
очки . . . . . eyeglasses

П

павильон . . . . . pavilion
пакет . . . . . package
пальто . . . . . overcoat
пансионат . . . . . pension, boarding house
парад . . . . . parade
парикмахерская . . . . . hairdresser
парк . . . . . park
парламент . . . . . parliament
партия . . . . . party
паспорт . . . . . passport
пассажир . . . . . passenger
перед . . . . . in front of
перо . . . . . pen
перчатки . . . . . gloves
перец . . . . . pepper
пианист . . . . . pianist
пиво . . . . . beer
пижама . . . . . pajamas
пикник . . . . . picnic
пилот . . . . . pilot
писать . . . . . to write
письмо . . . . . letter
пить . . . . . to drink
платформа . . . . . platform
плащ . . . . . raincoat
плита . . . . . stove
плохо . . . . . bad
пляж . . . . . beach
по . . . . . on
повторять . . . . . to repeat
под . . . . . under
подвал . . . . . basement
подушка . . . . . pillow
поезд . . . . . train
поездка . . . . . trip
пожар . . . . . fire
позвонить . . . . . to telephone/call
позиция . . . . . position
погода . . . . . weather
пожалуйста . . . . . please/you're welcome
полиция . . . . . police
половина . . . . . half
полотенца . . . . . towels
показывать . . . . . to show
покупать . . . . . to buy
понедельник . . . . . Monday
понимать . . . . . to understand
порт . . . . . port
портрет . . . . . portrait
посылать . . . . . to send
посылка . . . . . package
потолок . . . . . ceiling
потом . . . . . then
почему . . . . . why
почта . . . . . mail, post office
почтовое отделение . . . . . post office
почтовый ящик . . . . . mailbox
поэт . . . . . poet
правильно . . . . . correct
править . . . . . to drive
право . . . . . right
  направо . . . . . to the right
православная . . . . . Orthodox woman
православный . . . . . Orthodox man
практика . . . . . practice
прачечная . . . . . laundry
приезд . . . . . arrival
приезжать . . . . . to arrive
примеры . . . . . examples
приходить . . to arrive (trains, buses, ships)
программа . . . . . program
прогресс . . . . . progress
продавать . . . . . to sell
продмаг . . . . . food store
продукт . . . . . product
проект . . . . . project
профессия . . . . . profession
профессор . . . . . professor
процент . . . . . percent
прямо . . . . . straight ahead
пряники . . . . . pastries
путешественник . . . . . traveler
путешествовать . . . . . to travel
пятнадцать . . . . . fifteen
пять . . . . . five
пятьдесят . . . . . fifty
пятьсот . . . . . five hundred
пятница . . . . . Friday

Р

радио . . . . . radio
разговор по телефону . . . . . telephone conversation
размер . . . . . size
  Который размер? . . . . . Which size?
ракета . . . . . rocket
ранг . . . . . rank
рапорт . . . . . report
расписание . . . . . schedule
револьвер . . . . . revolver
революция . . . . . revolution
регистрация . . . . . registration
резервация . . . . . reservation
рекорд . . . . . record
религия . . . . . religion
ресторан . . . . . restaurant
родители . . . . . parents
родственники . . . . . relatives
розовый . . . . . pink
рубль/рубли . . . . . ruble/rubles

русский .... Russian
по-русски .... in Russian
русские .... Russians
ручка .... pen
рыбный рынок .... fish market
рыба .... fish
рынок .... market
рядом с .... next to

С

с .... with
сад .... garden
салат .... salad
салфетка .... napkin
самовар .... samovar
самолёт .... airplane
сандалии .... sandals
сапоги .... boots
свинина .... pork
сдача .... change
север .... north
северный .... northern
сегодня .... today
сезон .... season
секретарь .... secretary
секунда .... second
семинар .... seminar
семнадцать .... seventeen
семь .... seven
семьдесят .... seventy
семья .... family
сентябрь .... September
серебро .... silver coins
серый .... gray
сестра .... sister
сигара .... cigar
сигарета .... cigarette
симфония .... symphony
синий .... blue
сколько .... how much
Сколько времени? .... What time is it?
словарь .... dictionary
слово .... word
слон .... elephant
снег .... snow
собака .... dog
советский .... Soviet
Советский Союз .... Soviet Union
соль .... salt
сорок .... forty
спальня .... bedroom
спасибо .... thank you
спать .... to sleep
спокойной ночи .... good night
спросить .... to ask
я спрашиваю .... I ask
среда .... Wednesday
ставить .... park/put
стадион .... stadium
стакан .... glass
станция .... station
станция метро .... metro station
старый .... old
старейший .... oldest
старт .... start
стена .... wall
стирать .... to wash/clean (clothes)
сто .... one hundred
стоит .... costs
стол .... table
столовая .... dining room
стоянка .... parking lot, taxi stand
страница .... page
стригут .... (they) cut
студент .... student
стул .... chair
суббота .... Saturday
сувениры .... souvenirs
сумка .... purse/bag
суп .... soup

Счастливого пути! .... Have a good trip!
счёт .... bill
сын .... son

Т

табак .... tobacco
такси .... taxi
там .... there (is)
тарелка .... plate
театр .... theater
телевизор .... television
телеграмма .... telegram
телескоп .... telescope
телефон .... telephone
телефон-автомат .... public telephone
телятина .... veal
температура .... temperature
теперь .... now
терять .... to lose
тётя .... aunt
тихо .... softly
тогда .... then
тоже .... also
толстая .... thick
только .... only
томат .... tomato
тонкая .... thin
тост .... toast
трамвай .... street car/trolley
три .... three
тридцать .... thirty
тринадцать .... thirteen
триста .... three hundred
трубка .... receiver (telephone)
туалет .... toilet
туман .... fog
турист .... tourist
туфли .... shoes
тушёное .... stewed
тысяча .... one thousand

У

у вас есть .... you have
у меня есть .... I have
у нас есть .... we have
уезжать .... to leave
я уезжаю .... I leave
угол .... corner
удачи .... good luck
указания .... directions
укладывать .... to pack
я укладываю .... I pack
улица .... street
умывальник .... washstand
универмаг .... department store
универсальный магазин .... department store
университет .... university
утро .... morning

Ф

Фаренгейт .... Fahrenheit
фаршированый .... stuffed
февраль .... February
фильм .... film
фотоаппарат .... camera
фотограф .... photographer
фотомагазин .... camera store
фотоплёнка .... film
Франция .... France
по-французски .... in French
фрукт .... fruit
футбол .... soccer, football

Х

химически .... chemically
химчистка .... dry cleaner's
хлеб .... bread
холодильник .... refrigerator
холодная .... cold
хорошо .... good
не хорошо .... not good
хорошо сидит .... it fits well
хочу .... (I) would like
я хочу пить .... I have thirst

Ц

царь .... czar, tsar
цвет .... color
цветок .... flower
Цельсий .... Celsius
центр .... city center
церковь .... church
цирк .... circus

Ч

чай .... tea
час .... o'clock/hour
Который час? .... What time is it?
часто .... often
часы .... clock, watch
чашка .... cup
чемодан .... suitcase
четверть .... a quarter (toward)
четверг .... Thursday
четыре .... four
четырнадцать .... fourteen
чёрный .... black
числа .... numbers
чистый .... clean
читать .... to read
я читаю .... I read
что .... what
чулки .... stockings

Ш

шарф .... scarf
Швеция .... Sweden
по-шведски .... in Swedish
шестнадцать .... sixteen
шесть .... six
шестьдесят .... sixty
шкаф .... wardrobe/cupboard
школа .... school
шляпа .... hat
шоссе .... main road
штат .... state
шторм .... storm
шьёт .... sews

Э

экватор .... equator
экзамен .... exam
экономика .... economics
экспресс .... express
эра .... era
эскалатор .... escalator
этаж .... floor (of building)
это/этой/эти/этот .... that/this
Это всё .... That's all.

Ю

юг .... south
южный .... southern

Я

я I
яблоко .... apple
язык .... language, tongue
январь .... January
янтарь .... amber
Япония .... Japan
яхта .... yacht

DRINKING GUIDE

This guide is intended to explain the variety of beverages available to you while in the Soviet Union. It is by no means complete. Some of the experimenting has been left up to you, but this should get you started. One asterisk indicates a brand name, while two asterisks indicate a regional variety.

ГОРЯЧИЕ НАПИТКИ (hot drinks)

чай с лимоном............tea with lemon
чай с вареньем............tea with jam
чай с молоком............tea with milk
чай с мёдом............tea with honey

Чай was traditionally made in a samovar, **самовар.** A very strong tea was made in a teapot, which was kept warm on top of the samovar. A small portion of the tea was poured into a cup and diluted with hot water from the samovar.

кофе............coffee
- **кофе с молоком**............coffee with milk
- **чёрный кофе**............black coffee
- **кофе по-восточному**............Turkish coffee
- **кофе-гляссе**............coffee with ice cream

какао............cocoa

ХОЛОДНЫЕ НАПИТКИ (cold drinks)

молоко............milk
- **фруктовый коктейль**............milkshake
- **кефир**............sour milk (usually topped with sugar)
- **ряженка**............thick, sour milk

кисель............sour-fruit drink
лимонад............lemonade
байкал............cola drink
* **пепси-кола**............Pepsi-Cola
квас............kvass

Квас is a dark, non-alcoholic beverage made from yeast and black bread. Although it is not sold in restaurants, it is readily available from street vendors.

минеральная вода............mineral water
* **Нарзан**
* **Ессентуки**
* **Боржоми**

You'll find that most mineral waters in Russia are domestic, bottled from natural spring-water from the Caucasus.

фруктовый сок............fruit juice
- **апельсиновый сок**............orange juice
- **яблочный сок**............apple juice
- **виноградный сок**............grape juice
- **клюквенный морс**............cranberry juice
- **сливовый сок**............prune juice
- **абрикосовый сок**............apricot juice
- **гранатовый сок**............pomegranate juice
- **персиковый сок**............peach juice
- **томатный сок**............tomato juice

Don't miss a chance to sample Russian fruit juices. They are delicious. You'll find juice bars in the larger grocery stores.

ПИВО (beer)

светлое пиво............light beer
тёмное пиво............dark beer
* **Московское**
* **Ленинградское**
* **Двойное золотое**
* **Рижское**

Пиво is available in restaurants, but if you're visiting the Soviet Union during the summer, you'll want to visit the streetside beer stalls.

СПИРТНЫЕ НАПИТКИ (alcohol)

Both **спиртные напитки** and **вино** can be purchased by the bottle or by weight. A shot is 50 grams and a glass of wine is approximately 150 grams.

водка............vodka
* **Экстра**
* **Столичная**
* **Русская**
* **Пшеничная**
* **Смирновская**
* **Охотничья**

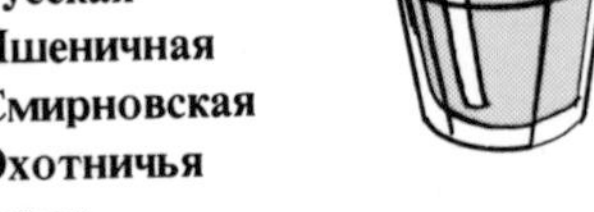

Коньяк............cognac
****Армянский коньяк**............Armenian cognac
****Грузинский коньяк**............Georgian cognac

виски............whiskey
джин............gin
ром............rum
аперитив............aperitif
ликёр............liqueur

ВИНО (wine)

красное вино............red wine
****Алазанская долина**............Georgian wine
****Мукузани**............Georgian wine
белое вино............white wine
****Цинандали**............Georgian wine
розовое вино............rosé wine
вермут............vermouth
портвейн............port
херес............sherry
шампанское............champagne
- **сухое шампанское**............dry champagne
- **полу-сухое шампанское**............semi-dry champagne
- **сладкое шампанское**............sweet champagne
- **полу-сладкое шампанское**............semi-sweet champagne

* **Игристое**
* **Золотое**

Russian champagne and **вино** from Georgia, a region in Caucasia, are considered to be some of the finest wines in the world. They are rated for their quality on a star system: seven stars indicates a superlative wine, while one star indicates a wine of lesser quality.

CUT ALONG DOTTED LINE, FOLD AND TAKE WITH YOU

Салат (salad)

салат из белых грибов	white-mushroom salad
салат из столичный	meat-and-vegetable salad
винегрет	vinaigrette of vegetables
соус винегрет	vinaigrette
соус фруктово-ягодный	berry, fruit sauce

Десерт (dessert)

мороженое	ice cream
ванильное мороженое	vanilla ice cream
шоколадное мороженое	chocolate ice cream
кисель	jello-style dessert
компот	compote
крем	whipped cream
пудинг	pudding
рисовый пудинг	rice pudding
лимон с сахаром	lemon with sugar
яблоки в вине	apples in wine
шоколадный соус	chocolate sauce
торт	torte, cake
кекс	muffin
пирог	pie
пряники	cookies
пирожные	pastries, small cakes
печенье	pastries, biscuits
коржики	shortcakes

Фрукты (fruit)

апельсин	orange
арбуз	watermelon
банан	banana
виноград	grapes
вишни	cherries
грейпфрут	grapefruit
груша	pear
дыня	melon
земляника	strawberries
дыня	cantaloupe
лимон	lemon
малина	raspberries
персик	peach
чёрная смородина	blackberries
яблоко	apple
ягоды	berries

FOLD HERE

Птица и Дичь (poultry and game)

курица/цыплята	chicken
гусь	goose
утка	duck
индейка	turkey
рябчик	hazel grouse
тетерев	black grouse
куропатка	partridge
вальдшнеп	woodcock
бекас	snipe
чирок	teal
перепел	quail
кролик	rabbit
оленина	venison
цыплята жареные	fried chicken
куриные крокеты	chicken croquettes
белое мясо курицы	breast of chicken
котлеты по-киевски	chicken Kiev

Овощи (vegetables)

баклажаны	eggplant
горох	peas
грибы	mushrooms
капуста	cabbage
красная капуста	red cabbage
цветная капуста	cauliflower
картофель	potatoes
картофель жареный	fried potatoes
картофель отварной	boiled potatoes
картофель пюре	mashed potatoes
картофель в сметане	potatoes in sour cream
кукуруза	corn
лук	onions
морковь	carrots
перец	pepper/green pepper
перец горький	pimentos
петрушка	parsley
помидоры	tomatoes
редиска	radishes
репа	turnips
свёкла	beets
шпинат	spinach

(pree-yaht-nah-vah) (ahp-peh-tee-tah)
Приятного аппетита!

FOLD HERE

Меню
menu

Завтрак? Обед? Или Ужин?

отварное	boiled
жареное	roasted
тушёное	stewed
запеченное	baked
фаршированый	stuffed
на вертеле	grilled on a skewer
в сметане	in a sour cream sauce
в томате	in a tomato sauce
паровой	steamed
мало прожаренный	rare
не сильно прожаренный	medium
хорошо прожаренный	well-done

Что мне нужно? (what do I need?)

масло	butter
сахар	sugar
варенье	jam
мёд	honey
соль	salt
перец	pepper
уксус	vinegar
растительное масло	oil
оливкое масло	olive oil
горчица	mustard
соус	sauce, gravy
сыр	cheese
вода	water
лед	ice
майонез	mayonnaise
сливки	cream
сметана	sour cream
кефир	sour milk
творог	cottage cheese

Закуски (appetizers)

икра	caviar
икра грибная	mushroom caviar
красная икра	red caviar
чёрная икра	black caviar
сардины	sardines
сельдь	herring
креветки	shrimp
балык	smoked sturgeon
сосиски	sausages
колбаса	cold cuts
копчёная колбаса	smoked cold cuts
паштет	pâté
студень	aspic
форшмак	potato-and-meat hash
бутерброды открытые	open-faced sandwiches
бутерброды закрытые	sandwiches

Хлеб (bread and dough dishes)

чёрный хлеб	black bread
белый хлеб	white bread
ржаной хлеб	rye bread
пшеничный хлеб	wheat bread
булочки	rolls
блины	pancakes
блины с маслом и сметаной	pancakes with butter and sour cream
пельмени	small dumplings
каша	buckwheat, cereal
манная	farina
пирожки	baked, stuffed dumplings
кулебяка	breaded fish loaf
рис	rice
макароны	macaroni
пирог с грибами	mushroom pie
пирог с капустой	cabbage pie
пирог с луком	onion pie
пирог с мясом	meat pie

Яйца (eggs)

яйца вкрутую	hard-boiled eggs
яйца всмятку	soft-boiled eggs
яичница	fried eggs
взбитая яичница	scrambled eggs
фаршированные яйца	stuffed eggs
яйца с икрой	eggs with caviar

FOLD HERE

Суп (soup)

борщ	borsch
борщ со свининой	borsch with pork
щи	cabbage soup
щи суточные	sauerkraut soup
уха	fish soup
лапша	noodle soup
молочная лапша	milk soup with noodles
суп-грибной	mushroom soup
суп-овощной	vegetable soup
суп-пюре из овощей	vegetable purée
суп молочный с овощами	cream-of-vegetable soup
суп из фасоли	bean soup
суп картофельный	potato soup
суп гороховый	pea soup
солянка	spicy, thick soup
рисовый суп	rice soup
бульон	bouillon
бульон с яйцом	bouillon with an egg
бульон с фрикадельками	bouillon with meatballs
рассольник	kidney-and-cucumber soup

Рыба (fish dishes)

треска	cod
камбала	flounder
карп	carp
лосось	salmon
кета	Siberian salmon
щука	pike
раки	crayfish
краб	crab
окунь	perch
судак	pike perch
палтус	halibut
форель	trout
осетрина	sturgeon
осетрина в томате	sturgeon in tomato sauce
осетрина под маринадом	pickled sturgeon
севрюга	type of sturgeon
осетрина „фри“	fried sturgeon
судак „фри“	fried pike perch

Мясо (meat dishes)

баранина	mutton
ветчина	ham
говядина	beef
свинина	pork
телятина	veal

FOLD HERE

Мясо (meat dishes)

бараньи котлеты	lamb chops
ветчина жареная	fried ham
колбаса жареная	fried sausages
мозги жареные	fried brains
телятина жареная	roast veal
мясо жареное в сметане с луком	meat roasted in sour cream and onions
ростбиф	roast beef
поджарка	roast pork
бефстроганов	beef Stroganoff
бифштекс	beefsteak
рагу	stew
говядина тушеная	beef stew
говядина в сухарях	breaded beef
рулет	meatloaf
гуляш	goulash
котлеты	chopped beef
шашлык	shashlik, kebabs
долма	stuffed grape leaves
голубцы мясные	stuffed cabbage
котлеты свиные отбивные	breaded pork chops
котлеты отбивные из баранины	breaded lamb chops
котлеты натуральные из баранины	grilled lamb chops
шницель	breaded veal cutlet
язык	tongue
печёнка	liver
сосиски	sausages
сардельки	small sausages
бекон	bacon
битки/биточки	meatballs
почки	kidneys
купаты	spicy pork sausage
плов	pilaf

Салат (salad)

салат из фруктов	fruit salad
салат из огурцов	cucumber salad
салат из помидоров	tomato salad
салат из фасоли	bean salad
салат из редиса	radishes with sour cream
салат картофельный	potato salad
салат из капусты с яблоками	cabbage-and-apple salad

(yah) *(zah-kah-zih-vah-yoo)* **я заказываю**	*(yah)* *(yeh-doo)* **я еду**
(yah) *(pah-koo-pah-yoo)* **я покупаю**	*(yah)* *(pree-yez-zhy-yoo)* **я приезжаю**
(yah) *(ee-zoo-chah-yoo)* **я изучаю**	*(yah)* *(vee-zhoo)* **я вижу**
(yah) *(pahv-tar-yah-yoo)* **я повторяю**	*(yah)* *(zhee-voo)* **я живу**
(yah) *(pah-nee-mah-yoo)* **я понимаю**	*(yah)* *(zhdoo)* **я жду**
(yah) *(gah-vah-ryoo)* **я говорю**	*(yah)* *(eesh-choo)* **я ищу**

I go

I order/reserve

I arrive/come

I buy

I see

I learn

I live

I repeat

I wait for

I understand

I look for

I speak/say

(yah) *(yem)* **я ем**	*(yah)* *(prah-dah-yoo)* **я продаю**
(yah) *(pyoo)* **я пью**	*(yah)* *(pah-sih-lah-yoo)* **я посылаю**
(yah) *(hah-choo)* **я хочу**	*(yah)* *(splyoo)* **я сплю**
(men-yeh) *(noozh-nah)* **мне нужно**	*(yah)* *(zvah-nyoo)* **я звоню**
(men-yah) *(zah-voot)* **меня зовут...**	*(die-tee)* *(men-yeh)* **дайте мне**
(oo) *(men-yah)* *(yest)* **у меня есть**	*(yah)* *(pee-shoo)* **я пишу**

I sell

I eat

I send

I drink

I sleep

I would like

I phone

I need

give me…

my name is…

I write

I have

(yah) (pah-kah-zih-vah-yoo)
я показываю

(yah) (lee-choo)
я лечу

(yah) (plah-choo) (zah)
я плачу за

(yah) (prahv-lyoo)
я правлю

(yah) (znah-yoo)
я знаю

(yah) (oo-yez-zhah-yoo)
я уезжаю

(yah) (mah-goo)
я могу

(yah) (dyeh-lah-yoo)
я делаю

(yah) (chee-tah-yoo)
я читаю

(yah) (dyeh-lah-yoo) (pyair-yeh-sahd-koo)
я делаю пересадку

(yah) (poot-yeh-shest-voo-yoo)
я путешествую

(yah) (oo-klah-dih-vah-yoo)
я укладываю

I fly	I show
I drive	I pay for
I leave	I know
I do/make	I can
I make a transfer	I read
I pack	I travel

(poh-yezd) (ah-pahz-dih-vah-yet) **Поезд опаздывает.**	*(yah) (zah-krih-vah-yoo)* **я закрываю**
(poh-yezd) (pree-hoh-deet) (vuh) **Поезд приходит в...**	*(yah) (aht-krih-vah-yoo)* **я открываю**
(poh-yezd) (aht-hoh-deet) (vuh) **Поезд отходит в...**	*(yah) (koor-yoo)* **я курю**
(yah) (stee-rah-yoo) **я стираю**	*(yah) (lyoob-lyoo)* **я люблю**
(yah) (tyair-yah-yoo) **я теряю**	*(yah) (sprah-shee-vah-yoo)* **я спрашиваю**
(yah) (rah-boh-tah-yoo) **я работаю**	*(yah) (nah-chee-nah-yoo)* **я начинаю**

I close	The train is late.
I open	The train arrives at…
I smoke	The train departs at…
I like	I wash
I ask	I lose
I begin	I work

(zah-nee-mah-yet)
занимает

(eez-vee-neet-yeh)
извините

(skohl-kah) (et-tah) (stoy-eet)
Сколько это стоит?

(ee-dyoht) (dohzhd)
Идёт дождь.

(kahk) (dee-lah)
Как дела?

(ee-dyoht) (snyeg)
Идёт снег.

(doh) (svee-dahn-yah)
До свиданья!

(see-vohd-nyah)
сегодня

(pah-zhahl-oos-tah)
пожалуйста

(zahv-trah)
завтра

(spah-see-bah)
спасибо

(vchee-rah)
вчера

excuse me

it takes

It is raining.

How much does this cost?

It is snowing.

How are things/ How are you?

today

good bye!

tomorrow

please/you're welcome

yesterday

thank-you

(zdah-rohv) *(bohl-yen)*
здоров - болен

(tohl-stah-yah) *(tohn-kah-yah)*
толстая - тонкая

(hah-rah-shoh) *(ploh-hah)*
хорошо - плохо

(nahd) *(pohd)*
над - под

(gor-yah-chah-yah) *(hah-lohd-nah-yah)*
горячая - холодная

(lyev-ah) *(prah-vah)*
лево - право

(tee-hah) *(grohm-kah)*
тихо - громко

(myed-lyen-nah) *(bis-trah)*
медленно - быстро

(kah-roht-kah-yah) *(dleen-nah-yah)*
короткая - длинная

(vwee-soh-kah-yah) *(nees-kah-yah)*
высокая - низкая

(vwee-soh-kah-yah) *(mah-lyen-kah-yah)*
высокая - маленькая

(stah-ree) *(mah-lah-doy)*
старый - молодой

thick - thin

healthy - sick

above - below

good - bad

left - right

hot - cold

slow - fast

softly - loudly

high - low

short - long

old - young

tall/high - small

(dah-rah-gah-yah) *(dyeh-shyoh-vah-yah)* **дорогая - дешёвая**	*(yah)* **я**
(bah-gaht) *(byed-yen)* **богат - беден**	*(ohn)* **он**
(mnoh-gah) *(mah-lah)* **много - мало**	*(ah-nah)* **она**
(aht-krit-tah) *(zah-krit-tah)* **открыто - закрыто**	*(mwee)* **мы**
(slahd-kee) *(kees-lee)* **сладкий - кислый**	*(vwee)* **вы**
(bahl-shoy) *(mah-lyen-kee)* **большой - маленький**	*(ah-nee)* **они**

Sunset
Proof-of-Purchase
ISBN 0-944502-45-8

I	expensive-inexpensive
he	rich - poor
she	a lot - a little
we	open - closed
you	sweet - sour
they	big - small